–

Demographic Challenges for the 21st Century

A State of the Art in Demography

–

Johan Surkyn, Patrick Deboosere & Jan Van Bavel (eds.)

–

Demographic Challenges for the 21st Century

A State of the Art in Demography

–

Conference organized as a tribute to the continuing endeavours
of Prof. Dr. Em. Ron Lesthaeghe in the field of Demography

Cover design: Koloriet, Sterrebeek
Book design: Stipontwerpt, Antwerpen
Print: Flin Graphic Group, Oostkamp

© 2008 VUBPRESS Brussels University Press
VUBPRESS is an imprint of ASP nv
(Academic and Scientific Publishers nv)
Ravensteingalerij 28
B-1000 Brussels
Tel. ++ 32 2 289 26 50
Fax ++ 32 2 289 26 59
E-mail info@vubpress.be
www.vubpress.be

ISBN 978 90 5487 447 8
NUR 756
Legal Deposit D/2007/11.161/037

Contents

Acknowledgements

This volume results from the colloquium Demographic Challenges for the 21st Century, organised by Interface Demography on the occasion of the retirement of Ron Lesthaeghe as a full professor of the Vrije Universiteit Brussel (VUB). It was held at the VUB-campus in Etterbeek, Brussels, February 15-16, 2007. In the first place, the organising committee wishes to thank Ron himself because, without his important and internationally renowned contributions to the field of population studies, we would never have been able to attract speakers and participants from so many different corners of the world to the conference.

Financial support was provided by the two major Belgian science foundations, i.e. the Francophone Fond National de la Recherche Scientifique (FNRS) as well as the Flemish Fonds voor Wetenschappelijk Onderzoek (FWO). In addition, we received funding from the Vrije Universiteit Brussel (VUB) and the government of the Capital Region of Brussels (Brussels Hoofdstedelijk Gewest/Region de Bruxelles-Capitale).

We express our gratitude to all members of scientific as well as the organising committee. Vicky Bastiaenssen, member of the organising committee, was one of Ron's last VUB-students. She deserves a special word of thanks for spontaneously taking many aspects of the practical organisation in good hands. Patrick Deboosere assured good overall co-ordination. We also remember the help kindly provided by former Interface Demography members Mirjam Klaassens and Tristan Bockstael, as well as by some enthusiast sociology students. The conference itself was chaired by Johan Surkyn, who has been Ron's collaborator for many years. Professor Frans Willekens (NIDI and University of Groningen) provided an excellent laudation for Ron's impressive career. The academic part of the conference benefited from an eloquent summing up by Professor John Hobcraft (University of York).

We highly appreciate the speakers at the conference and the authors of the chapters not just for their interesting contributions but also for their patience before seeing this book in print. We also apologize for the delay to people who pre-ordered a copy of this book. It should be made clear that the delay was due only to the academics involved in producing this book, not to the people at the publishing house. Many thanks to Gert De Nutte, managing editor of VUBPress, for his understanding and patience.

On behalf of the Interface Demography group,
Jan Van Bavel

About the Authors

FRANS J. WILLEKENS is director of the Netherlands Interdisciplinary Demographic Institute (NIDI) and professor of Population Studies, University of Groningen, The Netherlands. He is a member of Royal Netherlands Academy of Sciences (KNAW) and has been elected to the Cream of Science, which consists of about 200 top scientists in The Netherlands.
He studied agricultural sciences and economics at the University of Leuven, Belgium, and holds a PhD in Urban Systems Engineering and Policy Planning from Northwestern University, Evanston, Illinois, USA (1976). His current research interest is the modelling of life courses of individuals and groups as multistage stochastic processes. The models use longitudinal data and integrate insights from different disciplines. The research produces (synthetic) biographies of cohorts and individuals and provides a link between micro-level biographic change and macro-level demographic change.
Frans Willekens and colleagues took the initiative to establish the European Doctoral School of Demography (EDSD). Currently more than 20 universities and research institutes participate in the EDSD. The aim is a solid knowledge base to confront the demographic challenges Europe faces in the 21st century.

TOMÁŠ SOBOTKA is Research Scientist at the Vienna Institute of Demography of the Austrian Academy of Sciences and managing editor of the Vienna Yearbook of Population Research. He received his PhD in Demography from the Population Research Centre, University of Groningen (the Netherlands) in 2004. His main research interests are postponement of childbearing and very low fertility in industrialized countries, demography of Central and Eastern Europe, second demographic transition, cohabitation and changes in living arrangements, and childlessness.

GERDA NEYER is head of the Laboratory of Population and Policy at the Max Planck Institute for Demography, Rostock, Germany. Her research focuses on the interrelationship between welfare-state policies, gender policies, and fertility development in contemporary Europe.

JAN M. HOEM is Director at the Max Planck Institute for Demographic Research in Rostock 1999-2007, emeritus since mid-2007. Previously he founded and led the Socio-demographic Research Unit of the Central Bureau of Statistics of Norway, was Professor of Insurance Mathematics at the University of Copenhagen, and later Professor of Demometry at the University of Stockholm. Several research visits to the United States. Editor of the electronic journal Demographic Research 1999-2006. IUSSP Laureate 2006. He has published widely on methodological and empirical issues of demography.

AAT C. LIEFBROER received his PhD in Sociology from the Vrije Universiteit (VU) in Amsterdam. Currently, he is Head of the Department of Social Demography at the Netherlands Interdisciplinary Demographic Institute (NIDI) in the Hague. He holds a Professorship in Demography of Young Adulthood at the VU. Together with prof. dr. Francesco Billari, he is joint-chair of the Working Group on the Second Demographic Transition of the European Association for Population Studies. His main research interests all relate to social and demographic aspects of the life course, particularly among young adults. He has studied historical changes in the transition to adulthood, the impact of parental background, values and norms on life course decisions, cross-national differences in the transition to adulthood, the interplay between life-course events in different life-domains, and the consequences of life course transitions for well-being. He also continues to be involved in a number of large-scale data-collection efforts in the Netherlands.

TINEKE FOKKEMA received her PhD in Economics and Econometrics from the Vrije Universiteit (VU) in Amsterdam. Currently, she is a Senior Researcher at the Netherlands Interdisciplinary Demographic Institute (NIDI) in the Hague. She has participated in the development of the Generations and Gender Survey (GGS), one of the two pillars of the Generations and Gender Programme (GGP) designed to improve our understanding of demographic and social development across Europe and its determinants. She has been a member of the research team involved in the Population Policy Acceptance Study (PPAS), analysing values and attitudes towards fertility, parenthood and population related policies. Her principal research interests concern the ageing of populations, in particular the well-being and loneliness of older adults, and the patterns of intergenerational solidarity and exchange.

MICHEL POULAIN received his Masters (1978) and his PhD (1980) in Demography from the Catholic University of Louvain (UCL). Previously, he obtained a B.S in Astrophysics (1969) at the University of Liege. Since 1983, he has been professor at the faculty of Economic, Political and Social Sciences at UCL. Dr. Poulain is senior researcher at the National Research Institute (FNRS) and founder of the *Groupe d'étude de Démographie Appliquée* (GéDAP – Research Centre in Applied Demography). He has a great deal of experience in international projects. He was the project leader of THESIM (Towards Harmonised European Statistics in International Migration), an EU founded research project. He has contributed to EUROSTAT over the last two decades, working for improvements in international migration in Europe. He is scientific coordinator of FELICIE and MAGGIE, two EU founded projects, analysing the Future Elderly Living Conditions in Europe and associated Major Gender Gaps. In addition, he is involved in longevity studies in Belgium and also old age validation in Italy, Spain, Georgia and Japan. Dr. Poulain is also a well renowned specialist in applied ·demography heavily involved with policy support for many local administrations.

NICOLAS PERRIN, GéDAP, Université catholique de Louvain, Louvain-la-Neuve (Belgium) works on international migration, foreign populations and related statistical data sources.

ALBERTO PALLONI is Board of Trustees Professor of Population and Sociology at the Institute for Policy Resarch and Department of Sociology, Northwestern University. In 2006, he was also President of the Population Association of America. He received his PhD in Sociology (and Demography) in 1977 from the University of Washington and joined the University of Wisconsin Faculty in 1980. Previously he obtained his B.S / B.A from the Catholic University of Chile from 1967 to 1971. Currently his research explores health and inequality in developed countries, mortality and health disparities, statistical models for the analysis of self reported health data, aging in developing countries, effects of HIV/AIDS on families and households in Sub-Saharan Africa, relations between early health status and adult socioeconomic achievement and health status.

CAROLINA MILESI is a post-doctoral fellow at the Center for Human Potential and Public Policy at the Harris School of Public Policy Studies, University of Chicago. Carolina's research focuses on socioeconomic disparities in education and health. Her dissertation examined the trajectories youth follow in post-secondary education, and in particular the impact that increasingly alternative trajectories have had on the completion of a post-secondary degree. Her most recent work focuses on the impact that health conditions early in life have on the development of cognitive skills as children begin formal schooling. Carolina's research has been supported by the Spencer Foundation and the American Educational Research Association.

ROBERT G. WHITE is a doctoral candidate in Sociology and an affiliate of the Center for Demography and Ecology and the Center for Demography and Health of Aging at the University of Wisconsin, Madison. His research concerns health and social stratification and methods for lifecourse analysis and population health.

ALYN TURNER is a graduate student of Sociology at the University of Wisconsin-Madison. Her interests include social demography, stratification, sociology of education, and epidemiology. She defended her master's thesis in 2007, titled "Infant Health and Educational Success: Breastfeeding and High School Graduation." Her study assess the impact of infant health on adolescent educational success and identifies mechanisms that potentially mediate this relationship. Alyn is currently an Institute for Education Sciences Predoctoral Fellow at the Wisconsin Center for Education Research. She plans to finish her Ph.D. in Sociology at UW-Madison in the coming years.

VLADIMIR SHKOLNIKOV was trained as a mathematician at the Moscow Aerospace Institute and received his PhD in Social and Economical Geography from the Institute of Geography (Academy of Sciences of the USSR). In 1991 he became head of the Laboratory of Mortality analysis and Forecasting at the Center of Demography and Human Ecology in Moscow. In 2000, he joined the Max Planck Institute for Demographic Research in Rostock as a head of the Data Laboratory. His research focuses on demographic modeling, mortality differentials, macro- and micro-level epidemiological studies. He also coordinates mortality databases like Human Mortality Database, Human Life Table Database, Kannisto-Thatcher Database on Old Age Mortality and other data collection projects.

DMITRI JDANOV is a research scientist at the Data Laboratory of Max Planck Institute for Demographic Research in Germany. His main research interests are in mortality and health determinants in developed countries and in various mathematical models and methods for demographic data analysis (e.g. survival analysis and epidemiology, statistics of random processes, linear and nonlinear filtration of stochastic processes).

EMILY GRUNDY took the MSc in Medical Demography at the London School of Hygiene & Tropical Medicine and subsequently her PhD from the University of London.
She returned to the Centre for Population Studies (CPS) at LSHTM in 1998 as Reader in Social Gerontology. She was Head of the CPS from 2000 to 2003 and then was appointed Professor of Demographic Gerontology. She previously worked at the Age Concern Institute of Gerontology, King's College London, and prior to that in the Social Statistics Research Unit at City University and in the Department of Health Care of the Elderly University of Nottingham. Her research has focused on ageing, with main interests including families and social support in later life, especially in relation to health; trends and differentials in health and disability, and the long term consequences of marital and reproductive biographies for health and social support. Emily is involved in large collaborative projects, both within and outside Europe. She chairs the European Population Association working group on Demographic Change and Care for Older People and is Vice President of the British Society for Population Studies.

Preface

This book consists mainly of scientific contributions by a few of Ron Lesthaeghe's long time colleagues and friends. When invited to participate in the conference in Ron's honour, they accepted our invitation without hesitation, despite extremely busy schedules. Many others would have loved to join in as speakers (I must apologize to all of them), or have expressed sincere regrets that other obligations kept them from attending. Well known for his forthright approach, and never afraid to speak his mind, Ron was not an uncontroversial figure. It is all the more striking, that his name and presence continue to create an atmosphere of goodwill and cooperation. I consider myself very lucky to have worked and studied in that atmosphere during most of my professional life (and, as a matter of fact, for more then half of my natural life).

But is it possible to talk about Ron's personality without focusing on his professional accomplishments? And more importantly, would it capture the essence of him? I must admit to struggling with these questions! After all, in those years with Ron, first as a student and later as his teaching assistant and collaborator, teaching and research in demography were our main preoccupation. Having just finished two large scale surveys among the Turkish and Moroccan populations living in Belgium, even those holidays in Turkey and later in Morocco with the members of the research team had a scientific undertone. Had our stay been any longer, Ron would surely have become a leading expert in Greek and Roman civilizations in the Mediterranean, early Christianity in central Turkey, the Jewish heritage in Morocco and the Islamisation of Northern Africa. However, apart from his unstoppable intellectual curiosity, these trips did reveal the only entirely leisurely activity we have ever seen him indulge in: beach bumming.

At the university, Ron was appreciated as a gifted teacher. His legendary severity at exams was compensated for by the enthusiasm with which he transferred his knowledge and insight to his students. Many of them, struggling with the methodological aspects of demographic research, were enthused by his field experience and his sociological and anthropological views on the subject matter. Former students, including those who struggled most, often mention Ron's teachings as one of the highlights in their academic years.

As in everything he did, it seemed to come naturally, even effortlessly. However, after 35 years of teaching the same course he would hide away in his office half an hour before the lesson started, to prepare once more what he must by then have known by heart. This is typical of Ron: the results of his work were always more visible than the effort he put into it.

To complete this introduction, I must refer to the most influential concept that Ron (without, of course, forgetting Dick van de Kaa) developed: that of the Second Demographic Transition. It started to take shape during the first years I worked in the demography department of Brussels Free University. Demonstrating Ron's broad multi-disciplinary approach, it links earlier work on reproductive regimes, culture and social structure in sub-Saharan Africa, work on the first demographic transition in Belgium and his general interest in history and in secularization and institutional control spanning several centuries.

Two of the central values driving the Second Demographic Transition are the quest for self-actualisation and the rejection of (institutional and moral) control. In the following decade, Ron and several of his co-workers spent timeless hours searching through datasets of all kinds, to find indicators relating to these values and link them to family formation and demographic behaviour. It is certainly not a coincidence that it was precisely Ron who would play such a central role in discovering their importance for demographic change.

Ron, to put it mildly, you have always been an independent spirit and I have yet to discover the institution that has been able to impose it's moral control on you. As to self-actualisation, your hunger for more has never been satisfied.

For the future, whether lecturing before an international audience, publishing in top journals, or lying flat on your back in the sun on the beach, I'm sure that any or all of these will inspire your quest. And as to the individuals or institutions trying to get a firmer grip on your person or your thinking, I wish them courage and strength in accepting defeat.

Johan Surkyn

—

01 Laudation for Ron Lesthaeghe

Frans Willekens

Ron is one of the very few who shaped demography and population studies to what they are today. He continues to have a great impact on the way we think about fertility and the way we study demographic change. A survey carried out by CICRED in 2000 among more than 600 professional demographers worldwide indicated that professional demographers consider Ron among the 10 most influential demographers of the past half-century[1]. Ron, not only are you among the top 10 but you are also the youngest and you occupy a very central position in the networks that exist in demography.

Ron has published more than 150 papers, most in high-profile journals. The journals include Population and Development Review (8 papers) and Population Studies, but also Bevolking en Gezin (13).

Ron's influence extends beyond demography. Harry van Dalen and Kene Henkens from NIDI developed a method to assess the ranking of journals in demography and related fields in terms of the level of citations. Harry kindly agreed to apply his method to quantify the scholarly influence of Ron. Articles published by Ron in the 17 demographic journals that are included in the Social Science Citation Index (excluding Demographic Research that has been included only recently) have been cited close to 1,000 times in high-level journals. About 50 percent of the citations are in demography and about 40 percent in sociology and family studies. About 10 percent of the citations are in Population and Development Review (the highest-ranking journal in terms of the level of citations) and another 10 percent in Population Studies. Since citations to books and to publications in journals such as Demographic Research, Bevolking en Gezin and Mens en Maatschappij are not included in the SCSI and are excluded from this study, the total number of citations is several times larger than indicated here. The geographical distribution of the citations is interesting. 48 percent of the citations are by authors in the United States, 10 percent in England, 7 percent in the Netherlands and 6 percent in Belgium, the same as in Australia. The study also revealed who is citing Ron. The answer is simple: Ron is cited by top demographers publishing in top journals. Predominantly mid-career demographers and sociologists are citing Ron. It may be that mid-career scholars account for most of the publications in the past years, but it also demonstrates the strong intergenerational transfer of ideas, theories and methods generated by Ron.

1   The results of this study, carried out under the auspices of CICRED (Paris), can be found in J-C.Chasteland,
    M. Loriaux & L. Roussel (eds.), Démographie 2000, CICRED.

Ron's impact on the discipline has been acknowledged by a number of awards:

- The prestigious Irene Taueber Award (2003), awarded biennially by the Population Association of America (PAA) and the Office of Population Research of Princeton University 'in recognition of an unusually original and important contribution to the scientific study of population or an accumulated record of exceptionally sound and innovative research'.
- Ranked 10 among the most influential demographers in the world in the period 1950-2000 by respondents in the survey of professional demographers worldwide.
- Elected to the Belgian Royal Academy of Arts and Sciences (1996) and to the Netherlands Academy of Sciences (1999) (buitenlands lid; foreign member)
- The Ernest Solvay Prize (2005) awarded to a single person every five years by the FWO-Vlaanderen (Belgian Science Foundation - Flanders) for outstanding scientific career and contributions in the social sciences and humanities. The Ernest Solvay Prize is the highest award of the Belgian National Science Foundations for research in the social sciences and humanities.
- Visiting professorships at Paris (Colson Chair), Harvard (Erasmus Chair), UCL (Leclerc Chair) and Antwerp (Franqui Chair).

Ron, you reached the top relatively early in your professional life and you settled there. As a matter of fact, you feel quite confident and you seem to like it too. How did you get there? Would someone, say 30 years ago, have been able to predict your success and achievements? Let's look at how it started. Most of the information I use is published material accessible on the internet. Let's use that information to reconstruct Ron's professional biography. In their book Looking at lives: American longitudinal studies in the twentieth century (Russell Sage, 2002), Phelps, Furstenberg and Colby stress that lives are shaped by complex interplay with other people (families, communities, cohorts) and are shaped by contingencies in the context in which the life is lived (p. 8). The book describes the lives of social scientists involved in multiyear, often lifelong, projects. It illustrates how interests, personality and context shape a person's life.

In 1967, at the age of 22 Ron (born 2nd June 1945), obtained his university degree in political and social sciences magna cum laude from Ghent University. He had entered the university in 1963 at the age of 18 and completed the 4-year study programme in 4 years. That already is a good start. The study period in Ghent coincided with the student uprising in the late 1960s. At that time, many students not only selected to study political and social sciences but were also actively involved in the frequent protests. Ron was able to resist the lure of participatory observation of the exciting social changes going on at that time to concentrate more on the study of change instead. A strong character is a necessary condition to pursue a goal and to make a difference in life. During this period, Ron became interested in demography. The lectures of Martha Versichelen and particularly the book by Roland Pressat L'Analyse demographique (PUF, 1961) triggered the interest. Ron had a perfect start to become a demographer: Pressat's book, the opportunity to analyse large amounts of published and unpublished data at what is now Statistics Belgium (NIS) in Brussels (Mr. Schobbens), and the right mentors. That early project at Statistics Belgium is probably the start of a special relation with the NIS that will become very important later in his professional life and that has benefited both the university and Statistics Belgium.

Immediately after graduation at Ghent University Ron obtained a Fulbright Fellowship to continue his study in the United States and went to Brown University for a masters programme. The Fulbright Program is considered one of the most important investments the United States had made to build bridges between people and foster mutual understanding around the globe. Fulbright Fellowships were given to a very select group of students who had the potential to become leaders in science or government. At Brown Ron combined his study with a teaching assistantship in statistics and social science research methods. That teaching did not prevent him from getting the degree within a year (1968), at the age of 23. An exceptional accomplishment indeed and that was just the start. After graduation from Brown Ron took a summer job at the Population Council in New York to help analyse a demographic survey in urban Morocco. In that same year (1968) he published his first paper based on his work at the Population Council. The paper was on Africa (fertility in urban areas of Morocco) and was published in an African journal Bulletin Economique et Social de Maroc. Ron was the sole author. To me it demonstrates that he was motivated, willing to take risks, and had a good level of self-efficacy.

In September 1968, when the student revolt in Europe was at its peak, Ron returned to Ghent for PhD research, funded by an NFWO (Belgian National Science Foundation) fellowship. Professor Versichelen and Professor Picard, who had been on the jury of his undergraduate thesis, were his supervisors. Loyalty is characteristic for Ron. The dissertation was on mathematical demography: the Leslie matrix and the theory of stable and quasi-stable populations. That theory was applied to assess the impact of the fertility transition on the age structure of a population. Ron completed the dissertation in less than two years and obtained his PhD degree from Ghent University in June 1970 (maxima cum laude) in precisely the same month he celebrated his 25th birthday. To summarize, in the month Ron reached 25, he had completed a university degree, an MA degree in an Ivy League university in the United States, and a PhD degree maxima cum laude. He had also accumulated working experience in Brussels (NIS) and at two different places in the United States, including New York. And he had published internationally. These developments early in life must have strengthened his belief about his capabilities to produce high levels of performance and his ability to influence events that affect the course of life, the basic ingredients of self-efficacy.

Ron, if at that time someone would have been asked to predict your career path, given that empirical evidence on the early stage of your professional life and what we know today about the effects of early-life experiences on values, orientations, attitudes and behaviour in later life, he or she would probably have predicted your life course within a certain margin of error. Recipients of a Fullbright Fellowship are known to demonstrate academic excellence and strong leadership in their respective fields. It is a strong predictor of success. The sequence and timing of events during the transition of adulthood are also good predictors. The preconditions for success - being talented and intelligent, energetic and ambitious - were present and certainly helped you along your career path. You have an independent mind, which is a prerequisite for creativity, and you are persistent and selfconfident, prerequisites for innovation. These are necessary conditions for success but they are not sufficient. Being at the right place at the right time is important too, as we will see.

After completing your PhD in 1970, you became Research Assistant at the Centre for Population & Family Studies (CBGS), Ministry of Public Health, Brussels. At CBGS, you worked on social housing in Belgium and, with Rob Cliquet and others, on developing an interdisciplinary research project on fertility and partner relations that was published in Bevolking en Gezin/Population et Famille. I guess that few people expected you to stay in Belgium, given your life course up to the age of 25.

1971 is the year of random events that will determine your subsequent lifepath. Shortly after you started at CBGS, your dissertation De ergodiciteit van de leeftijdsstructuur en demografische transitie (Age structure ergodicity and demographic transition) caught the attention of people at the Office of Population Research (OPR) at Princeton University. You had sent copies to several Belgian demographers, and one reached Ansley Coale through Etienne van de Walle, a Belgian demographer affiliated with OPR. Ansley Coale was involved in an ambitious study of the decline in fertility in a number of European countries and the reconstruction of the demographic transition at subnational level (provinces). The aim was to determine under what conditions the decline of fertility in each province occurred. The Princeton European Fertility Project had started in 1964 and had already resulted in a book by Massimo Livi Bacci on Portugal (1971) and three others were underway: John Knodel on Germany (1974), Etienne van de Walle on France (1974) and Massimo Livi Bacci on Italy (1977). You left for Princeton as a Visiting Research Associate. During your stay at Princeton, you met Hilary.

The period in Princeton resulted in your first publication in Population Studies (1971) and a report to the United Nations, co-authored by Etienne van de Walle.

In the fall of 1971 you were appointed lecturer in Social Science Research Methods at the Free University of Brussels and returned to Belgium. One of the outcomes of the students' uprising in the 1960s was that the university of Brussels was split into two independent universities: a French-speaking university and a Dutch-speaking university, the VUB. The VUB was established in 1970. That created career opportunities for promising young scholars. Your appointment in 1971 would be the beginning of a career at the Free University with a professorship in 1977 at the age of 32. The assignment was to teach methods courses to students in the social and behavioural sciences. Demography was not part of your teaching assignment, but that would change later and your research in demography continued to develop in the meantime. In the early days, the VUB was located in the Glaverbel building at Watermaal-Bosvoorde. I was told that you frequently stayed overnight to complete your work. Also that you combined work at the university with your military service. Given your previous life course, that does not come as a surprise. You had already demonstrated that you are able to manage several activities simultaneously.

In the fall of 1971 you got an established position at the university. On 25 December 1971, you and Hilary married. You did what was expected at that time: first build a career and then marry.

After returning to Belgium in 1971 the work on the Princeton project continued. It resulted in the book: "The Decline of Belgian Fertility, 1800-1970", Princeton Univ. Press (1977) and in 8 articles and chapters, occasionally co-authored (C. Wilson, E. van de Walle, J. Duchène). More importantly, you showed that secularization, the breakdown of traditional religious authority and the decrease of adherence to organized forms of religion and the associated rejection of traditional values and modes of thinking, is equally important as economic factors in explaining changes in fertility behaviour. Secularization (measured by voting behaviour) is singled out as the most important variable at the onset of fertility decline and the one with the longest lasting effect or the highest degree of persistence (1977, p. 230). Secularization will remain a dominant variable in your research.

At the VUB, you had a heavy teaching load. The main duty of a professor at a Belgian university at that time was not research but teaching, and preferably teaching large groups of students. You managed to continue your research and to obtain external funding to support a research team. From the mid-seventies to the mid-eighties, the CBGS was a partner in research. With funds from the CBGS, you and your team developed the first demographic-economic model of Belgium and estimated the social and economic consequences of alternative demographic futures (Janus project). The model, which resulted in a major publication in 1979, showed the National Bureau of Economic Analysis (Planbureau) the way to model the interaction between demographics and the economy. The model was later used (in collaboration with Johan Surkyn) to assess the demographic consequences of immigration (several years before the United Nations report on replacement migration, published in 2000), and (in cooperation with Meeusen and Van de Walle of the University of Antwerp) to study the consequences of changes in fertility, mortality and migration on the economy and the welfare state. Ron, you are an exceptional scholar with a broad interest who reaches out to other disciplines and who is able to maintain the focus that is needed to produce results.

In 1975, Africa called. Hilary got you interested in Africa. You and Hilary became the Population Council representatives in Lagos for programmes in Western Africa broadly defined. Around that time, John Bongaarts of the Population Council was developing models of the intermediate fertility variables to disentangle the effects of different proximate determinants on fertility decline in developing countries. A questionnaire was developed and a survey organized in Lagos. The Lagos survey was a prototype for parts of the World Fertility Survey (WFS) organized in a large number of developing countries from 1976 to the 1980s - when the WFS was replaced by the Demographic and Health Surveys (DHS) that continue today to be organized in developing countries and countries in transition. When you returned to Brussels in 1977, the WFS was well underway and your team at the VUB participated actively in the analysis, funded by mainly American funds. That resulted in two books Child spacing in tropical Africa (1981) and Reproduction and social organization in sub-Saharan Africa (1989) and numerous articles. At WFS headquarters in London, you and Hilary provided training in questionnaire design and data analysis.

The Africa experience, the WFS data waiting to be analysed and the composition of your team at the VUB with Philip van Praag, Stan Wijewickrema (from 1972), Hilary (from 1977) and others was a perfect condition to start a training programme oriented towards students from developing countries. In 1977 the Interuniversity Programme in Demography (IPD) was established. The first cohort of master students enrolled in February 1977, 13 in total (3 from Belgium and 9 from developing countries). Three of these students will subsequently continue for a PhD. Today, they are internationally acknowledged demographers: Oleke Tambashe, Iqbal Shah and P.S. Nair. IPD was a joint venture of the VUB, CBGS and the universities of Leuven and Ghent. The Belgian government provided fellowships. The programme included courses on demographic analysis, mathematics, statistics, computer programming, epidemiology, psychology, sociology and economics. IPD was a unique experiment. I was very fortunate to be part of IPD from 1978 to 1982. IPD generated several other excellent PhD candidates until the programme was discontinued and replaced by the Interface Demography, the new unit for population research at the VUB (1988). Interuniversity cooperation is extremely difficult, as many who tried have experienced. When the University of Groningen established the international master and PhD programme in Population Studies, IPD was the model.

After the IPD experience, two new developments were initiated. The first development was initiated by the observation that you could study third-world populations right here in Belgium. You and Hilary had seen that migration and minority populations will become an important issue in Belgium and much of Europe. Your attention shifted to minority populations in Belgium, mainly the populations of Turkish and Moroccan origin. That research got a push when in 1989 the extreme right party Vlaams Blok made a major leap forward. The federal government (DWTC) contributed significantly to a major interuniversity research programme on integration and you were ready, willing and able to do the research (in cooperation with colleagues at the VUB and Hilary and her associates at Ghent University). The empirical evidence was collected in surveys among Turkish and Moroccan women and (later) men. Two books were the result: Diversiteit in sociale verandering: Turkse en Marokkaanse vrouwen in Belgie (1997), Communities and generations: Turkish and Moroccan populations in Belgium (2000) and the edited volume Denken over migranten in Europa (Reflections on migrants in Europe) (1993) and several articles.

The second development was triggered, also in the mid-1980s, by a decision of the editor of the sociology journal Mens en Maatschappij to a produce a special book volume of the on demographic developments in the Low Countries (Special issue – Groei en Krimp). Dick van de Kaa was approached to edit the volume with the suggestion that perhaps he could work with Lesthaeghe to produce a well-balanced book. The editor of Mens en Maatschappij did probably not realize that the decision to bring these two outstanding people together to edit a volume would produce a paradigm shift in demography. Fertility and marriage variables indicated that from the mid-sixties onward a fundamental change had taken place in fertility and marriage behaviour. Fertility had steadily declined, the age at marriage was rising, childbearing occurred at higher ages, cohabitation and extra-marital fertility were on the increase and using efficient contraception seemed to become the rule. A shift in the demographic regime of the developed countries of Europe had occurred and that shift was linked to changes in the dominant family model. The traditional family model was being replaced by 'an individualistic family model' with an emphasis on self-development, individual autonomy and gender equality. Individual choice within a wider range of family forms and wider variations in family life courses were becoming accepted. Better educated men and women held secular and anti-authoritarian sentiments and had stronger "postmaterialist" political orientations demonstrated by their voting behaviour. As a result of these changes, the traditional links between sexuality, marriage and childbearing weakens substantially and the child occupies a smaller place in a marriage than before (Aries). The expectation was that the very low, below replacement levels of fertility observed at that time would not be a temporary phenomenon but would be here to stay. A new demographic transition seemed to be on its way. The paper in Mens en Maatschappij was given the title 'Twee demografische transities?' (Lesthaeghe and

Van de Kaa, 1986). The concept of the Second Demographic Transition was launched and it became the dominant model to address issues of sub-replacement fertility. The concept has been used in hundreds of articles and papers.

Ron, you were able to demonstrate the significance of ideational factors in behavioural change, in addition to technological and structural (e.g. economic) factors. You demonstrated a two-way interaction between value change and behavioural change: value change leads to behavioural change and behavioural change enforces value change (= selection). It is a source of inspiration for many in Europe and beyond. Two Euresco conferences have been devoted to the subject (in Bad Herrenalb and Spa) followed by conferences in Vienna (2005) and Budapest (2007). Even the United Nations adopted the concept to comprehend demographic changes in the developed world. The theory applies, not only in Europe, but in different societies around the globe including Japan, South India and the United States. Twenty years after launching the concept of the Second Demographic Transition, it becomes clear that the transition is not a European phenomenon but a global phenomenon that is tied to the adoption of values of individual autonomy, not only for men but also for women.

The theory has important implications for the future of the world and of Europe in particular. If a causal link exists between the position of the individual in society and the postponement of childbearing, fertility decline to sub-replacement levels may be expected in societies that promote individual rights and responsibilities. The impact of the Second Demographic Transition is significant (Lesthaeghe and Surkyn, 2006, Justitiële Verkenningen):

• Ageing as a result of sub-replacement fertility
• Greater dependency on immigration leading to multi-ethnic societies
• Limited emphasis on social cohesion
• Instability of the family

The concept of the Second Demographic Transition inspired scholars in other disciplines, such as epidemiology. The concept of the Second Epidemiological Transition (SET) was introduced by Rudi Westendorp in his inaugural lecture at the University of Leiden (15th June 2001) and is spreading. It contrasts the First Epidemiological Transition, marked by the emergence of infections. In the SET, public health measures, improved nutrition and medicine result in declines in infectious disease and a rise in chronic and degenerative diseases. The acceptance of the concept of SET is no way near that of the Second Demographic Transition (SDT). A Google search produces more than 35,000 hits for the SDT (1,200 in Google Scholar) and 48 for the SET.

On October 1, 2005, after 34 years of teaching and research at the frontier of demography, you decided to leave teaching to the younger cohort and to focus on research instead. You are one of the most eminent scholars the VUB ever had. On several occasions, renowned universities and institutions in the world tried hard to lure you away from the VUB, including Princeton in the mid-1980s. But you remained. You contributed significantly to the university's reputation internationally. Many people in the world know and acknowledge the VUB because of you. Your retirement from the VUB does not imply a retirement from academia and from research. You seem to be busier than ever.

L'Analyse demographique by Roland Pressat and the undergraduate lectures in demography given by Martha Versichelen in Ghent triggered your initial interest in demography, and that interest subsequently had an effect on the discipline no-one at that time would have been able or willing to predict. Several events along the way challenged you to use your talents and your energy, which you did to the benefit of the entire demographic community today and tomorrow. An exceptional accomplishment by an exceptional person. Ron, on behalf of that community and on my own behalf, a special thank you.

–

02 Does persistent low fertility threaten the future of European populations?

Tomáš Sobotka

1. Introduction

Three stylised demographic facts are nowadays taken for granted by many Europeans: First, European birth rates are very low and further declining. Second, the currently low fertility will inevitably lead to rapid population ageing and population decline in the future. Third, these trends are unsustainable in the long run and constitute serious threats to the economy, the labour market, the welfare system, and to the foundations of European societies. Politicians and demographers are particularly concerned about this perspective. In the Green Paper on "Confronting Demographic Change", an official discussion document of the European Commission published in 2005, the low birth rate is mentioned as a "challenge for the public authorities" (p. 5) and a "return to demographic growth" as the first out of three "essential priorities" which Europe should pursue to face up demographic change. Perhaps no one summarised the fears of shrinking Europe more succinctly than Pope Benedict XVI during his Christmas address to the Roman Curia in December 2006: "...the problem of Europe, which it seems no longer wants to have children, penetrated my soul. To foreigners this Europe seems to be tired, indeed it seems to be wishing to take its leave of history" (Vatican 2006). The Pope linked this perceived lack of interest in children to several factors, which are familiar to scholars studying contemporary family and fertility change. He posited that "contemporary man is insecure about the future," unsure about the norms and rules for life. Furthermore, he mentioned a 'problem' of definitive decisions, before lamenting the "relativisation of the difference between sexes". Were he a secular person talking to a different audience, he might also have said that changed norms and values are intrinsically linked to the lack of interest in childbearing among contemporary Europeans. This argument finds parallels in the concept of the second demographic transition (SDT) whose two main protagonists, Ron Lesthaeghe and Dirk van de Kaa, have repeatedly linked the declining fertility rates observed in most regions of Europe in the 1970s and later to broad societal and cultural changes, marked by a rise of secular individualism, the quest for individual self-fulfilment, and a decline of the traditional 'bourgeois' family.

The fears of a population and fertility slump in Europe are not new and have been repeatedly voiced since the late 19th century (Teitelbaum and Winter 1985), especially in times when birth rates in many European societies declined rapidly. Some well-known alarmist examples in this respect are books like "The Decline of the West," published first in 1918 by German philosopher Oswald Spengler, "The Twilight of Parenthood," published in 1934 by Enid Charles, a lecturer at the London School of Economics (and later republished under the title "The Menace of Under-population") and Debré and Sauvy's (1946) laments about the aged, sclerotic, and shrinking French population. A new wave of such publications has come up since the 1970s, concomitant to the rapid decline in fertility rates in most European societies. Already in 1984, the European Parliament passed a resolution calling for "measures to combat this marked trend towards population decline, which is common to all the member states" (by then comprising ten countries; PDR 1984). And even in the United States, where fertility rates are well above those of any larger country of Europe except France, books such as "The Empty Cradle" by Philip Longman (2004) warn of rapidly ageing societies challenged by the loss of economic prosperity and innovativeness. Jean-Claude Chesnais, a prominent French demographer, in 2001 suggested that after experiencing the population explosion of the 20th century, the 21st century might be a period when mankind will experience a population implosion, and this implosion may be particularly pronounced in Europe.

Should these renewed fears of childless, aged and shrinking societies be renounced as unwarranted and exaggerated, similar to those painting a gloomy portrait of European population decline just a few decades before the baby boom of the 1950s and 1960s took place? There are many good reasons to be seriously concerned about the future fertility and population trends in Europe. In contemporary European societies voluntary childlessness is commonly accepted as a lifestyle choice, whereas large family sizes have become unusual. Many countries have experienced several decades of very low fertility levels and some have already seen extended periods of population decline (Eurostat 2006a). Three-quarters of Europeans in 2005 lived in countries with period total fertility rates (TFR) below 1.5 (Eurostat 2007). Today we have at our disposal better data, analytical tools and projection methods that avoid many errors that were inherent in the first forecasts done more than half a century ago. And contemporary projections do support many fears commonly voiced about Europe's demographic future. The population momentum inherent in the current age structure that has developed during the previous decades of low fertility will eventually bring negative rates of natural increase in most European countries and in Europe as such (Lutz, O'Neill and Scherbov 2003). Likewise, a relatively rapid population ageing will inevitably occur in the coming decades and the official projection of Eurostat (2006c) envisions that the European population will start shrinking after 2025. Working-age population is also projected to decline rapidly. On a global scale, a demographic marginalisation of Europe is well underway (Demeny 2003) and this may lead to a rapid decline in the future cultural and economic importance of Europe.

Yet, despite this list of likely demographic troubles to come, which could be further expanded, there are also reasons for a less gloomy evaluation of some current and the likely future population trends in Europe. This contribution focuses on selected trends and cross-country differences in fertility, many of which are commonly seen as the main 'causes' of the envisioned future demographic decline of Europe. In addition, the article assesses the importance of observed fertility trends in conjunction with migration which has a rising influence on European population. It does not attempt to provide a comprehensive review of all the important changes in fertility in different parts of Europe and the factors behind them—such an overview would be excessively large and would repeat much of the valuable analysis provided in a number of other publications (e.g., Engelhardt and Prskawetz 2004; Lesthaeghe and Moors 2000; Kohler, Billari and Ortega 2002; Morgan 2003; Billari and Kohler 2004; Sobotka 2004a; Billari 2005; Frejka and Sardon 2004; Morgan and Taylor 2006). Instead, I look at selected important developments and factors which have been rather neglected in contemporary literature on European fertility but which are important for our assessment of future fertility trends. In doing so, I pay little attention to a number of factors affecting fertility which are well represented in recent studies, among them the topics of women's labour participation, family policies, gender equality and reconciliation of work and childbearing, the influence of welfare state regimes, and the effects of education on fertility (some of them are discussed in the concluding section). To further narrow down the scope of this contribution, I also omit the discussion on the specific factors affecting fertility trends in the former Communist societies during the transformation period after 1989 (see chapters 7-8 in Sobotka 2004a).

Throughout this paper I aim to pursue the following hypotheses:
• Extremely low period total fertility rates, observed at present in many parts of Europe, are linked to the rapid postponement of childbearing, and are likely to be temporary;
• Very low fertility rates are often related to economic, cultural and institutional constraints which may be reduced in the future;
• The second demographic transition is closely linked to fertility postponement, but not necessarily to below-replacement fertility level;
• Pronounced differences in low fertility are characteristic of contemporary Europe and are likely to prevail;
• If migration is taken into account, population replacement rates are close to the threshold necessary for stable or increasing population in most regions of Europe;
• Therefore, very low fertility and the threat of marked population decline constitute a regional problem rather than a threat for the whole of Europe.

Overall, this contribution argues that the occasionally predicted spiral of declining number of births and declining population size is not an inevitable future of European population, especially when the European Union as a whole is considered. While some regions are likely to experience considerable and long-lasting population decline, other regions may see continuing population increase, extended well beyond the mid-21st century. A slight increase in fertility combined with relatively high immigration may be the major factors to bring about such developments.

This article is structured as follows. The second section analyses the recent spread of low and lowest-low fertility in Europe and outlines the persistent trend towards delayed childbearing. Selected insights from cohort analysis are used to illustrate the long history of sub-replacement fertility and the variability in contemporary low fertility in Europe. The third section reviews changes in the family context of childbearing and discusses the effects of union instability, the decline of marriage as well as the suggested retreat from fatherhood, on fertility. The fourth section shows that the second demographic transition has become positively linked to fertility in a cross-country perspective. The fifth section assesses the importance of migration for European fertility and the role of migration for sustaining population size in many European countries. The final section discusses the current positive association between the second demographic transition and fertility, summarises reasons why European fertility rates might increase in the future, and reiterates the importance of migration for European population trends.

2. Selected trends and features of contemporary fertility in Europe

2.1. The spread of low and very low fertility in Europe

Trends in the most commonly used indicator of period fertility—the total fertility rate (TFR)—seem to leave little doubt about the unprecedented extent of currently very low fertility in Europe. In 2005, 25 out of 39 European countries with population above 100,000 recorded TFR below 1.5 (see Figure 1). These countries represent almost three quarters of the European population. All countries of Europe reached below-replacement fertility, with the TFR lower than 2.0. In comparison, no European country had a period TFR below 1.7 in 1970. Furthermore, since the early 1990s, an increasing number of countries of southern and central-eastern Europe experienced a decline of the period TFR towards the 'lowest-low' levels below 1.3 (Kohler, Billari and Ortega 2002). This trend has culminated in 2002, when one-half of Europeans lived in societies with such low TFR levels.

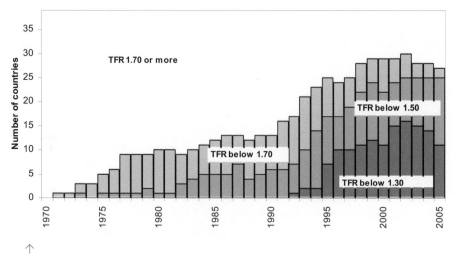

↑

Figure 1: Number of European countries with the period TFR below 1.7, 1.5 and 1.3 in 1970-2005 (out of 39 countries with population above 100,000)

Source: Computations based on Eurostat (2007) and Council of Europe (2006).

Note: Montenegro and Kosovo counted as a part of the former republic of Serbia-Montenegro

This general picture may be misleading, however. Extreme low levels of the period TFR are closely associated with a rapid postponement of parenthood towards higher reproductive ages and are likely to be temporary (see section 2.3 below). Furthermore, contemporary low fertility in Europe is regionally differentiated. Many countries of western and northern Europe that had experienced rapid falls in the TFR below 2.0 already in the early 1970s subsequently retained the TFR relatively close to this threshold, with a recent increasing tendency (Figure 2). France stands out as the only larger European country that recorded a rise in the TFR to 2.0 in 2006. In contrast, German-speaking countries (Austria, Germany and Switzerland), southern Europe and, most recently, countries of central-eastern Europe have seen much deeper falls in the period TFR. Numerous cultural, institutional and economic factors have been proposed to explain these regional divides (Esping-Andersen 1999; Caldwell and Schindlmayr 2003; McDonald 2000; Rindfuss, Guzzo and Morgan 2003; Adsera 2004; Billari and Kohler 2004). Nevertheless, a proper understanding of the emerging cross-country differences in fertility rates cannot be achieved with crude and rather simplistic measures such as the TFR. Cross-country diversity needs to be assessed with parity-specific period and cohort fertility rates, which are briefly analysed in section 2.4 below.

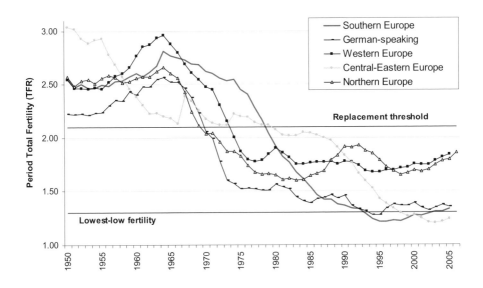

↑

Figure 2: Period total fertility rate in European regions, 1950-2006

Source: Computations based on Eurostat (2007), Council of Europe (2006), Festy (1979),
Chesnais (1992) and national statistical data.

Notes: Data are weighted by population size of given countries and regions.

Countries are grouped into regions as follows:

Western Europe: Belgium, France, Ireland, Luxembourg, the Netherlands, United Kingdom;

German-speaking countries: Austria, Germany, Switzerland;

Northern Europe: Denmark, Finland, Iceland, Norway, Sweden;

Southern Europe: Cyprus, Greece, Italy, Malta, Portugal, Spain;

Central-eastern Europe: Croatia, Czech Republic, Estonia, Hungary, Latvia, Lithuania,
Poland, Slovakia, Slovenia, Bosnia-Herzegovina, Bulgaria, Macedonia, Montenegro, Romania,
Serbia (recent data exclude Kosovo).

2.2. Persistent delay of childbearing and rising social status heterogeneity in first birth

Lesthaeghe and Moors (2000) have suggested that the postponement of parenthood
has become the hallmark of the second demographic transition. Whereas many
interrelated social, economic and lifestyle changes have been identified as the driving
forces of the shift towards delayed entry into parenthood (Sobotka 2004a, chapter 2),
late childbearing also constitutes a strategy that is consistent with the expected decline
in the relative importance of children and family life for individuals' self-realisation.
Initiated in the early 1970s in western and northern Europe, the shift towards later
parenthood had reached all corners of Europe by the late 1990s. Women in Greece,

Italy and Spain and most countries of western and northern Europe give birth to their first child at ages 28-29 on average, up from age 24-25 in the early 1970s (Figure 3). The overall mean age at childbearing has surpassed 30 in the majority of these countries. The frequency of 'late' births (births to women over age 40) has increased sharply since the late 1980s, especially in the case of first births, bringing a reversal to the long-standing downward trend initiated by the first demographic transition (Sobotka, Kohler and Billari 2007). At the same time, the pace of first-birth postponement has been slowing down since the late 1990s in all parts of Europe except the post-communist countries of central-eastern Europe where childbearing postponement has become particularly pervasive. Although young cohorts of women in northern, western and southern Europe do not show signs of much additional delay of childbearing, there is still scope for a further shift towards later parenthood (Goldstein 2006): most women can fulfil a typical desire for a two-child family even when they have a first child after age 30.

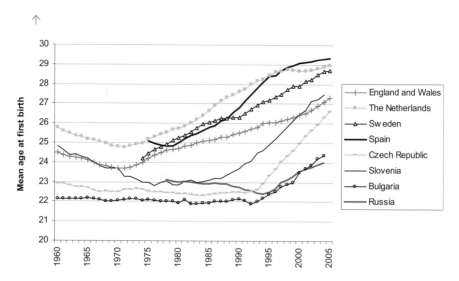

Figure 3: Mean age of mother at birth of first child, selected countries of Europe (1950-2005)
Source: Computations based on Eurostat (2007), Council of Europe (2006), Smallwood (2002), Vishnevski (2006) and national statistical data.

Not all social groups have postponed parenthood to the same extent: women with tertiary education have frequently shifted birth of their first child after the age of 30, whereas women with low qualification usually give birth to their first child at an early age, often as teenagers (McLanahan 2004). The resulting rise of social status heterogeneity in the timing of first birth has been most pronounced in countries with 'liberal' welfare regimes that are characterised by larger social disparities—England and Wales, Ireland and, outside Europe, in the United States (Sobotka 2004a: Table 3.5). This trend is a part of a broader shift towards the 'polarisation' in the timing and pathways to parenthood (Ravanera and Rajulton 2004). McLanahan (2004) argues that the increasing divergence in partnership, family, and work trajectories of low-educated and highly educated women and their partners is linked to an increasingly disadvantaged economic position of the former group.

2.3. Delayed childbearing and very low fertility

Fertility postponement negatively affects both the observed number of births and the commonly used fertility indicators as some of the births that would have been realised in a given period were put off into the future. This distortion, frequently called 'tempo effect' is temporary and persists only as long as the shift in fertility timing takes place. However, contemporary progression of delayed parenthood is unique in its intensity and duration—in some countries continuing for more than three decades. Not surprisingly, there are sceptical voices suggesting that the envisioned 'recovery' in period fertility may not take place. For instance, McDonald (2006: 487) noted that waiting for the tempo effect to disappear is "beginning to look like waiting for Godot." The possibility that the end of fertility postponement may not be linked to a notable rise in period fertility rates cannot be ruled out: Bongaarts (2002) outlines a scenario in which a parallel decline in the underlying fertility level may erase most of the gains associated with the ending of fertility postponement.

However, recent experience of many advanced societies shows that the cessation, or slowing down, of childbearing postponement, as reflected in the stabilization of the mean age at first birth, is linked to a significant rise in the ordinary TFR. The decline in the intensity of fertility postponement after 2000 is probably the main factor explaining the recent modest increase in the TFR in many countries of Europe. But how much can the TFR increase once the postponement stops in all parts of Europe? Lesthaeghe and Willems (1999) emphasised that it is highly unlikely that total fertility would bounce back to the replacement level. On the low side of fertility spectrum, my analysis (Sobotka 2004b) suggested that the end of fertility postponement in the countries with the lowest-low period TFR below 1.3 would probably bring an increase above this level in all parts of Europe. Table 1 presents an update of this analysis, using estimates of the adjusted TFR proposed by Bongaarts and Feeney (1998) and computed by the Vienna

Institute of Demography for the period 2001-2003 (VID 2006). This method estimates the period TFR that would have been achieved in the absence of tempo effects. Because the adjusted TFR is based on several assumptions and may fluctuate considerably for individual countries, I provide a summary of results for different regions of Europe and do not show data for individual countries.[1]

Table 1: Period TFR and tempo-adjusted TFR in European regions, 1995-2000 and 2001- 2003
↓

	Population size, mill.	TFR		Adjusted TFR (Bongaarts-Feeney)		Cohort TFR
	2002	1995-2000	2002	1995-2000	2001-2003 or most recent	1960 cohort
Western Europe	149.3	1.71	1.75	1.88	1.92	2.02
Northern Europe	24.3	1.70	1.70	1.94	1.96	2.00
German-speaking countries	97.8	1.35	1.32	1.52	1.53	1.67
Southern Europe	120.4	1.23	1.28	1.59	1.43	1.74
Central-eastern Europe	77.6	1.40	1.25	1.74	1.66	2.10
South-eastern Europe	43.7	1.43	1.33	1.67	1.64	2.14
Eastern Europe	205.8	1.25	1.25	1.46	1.45	1.85
EU-15	378.6	1.47	1.49	1.70	1.67	1.84
EU-12 new (2004 & 2007)	104.1	1.36	1.24	1.67	1.63	2.10
EU-27	482.6	1.45	1.44	1.69	1.66	1.89
Europe	722	1.46	1.39	1.63	1.61	1.89

Source: Computations based on VID (2006), Eurostat (2007), Council of Europe (2006), Sobotka (2004b) and national statistical data.

Notes: Data are weighted by population size of given countries and regions. Countries are grouped into regions as follows: Eastern Europe: Belarus, Moldova (excluding Transnistria),

---

1   Among various adjustment methods, Bongaarts-Feeney's adjustment is the least data intensive and easiest to compute. Various papers have discussed or questioned its results and theoretical assumptions (e.g., Lesthaeghe and Willems 1999; van Imhoff 2001). Given the limited data availability for computing more sophisticated indicators, I consider this indicator a reasonably good approximation of fertility quantum, especially when summarised for longer time periods or for regions broader than individual countries. The relative stability of this measure between 1995-2000 and 2001-2003 in most regions of Europe lends support to this argument.

Russia (including Asian part), Ukraine.
Central-eastern Europe: Croatia, Czech Republic, Estonia, Hungary, Latvia, Lithuania, Poland, Slovakia, Slovenia.
South-Eastern Europe: Bosnia-Herzegovina, Bulgaria, Macedonia, Montenegro, Romania, Serbia (except Kosovo).
For other regions see Figure 2.

The Table shows much stability in both the ordinary TFR and the adjusted TFR during the analysed period (more recently the TFR has increased in most regions, see Figure 2). While the TFR further declined in the former communist countries of central-eastern and eastern Europe, the adjusted TFR declined in southern Europe and central-eastern Europe. The European Union (27 countries) had the adjusted TFR at 1.66 in 2001-2003, with both old members (EU-15) and the new member states recording very similar levels. This contrasts with the ordinary TFR which—due to intensive fertility postponement—is much lower in the new member countries that accessed the EU in 2004 and 2007 (1.24). The Table also corroborates previous findings on regional fertility contrasts in Europe. Northern and western European countries have the highest levels of both TFR and adjusted TFR, with the latter reaching above 1.9. Remarkably, the adjusted TFR in these regions comes relatively close to the replacement level as well as to the cohort TFR of women born in 1960 (2.0 on average). This suggests that fertility quantum has been relatively stable there in the last two decades. In contrast, eastern European countries of the former Soviet Union, southern Europe and the German-speaking countries of central Europe have a much lower adjusted TFR, hovering at or slightly below 1.5 in 2001-2003.

2.4. Completed fertility and parity progression ratios

Long-term data on cohort fertility put period fertility trends into a broader perspective. Figure 4, comparing completed fertility of women born since the early 20th century in selected countries of Europe, brings a number of important observations:

- Low completed fertility is not a new phenomenon emerging with the second demographic transition. At least four out of nine countries shown in Figure 4—Austria, Czech Republic, England and Wales and Sweden—achieved low cohort fertility (below 2 children per woman) among the early 20th century cohorts. In England and Wales and in Sweden, women born in the early 1960s reached higher completed fertility than the cohorts of their grandmothers born in 1905-1910;

- Relative to the replacement level threshold, cohort fertility rates of women born in the first two decades of the 20th century were lower than among those born in the 1960s in many countries of Europe. For instance, the ratio of observed cohort TFR to the replacement-level cohort TFR was 0.76 in France in the 1901 cohort, but 0.96 in the early 1960s cohorts (replacement-level cohort TFR for France is plotted in Figure 4);

- Although a majority of European countries experienced a significant fall in completed TFR among women born during the 1950s and 1960s (Frejka and Sardon 2004), there are several interesting cases that do not conform to this trend: Completed TFR of Danish women has increased slightly in the post-1955 cohorts, whereas French women born in the early 1970s are projected to achieve a stable fertility level of 2.0 (Prioux 2006). On the other hand, women in southern Europe experience a particularly pronounced decline in their completed fertility and German women born in the early-1960s have seen a fall in completed TFR below 1.6.

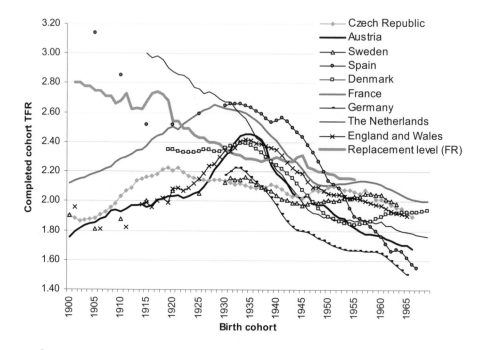

Figure 4: Completed fertility in selected countries of Europe (cohorts 1900-1968) and replacement-level fertility in France
Sources: Festy (1979), Sardon (1991), Frejka and Sardon (2004), INSEE (2007) and own computations based on Eurostat (2007) and national statistical data.

Admittedly, women born in the early 20th century experienced low fertility rates due to a combination of several factors (especially the First World War and the economic depression of the 1930s) that negatively affected their partner choice and their economic circumstances. Although this early emergence of sub-replacement fertility in Europe was closely linked to negative economic conditions (see, however, Van Bavel

2007), it also shows that under such circumstances many women and men were 'ready, willing and able' to reduce their family size to one child or abstain from having children altogether well before the onset of the second demographic transition.

Low fertility in the early 20th century cohorts was not achieved through a universal spread of low fertility: family size distribution varied greatly and both very small and large families were relatively common. In Austria, for instance, almost one-half of the women born in 1910 had no child or one child only, whereas 28 per cent of women had three or more children (data based on the 1991 Population Census). In contrast, the current low fertility is linked to a low prevalence of 'large' families (3 and more children), a strong adherence to a two-child family norm (e.g., Shkolnikov et al. 2007), and a gradual increase in the proportion of childless women and women with one child. Although childlessness has gradually increased in almost all European countries and this increase is likely to continue among women born in the 1970s (Sobotka 2005), most of the cross-country differences in completed fertility are due to differences in second-birth progression rates rather than due to an increasing rejection of parenthood. Most countries with low or rapidly declining completed fertility also have low progression rates after the first child (Billari and Kohler 2004). This pattern is typical of southern Europe, many ex-Communist countries of central and eastern Europe, and the Balkan countries. Only German-speaking countries do not fully adhere to this pattern: there, relatively low cohort fertility is closely linked to high childlessness,[2] but not to particularly low second and third-birth rates. Third-birth rates, which had been declining in all parts of Europe for many decades, recently appear to stabilise or even increase slightly in some countries of western and northern Europe, partly fuelled by the rising share of immigrants with higher fertility preferences (see also section 5 below).

It is notable that many countries of northern and western Europe manifest relatively high second-birth rates combined with a persistent preference for a family with two to three children (e.g., Testa 2006). Another remarkable feature is the apparent absence of the postponement-quantum effect in several countries that have experienced fertility delay since the early 1970s. At an individual level, later age at first birth is negatively associated with completed fertility (Toulemon 2004a) as women face declining fecundity rates, especially past age 35 (Menken 1985). A simulation model by Billari and Borgoni (2005) demonstrates that first-birth postponement leads to a rapid decline in the predicted second-birth progression rates and has a negative effect on overall completed fertility rates, especially at the 'lowest-low' fertility levels. In view of these findings it is surprising that several countries with intensive fertility delays have

---

2   Childlessness is especially high in West Germany, probably reaching above 25 percent among the mid-1960s and younger cohorts (Engstler and Menning 2003; Duschek and Wirth 2005)

not experienced a decline in second-birth rates for the cohorts born in the 1950s and 1960s. In Sweden, for instance, there was no detectable tempo-quantum effect on first, second, or third-birth rates for the cohorts of 1940-65 (Figure 5). Similar findings were also reported for Denmark, France (Toulemon and Mazuy 2001) and for second-birth rates in Austria (Prskawetz et al. 2008). In these cases, the decline in fertility rates due to postponement was counterbalanced by an increase in childbearing intensity among women past age 30. The negative effects of postponement may become more visible among younger cohorts that have further shifted childbearing to a later age. An absence of such an effect in some countries suggests that other factors than postponement were decisive in pushing second-birth rates downwards in southern Europe and elsewhere and that the decline in completed fertility observed in most countries of Europe cannot be explained by fertility postponement.

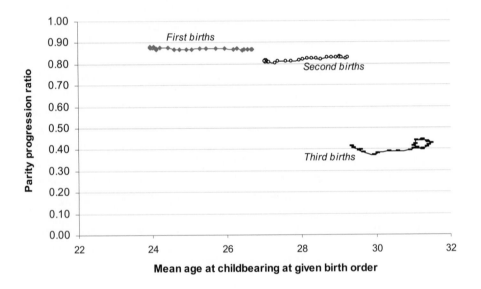

↑

Figure 5: Age at childbearing by birth order and parity progression ratios among women in Sweden born in 1940-65

Source: Author's computations based on Johansson and Finnäs (1983) and Eurostat (2007).

3. Women, men and childbearing: do family and partnership changes negatively affect fertility?

3.1. Changing living arrangements, family instability and the rise of non-marital childbearing

The postponement of entry into marriage and the decline in the proportion of people marrying are coupled with the rise of cohabitation and single living among younger persons and, in some countries, also with a delayed leaving from the parental home (Billari and Wilson 2001; Corijn and Klijzing 2001). Together with the growing instability of partnerships and unions these developments are among the behavioural cornerstones of the second demographic transition. The rise of cohabitation, documented in detail for western and northern Europe (e.g., Prinz 1995; Nazio and Blossfeld 2003; Kiernan 2004), is particularly illustrative: the prevalence of cohabitation differs between societies, but also across ages and various social groups. Among people below age 35, cohabitation has become more widespread than marriage in most western and northern European countries (Kiernan 2004: Figure 1). Heuveline and Timberlake (2004) show how the prevailing character of informal unions ranges from a relatively marginal phenomenon such as in Poland or a prelude to marriage (e.g., in Switzerland) to an alternative to marriage (e.g., in France) or a status, which has become undistinguishable from marriage (Sweden). The importance of cohabitation for childbearing depends on the extent to which cohabitation becomes a substitution for marriage and thus widely accepted and regarded as a childbearing institution (Heuveline and Timberlake 2004). The growing instability of both formal and informal unions has been one of the major forces contributing to the spread of solo parenting in many advanced societies (Heuveline, Timberlike and Furstenberg 2003).

The disconnection of childbearing from marriage is most clearly illustrated by a steep rise in the proportion of non-marital births over the last three decades which, after reaching historically low levels in the 1950s and 1960s took place since the early 1970s (earlier in northern Europe, see Figure 6). This change has accelerated in central and eastern Europe after the breakdown of the communist system in 1989 and in Italy and Spain after 1995. The recent rapid rise in extra-marital childbearing in the latter two countries may be seen as a surprise in the light of the persistent importance of marriage and traditional family bonds in these societies (Reher 1998; Dalla Zuanna 2001). It is linked to the recent rise in cohabitation (see Rossina and Fraboni 2004 for Italy), but also to an influx of immigrants from the countries where extra-marital childbearing is common (see Delgado, Meil and Zamora López 2008 for Spain). In most societies where childbearing outside wedlock had remained rare until recently, such as Belgium, Italy, or Poland, it has become a common phenomenon now. Only in Cyprus and Greece extra-marital births remain marginal, accounting for 4-5 per cent of all births in 2005. Moreover, a growing number of countries and regions register a majority of births taking place outside marriage: in 2005, Estonia, Iceland, Norway, Sweden as well as former GDR (East Germany) were in this group, whereas Bulgaria, France and Slovenia are likely to exceed the 50 per cent threshold soon as well.[3] Especially first births frequently take place outside marriage. In total, one-third of all births in the EU-25 occurred outside marriage in 2005, up from 5 per cent during the 1960s, and 18 per cent in 1990. Since 1980 this proportion has been rising steadily by about 1 per cent per year, so far without any sign of slowing down. However, if northern Europe shows the likely future trend, it reminds us that there are also limits to this increase: having reached about half of all births outside marriage, most Nordic countries experienced a stabilisation in this proportion since the late 1990s.

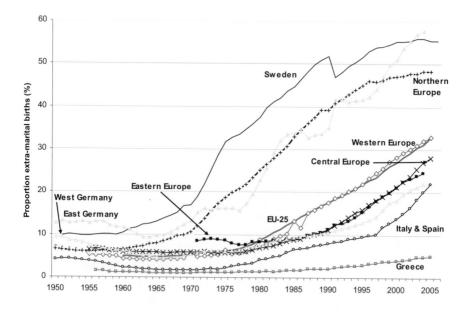

Figure 6: Proportion of children born outside marriage in selected countries and regions of Europe (1950-2005)
Sources: Council of Europe 2006, Eurostat 2006a and 2006b, Grünheid 2006.

---

3   Country-specific trends in non-marital childbearing conceal huge regional diversities, the roots of which frequently date back to the first demographic transition (Lesthaeghe and Neels 2002). Probably the most peculiar example of path-dependent persistence of two widely different patterns is the case of East and West Germany after German unification, when the proportion of non-marital births in East Germany, already high in 1989 (34 %) further skyrocketed and reached 58 % in 2004, contrasting with 22 % in West Germany (Grünheid 2006 (data exclude the Berlin region); see also Konietzka and Kreyenfeld 2002 and Sales 2006).

Note: Countries are grouped into regions as follows: Western Europe: Austria, Belgium, France, Germany, Ireland, Luxembourg, the Netherlands, Switzerland, United Kingdom. Northern Europe: Denmark, Finland, Iceland, Norway, Sweden. Eastern Europe: Belarus, Moldova (excluding Transnistria), Russia (including Asian part), Ukraine. Central Europe: Croatia, Czech Republic, Hungary, Poland, Slovakia, Slovenia.

Childbearing outside marriage covers various family forms, which have different implications for economic position and well-being of parents and their children (Heuveline, Timberlike and Furstenberg 2003; Kiernan 2004). In north-western Europe most extra-marital births are planned, intended by both parents and take place within the context of stable cohabiting unions. In Sweden, where the proportion of extra-marital births has been the second highest in Europe for many decades (after Iceland), only around one-tenth of births occur to single mothers and many couples marry after having their first or second childbirth (Oláh and Bernhardt 2008). In contrast, in central and eastern Europe a large portion of extra-marital births occurs to single mothers (Heuveline, Timberlike and Furstenberg 2003). Coleman 2006a posits that such patterns are partly fuelled by specific welfare policies providing support to single mothers (see also Gonzáles 2005). Data for England and Wales (Population Trends 2006) give a glimpse at the diversity of extra-marital childbearing over time (Figure 7). In times when extra-marital childbearing was rare, it was typically linked to solo motherhood; in 1971 only 8.4 per cent of all births in England and Wales were realised by unmarried women, but a majority of them took place among solo mothers. This pattern was documented for many parts of Europe: non-marital sexual activity often resulted in an unintended pregnancy, which led in most cases to a sudden rush to marry in order to 'legitimise' the soon-to-be-born child. In the span of one generation, cohabitation spread rapidly and childbearing outside marriage became common as well. Between 1971 and 2000 the proportion of extra-marital births in England and Wales increased five-fold, reaching 42.8 per cent. However, the absolute proportion of solo mothers remained stable over time, rising slightly between 1971 and 1986 (from 4.6 to 7.2 per cent) and hovering around that level ever since. Thus, in England and Wales as in other countries of western and northern Europe, the spectacular rise of extra-marital childbearing is mostly attributable to cohabiting couples or mothers having a non-cohabiting relationship with a partner who is ready to recognise his child. The 'normalisation' of extra-marital childbearing is also mirrored by a rising recognition of children by their fathers in other countries of Europe. In France, for instance, 92 % of children born outside marriage in 1994 were recognised by their fathers, up from 76 % in 1965 (Munoz-Perez and Prioux 2000).

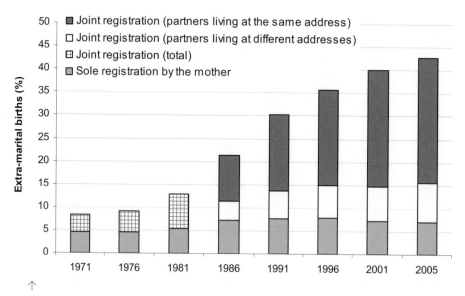

Figure 7: Proportion of non-marital births in England and Wales by the type of their registration, 1971-2005

Source: Own computations based on Population Trends 2006.

3.2. Partnership instability, decline of marriage and fertility

How are the rising instability of partnerships and the retreat from marriage linked to fertility trends? Should we worry that unstable partnerships will prevent many couples from having children? Paradoxically, some evidence points in the opposite direction: in many countries, partnership instability appears to be linked to the overall higher level of fertility. A cross-country analysis by Billari and Kohler (2004) revealed that the once powerful association between fertility rates, first marriage rates and divorce rates ceased to exist by the late 1990s. In fact, if any relationship could be observed between these indicators, it is the reversal of the pattern typical for the period of the 1960s through the 1980s: divorce rates are now positively associated with the total fertility rates (TFR), whereas first-marriage rates are slightly negatively associated with the TFR. In addition, the proportion of non-marital births has also become positively linked to the TFR. Although some of these associations might be temporary and spurious, it became apparent that the spread of alternative family forms and the rising divorce and partnership dissolution do not necessarily imply very low fertility. To the contrary, many countries which have advanced furthest in the decline of traditional family and the spread of less conventional and less stable living arrangements, record relatively high fertility when judged by contemporary European standards. The United Kingdom, France, Norway and Sweden share not only total fertility rates of 1.8-2.0 in 2006, but also close to one-half of all children being born outside marriage, very low marriage rates and total divorce rates approaching 50 per cent.

Expanding research on stepfamily fertility provides further evidence on the link between the formation of the second and later unions and fertility. Vikat, Thomson and Hoem (1999) found that Swedish couples want to have a shared child irrespective of how many children they have had in their previous union. Other studies concluded that the number of pre-union children does influence a couple's likelihood of having a shared child, especially if the partners already have two or more children (Buber and Prskawetz 2000), but the effect of these pre-union children is typically much smaller than the effect of their shared children (Thomson et al. 2002). In other words, both men and women have a considerably higher propensity to have another child when they form a new union—their shared child 'cements' their union and signals their commitment to each other (Griffith, Koo and Suchindran 1995). In addition, there is some tentative evidence on the increasing willingness of many couples to have a child in unstable partnership situations: Kravdal (1997: 289) reports that a substantial proportion of Norwegian couples deliberately enter parenthood "in unions that surely must be perceived as relatively likely to be broken." Motivation for motherhood may be strong also for some women who do not plan to enter a stable union, either due to their perceived inability to find a suitable partner or because of their unwillingness to enter a long-term committed relationship. Sobotka and Testa's (2008) comparative analysis found that a quarter of childless women aged 18-39 who expressed their preference for living single or having a non-cohabiting relationship also stated that they prefer this arrangement with children.

The overall net effect of increasingly unstable and complex partnership biographies on fertility remains unclear. This effect depends on a combination of many other factors than childbearing intensities in newly formed unions of couples with pre-union children. The most important factors include the proportion of divorcees who do not enter any stable union, the pace at which individuals who experienced union break-ups enter new unions and how much their previous fertility history differs from those who remained in their first parental union. Eckhard (2006) suggests that a shift towards a series of shorter, less stable, partnerships, increasing partnerlessness and the resulting increase in the number of years spent outside partnership before age 30 may partly explain declining cohort fertility in Germany. However, these effects may be country-specific. Prskawetz et al. (2003), focusing on cohorts born in the 1950s and the early 1960s, show huge cross-country differences in the proportion of women experiencing a second union as well as in the proportion of women already having a child when entering their second union. In many societies, union instability and stepfamily fertility may sustain higher-order fertility rates as many people have a strong motivation to have another child, above the usual two-child family norm, when they enter their second or third union. This hypothesis is confirmed by Prskawetz's at al. (2007) micro-simulation study of French fertility and Thomson's (2004) study of childbearing desires.

Data for Danish men born in 1960-65 illustrate the importance of multiple partner fertility for higher-order births (Table 3). A substantial fraction of Danish men with three or more children have them with two or more partners. Among a very small and select group of men having 5 or more children, a majority have children with at least two partners and one-fifth with three or more partners. Curiously, if more and more couples limit their childbearing aspirations to one child only—as it is the case in southern and eastern Europe—rising union instability may be seen as a way out of the 'low fertility trap.' As Billari (2005: 80) points out in a slightly provocative way, "If the rule is 'one child per couple', the only way to reach replacement is to have individuals experience two couple relationships!"

Table 3: Number of children among native Danish men (birth cohorts 1960-65) and the number of partners they have children with
↓

Number of children	Proportion of men	Of which having children with		
		1 woman	2 women	3+ women
0	24.5	x	x	x
1	17.0	100.0	x	x
2	38.3	92.9	7.1	x
3	15.8	78.4	20.0	1.5
4	3.6	60.8	32.0	7.2
5+	0.8	44.0	36.0	20.0
Total	100.0	67.6	7.3	0.6
Total fathers	75.5	89.5	9.7	0.8

Note: Fertility is recorded for the period through 2003; a significant portion of childbearing will be realised after that year. This will further increase the prevalence of multiple-partner fertility. No data about fathers are available for a small proportion of children (3.6 % for the children born in 1973-89).
Source: Author's computations based on Danish registry data.

3.3. Are men to be blamed for low fertility?

Rather limited empirical evidence pertains to the notion of men's retreat from parenthood and their inadequate parental commitment, voiced occasionally in the demographic literature (Jensen 1995; Goldscheider and Kaufman 1996). In part, these arguments are grounded on the notion that men may lack sufficient 'innate' motivation for fatherhood. This may be in contrast to women, who, according to Foster (2000) have an inherited biological predisposition to nurturing behaviour, which provides a strong incentive to motherhood. Thus, once efficient contraception broke the link between sex and childbearing and the normative pressure to follow traditional family behaviour diminished, many men may be unwilling to make long-term binding commitments related to marriage and childbearing. In addition, women's emancipation and their lifelong work participation coupled with the social security net of modern welfare states liberated them from long-term dependence on male breadwinners. Men became less needed for reproduction and their diminished economic activity and deteriorating relative income at younger ages made them less attractive for marriage—at least in the US (Oppenheimer 1994; McLanahan 2004), but probably also in many parts of Europe.

This effect does not need to have a large impact on fertility as long as women are ready to have children irrespective of whether they can or cannot find a suitable partner. But since a large majority of women perceive having a suitable and committed partner as a precondition to parenthood, men's attitudes and intentions do matter. Their importance is also fuelled by the rise of a reflexive model of partnerships, where emotional communication, intimacy and sexual affection become the key elements cementing the relationship (Giddens 1992) and childbearing ceases to be a self-understandable choice. It becomes one of the options on the road to self-fulfilment (van de Kaa 2004) and thus open to mutual negotiation between partners. It can be argued that the rise of reflexive and egalitarian model of partnerships has increased men's decision-making power about childbearing and, whenever conflicting preferences between partners arise, the resistance against having a child prevails (Voas 2003). A strong support for this 'double-veto model' was found in a study by Thomson and Hoem (1998) based on Swedish data. Some other studies provide a more nuanced view: Corijn, Liefbroer and de Jong Gierveld (1996) illustrate that the influence of both partners is highly contingent on the social context in which childbearing decisions take place. In addition, Berrington's (2004) study of British panel data shows that the effect of men's disagreement may be parity-specific: for childless women in their thirties, partner's disagreement did not have a strong effect on the actual likelihood of childbearing.

Men can negatively influence women's childbearing decisions and thus also the aggregate fertility trends in the following ways: a) by their frequent preference of less committed forms of partnerships that are not well compatible with childrearing; b) by their higher preference for childlessness and smaller family size; and c) by their preference for a more pronounced postponement of parenthood. This latter point might be especially important as men could be less concerned about delaying childbearing than women, whose ability to reproduce remains strictly limited by age. A recent study of 13 European countries (Sobotka and Testa 2008) has found some support for hypotheses a) and b). Childless men below age 39 had on average somewhat higher preferences for less traditional and less binding living arrangements (lifelong cohabitation, living-apart-together relationship and single living) than women. More pronounced differences were found in the intentions to remain childless and uncertainty about childbearing intentions. Childless men in all analysed countries except Latvia and Slovenia displayed higher levels of combined intended childlessness and intention uncertainty. When these intentions are related to all men and women below age 40, intended childlessness and uncertainty about childbearing intentions reached 23 per cent among men (average value for 13 countries) and surpassed that of women by a factor of 1.8 on average. These results should be interpreted with some caution. Rindfuss, Morgan and Swicegood (1988: 193-194) indicate that men are more ambivalent about parenthood than women, but their intentions are also less firm, possibly because parenthood usually places less constraints on men's lives. Moreover, men's intentions are frequently related to their current partnership status. Sobotka and Testa (2008) found that living alone and not having a steady partner was the most frequent reason cited by men who stated they intend to remain childless or expressed uncertainty about their intentions. Once having a steady partner, many men may warm up to parenthood: Liefbroer (2005) found that Dutch men perceived greater rewards and smaller disadvantages from having a child than women and they also expected a stronger increase in the quality of their partnership.

4. Second demographic transition and fertility: a positive link?

The concept of the second demographic transition (SDT) as developed by Dirk van de Kaa and Ron Lesthaeghe (e.g., van de Kaa 1987; Lesthaeghe 1995; van de Kaa 2001) is related to fertility levels and trends in three distinct aspects. First, it envisions a massive postponement of parenthood which is facilitated by the widespread use of modern contraception and which enables couples to concentrate on pursuing other goals earlier in life (see also section 2.2 above). Second, as a result of spreading cohabitation and rising union instability, the SDT leads to a marked rise in the proportion of non-marital births, which has been documented in section 3.1 above. Third, it foresees a decline of period and eventually also of cohort fertility below the replacement threshold and a rise in voluntary childlessness. In an 'ideal scheme' of 15 stages of the SDT, van de Kaa (2001: 302) outlines the following development: The fall in period fertility is first fuelled by a reduction in higher-order fertility, and later by the postponement of parenthood. At the end, some recuperation occurs once women who had postponed births have children at later ages. This recuperation is not sufficient and results in a "structural long-term subreplacement fertility" (Lesthaeghe and Neidert 2006: 669). Although neither Lesthaeghe nor van de Kaa anticipated the massive spread of the 'lowest-low' fertility in Europe during the 1990s, the SDT is commonly and at times simplistically associated with very low fertility rates.

The relatively high period total fertility rate (TFR) in the United States, which has been hovering around 2.0 since 1989, represents one out of several important indicators that seem to suggest that the US may constitute an exception among the industrialised countries where the SDT has not taken firm roots. Ron Lesthaeghe and Lisa Neidert's (2006) study shows that regional-level TFR in the US is negatively correlated with a set of variables representing the SDT on a county level (3141 counties), whereas on a state level (50 states) the TFR shows a small, but positive correlation with the SDT. Data for European countries lead to the suspicion that at present, when the second demographic transition has penetrated all corners of Europe, it may have become positively associated with fertility. Several countries which have been the forerunners in the progression of the SDT retain period and cohort fertility close to the replacement level (section 2). In addition, the recent positive correlation between the TFR and non-marital births, documented by Billari and Kohler (2004) suggests that at least some dimensions of the SDT in Europe have become positively linked to the TFR. Likewise, the lacking evidence for a negative impact of union instability on fertility (section 3.2) and the absence of a negative association between delayed childbearing and first and second birth progression rates in several countries (section 2.4) indicate that some of the main features of the transition are not closely related to fertility change. Finally, Liefbroer and Fokkema (this volume) have found that attitudes towards parenthood are not related to contemporary fertility behaviour in Europe. David Coleman (2004: 18) proposed that the SDT "manifestly has nothing to do with low fertility on a cross-national basis today." This is surprising, since, as he further argues, the underlying theory should imply for "populations that score highest on post-materialist ideational responses and which manifest strongly the other SDT attributes to have the lowest fertility as well." Dirk van de Kaa's (2001) analysis did not reveal any significant correlation of the TFR in European countries in 1992 with post-materialism or subjective well-being. In individual countries young women with post-materialist value orientation had higher family size ideals than materialist women, whereas fertility intentions did not differ between these two groups. However, van de Kaa also found that at a later age (30-34) post-materialists lagged behind materialists in their realised fertility, suggesting that they may overestimate their ability to have children at higher ages.

To investigate the association between second demographic transition and fertility in Europe I develop two indexes of the SDT which represent its two major dimensions—behavioural (demographic) and value orientation. Individual components of these indexes were rescaled to a range of 0 to 10, where the maximum value of 10 corresponds to a very advanced SDT.[4] Each of the two SDT indexes is derived as a mean value of its individual components and thus can also range between 0 and 10. The first index, denoted SDT1 and computed for 34 countries, combines six components of family-related behaviour in 2004: mean age at first birth and at first marriage, teenage fertility rate, proportion of non-marital births, total divorce rate and total first marriage rate for women. Ideally, this component would also include data on living arrangements, which are not available for many European countries. To account partly for the spread of cohabitation, the overall index SDT1 was adjusted upward by 0.5 for countries where cohabitating unions account for more than one-tenth of all unions (according to the 2001 census data assembled by Philipov 2005: 31, Table 2 and national data sources). The second index, SDT2, reflects attitudes and value orientation, based on eight selected questions recorded for 29 countries in the European Values Study in 1999-2000 and tabulated in Halman (2001). These items cover a broad range of values and attitudes linked to the SDT, including family attitudes, non-conformism and secularisation (see Appendix). In a crude fashion, they capture a number of items used in a multidimensional analysis of non-conformist values and living arrangements in Europe by Surkyn and Lesthaeghe (2004). The two dimensions reflected by the SDT1 and SDT2 indexes are very closely correlated (correlation coefficient of 0.84). This is an important finding, supporting the notion that values and family behaviour are tightly linked, at least in a cross-country perspective. Both indexes combined, an overall SDT index was derived for 29 countries analysed in the EVS survey. This combined index has a mean value of 5.3 and ranges from 2.5 (SDT score for Romania) to 8.6 (SDT score for Sweden). All four countries that rank above 7—Denmark, Finland, the Netherlands and Sweden belong to the 'usual suspects' of the advanced second demographic transition (in addition, Norway reached 8.0 in the SDT1 index, but no data were available to construct the SDT2 and SDT indexes). A more detailed overview of data and results is provided in Appendix.

Figure 8a plots the combined SDT index against the period TFR in 2004. The correlation is fairly strong (r=0.71) and further increases to 0.76 when the most important outlier, Ireland, which has high fertility combined with a low SDT score, is excluded. Surprisingly, out of the two dimensions studied, the values dimension SDT2 is more closely correlated with the TFR (r=0.71) than the demographic dimension SDT1 (r=0.58). It is possible that the correlation is spurious in that the scatterplot appears to feature two distinct clusters,

---

4   For an illustration, consider an example of the proportion of non-marital births, which is one component of
    the first (demographic) SDT1 index. The lowest value, 0, would be assigned to a country with no non-marital
    births, 5 to a country with 30 % non-marital births and 10 to a country where the proportion of non-marital
    births exceeds 60 %. In 2004, Greece reached the score of 0.5 (4.9 % non-marital births) whereas Iceland
    reached the score of 10 (63.7 % non-marital births) and the mean value for all European countries was 5.3.

one with the TFR below 1.5 and another, with the TFR above 1.6, within each of which the link between the TFR and SDT becomes much weaker. Likewise, one might argue that the association might be influenced by a different pace of fertility postponement which disproportionally affects the period TFR in some countries and thus distorts the association between the TFR and SDT score. This concern might be partly addressed by plotting the SDT index against the tempo-adjusted TFR level estimated for the period of 2001-2003 (VID 2006). As shown in Figure 8b, the correlation weakens somewhat, but remains notable (r=0.58). Moreover, the 'low' and 'high' fertility clusters move closer to each other and the gap between them becomes less apparent. The correlation with the values component SDT2 remains very similar (r=0.56) and further increases when Ireland is removed from the analysis.

Does a similar positive association hold for intended fertility? Figure 8c, using recent data on the mean intended family size for women aged 25-39 (based on the Eurobarometer 2006 survey tabulated by Testa 2006) indicates that the correlation becomes considerably weaker. In the 25 member states of the EU, family size aspirations are positively, but only loosely, linked to their score in the SDT index (r=0.30). Again, this correlation remains almost identical when only the demographic SDT1 index or the values-related SDT2 index is used. Finally, the SDT2 index also shows a close association with mean age at first birth (r=0.66), which is the most important indicator of delayed childbearing. This relationship is not surprising, since fertility postponement is one of the major features of the SDT concept.

Naturally, caution is needed in any interpretation of such cross-country correlations. Familiar concerns about ecological fallacy remain valid and it is very likely that there are unobserved underlying factors influencing both the SDT score and fertility levels. Moreover, the observed spatial correlations may be temporary and might disappear if the data were analysed for smaller regions or if they looked at trends over time. At this point, however, we may speculate about the possibility that once the SDT progresses to an advanced stage, it becomes positively linked to fertility levels. Such a possibility invites a number of exciting interpretations and speculations pertaining to the social change and institutional conditions conducive to the second demographic transition. I return to these issues in the concluding section 6.1.

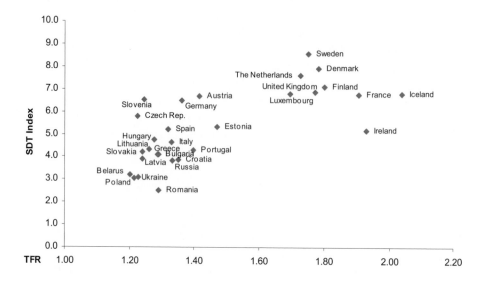

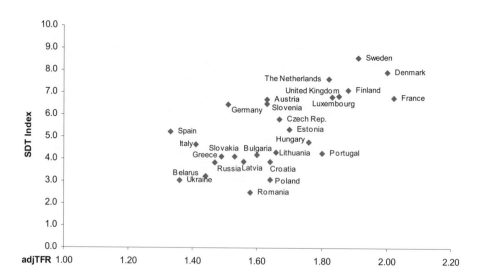

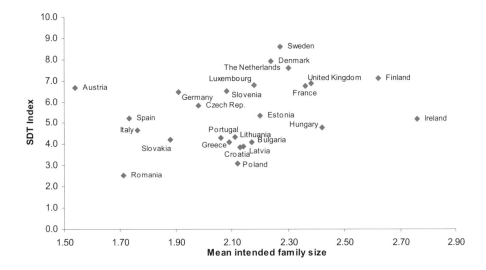

↑
*Figure 8a-c: Index of the second demographic transition, total fertility, adjusted total fertility and
the mean intended family size in 29 countries of Europe in the early 2000s*

5. Migration, childbearing and population change in Europe

During the last four decades, the European Union has become established as a region
of immigration, where migration plays an increasingly important role in population
trends. In their recent work, Van de Kaa and Lesthaeghe have repeatedly posited that
migration and the growing need for 'replacement migration' in developed countries
have become important components of the second demographic transition (e.g., van
de Kaa 2002; Lesthaeghe and Neidert 2006). Here I focus on two aspects of migration:
first, on its rising influence on childbearing trends in Europe and, second, on its rising
importance for the overall population change and for counterbalancing negative effects
of sub-replacement fertility on population and labour force size.

5.1. The rising importance of immigration for childbearing trends
The limited amount of data coupled with different concepts of migrant populations
hinders cross-country analysis of the impact of migration on fertility and childbearing
trends. To evaluate the contribution of migrants to childbearing and fertility rates I
review the statistics on the proportion of births to immigrant and foreign women and
the data on fertility differentials between migrant and 'native' women in selected
European countries. Because only few countries of Europe publish statistics for the
first generation of immigrants (i.e., for all residents born outside a given country), I
also analyse data for foreign women, who constitute a select group of immigrants (they

exclude 'naturalised' migrants who already obtained the citizenship of their current country of residence) and some of whom might have been born in their country of residence. The data on foreign women provide only a rough picture on migrants' contribution to childbearing and fertility and should be treated with caution. I shall give a more detailed analysis of immigrants' fertility and a discussion on the data and measurement issues in a separate article (Sobotka 2008).

Table 3 summarises main indicators of the contribution of immigrant women to childbearing in nine countries of western, northern and southern Europe. The overall proportion of births to immigrant women is substantial in all the analysed countries (irrespective of whether data pertain to all immigrants or to foreign women only) and frequently reaches one-fifth of all births (e.g., in England and Wales and Sweden). In Switzerland, births to mothers with foreign nationality make up more than a quarter of all births. Even in southern European countries, where births to foreign women were less common until recently, immigrants make a steadily rising contribution to the total births. This trend is most pronounced in Spain, where births to foreign women accounted for 15 per cent of all births in 2005, up from 3 per cent in 1996. However, data for foreign women seriously underestimate the share of immigrants in total number of births, as many migrant women are naturalised relatively soon after their arrival.

Immigrant and foreign women also usually display considerably higher period fertility rates than the 'native' women. The TFR of immigrants typically reaches close or somewhat above the replacement level (e.g., England and Wales and Sweden), even in the countries with lowest-low period fertility rates, such as Spain. This overall indicator of migrants' fertility hides a huge heterogeneity in childbearing patterns of different groups of migrant women. Data for foreign-born women tend to exaggerate migrants' TFR as foreign, non-naturalised women form a select group with higher fertility: many of them have arrived for the purpose of marriage or family formation, they typically have a relatively short duration of stay and display a lower degree of assimilation than those that have been 'naturalised'. Trends over time differ between countries, but typically indicate a gradual diminishing of differences between fertility levels of immigrants and foreigners on one side and natives on the other side.

Table 4: Proportion of children born to immigrant or foreign women, TFR of immigrant (foreign)
and 'native' women and the net impact of immigrants' fertility on the TFR.
↓

Country	Period	Type of data	Births to immigrant women (%)	TFR 'native' women	TFR immigrant women	Net impact of migrants on the TFR	Source
Austria	2005	F	11.7	1.31	2.00	0.10	Kytir 2006
Belgium (Flanders)	2003-4	F	12.4 (F),16.8[1]	1.51	3.07	0.10	Van Bavel and Bastiaenssen 2006, VAZG 2007
Denmark	1999-2003	I	13.5	1.69	2.43[2]	0.075	Statistics Denmark 2004
England and Wales	2005	I	20.8	1.6 (2001)	2.2 (2001)	0.07 (1996)	ONS 2006; Coleman et al. 2002
France	1991-98	I	12.4	1.65	2.5	0.07	Toulemon 2004b
The Netherlands	2005	I	17.8	1.65	1.97	0.078	CBS Statline 2006
Spain	2002	F	15.0 (2005)	1.19	2.12	0.08	INE 2006; Roig Vila and Castro Martin 2005
Sweden	2005	I	19.5	1.75	2.01	0.053	Statistics Sweden 2006
Switzerland	1997	F	26.3 (2005)	1.34	1.86	0.14	SFSO, Wanner 2002

Type of data: I – data pertain to all immigrant women (first generation); F – data pertain
to women with foreign nationality only (excluding 'naturalised' immigrants and including
foreign-nationality women born in the country)
Notes: 1) Births to women with other than Belgian nationality at the time of their birth. This
share excludes immigrants born with Belgian nationality and births to women with unknown
nationality at their birth (6.2 per cent). 2) Excluding immigrant women born with Danish
nationality.

Immigrants often differ from the native population in many other fertility characteristics.
Migrants from more conservative non-European settings frequently display an early
start of childbearing, markedly lower levels of childlessness and higher progression

rates to third and later births, higher ideal family size and very low non-marital fertility (Compton and Courbage 2002). Because of the progressive assimilation among subsequent generations of immigrants in their union formation and childbearing and, in a broader sense, their language and ethnic identity, the analysis of long-term effects of migration is very sensitive to the assumptions on migrants' assimilation and mixed-origin populations (Coleman 2006b).

The aggregate net impact of migrants on the observed trends and levels in period fertility appears to be relatively small despite their fertility rates well exceeding those of the native populations. In all countries analysed in Table 4, fertility of immigrant or foreign women had a slight upward effect on the period TFR. Except for Switzerland, this effect was comparable across countries: it shifted the period TFR upwards by 0.05-0.10 (i.e., by 3-7 per cent). This analysis indicates that immigration has played a relatively minor role in the recent upswing in the period TFR in some countries of Europe and that this upswing was mainly due to the rise in the TFR of native women, partly associated with a slowing-down of fertility postponement. The data for the Netherlands support this point: between 1996 and 2002, when the period TFR for all women increased from 1.53 to 1.73, the TFR among women born in the Netherlands rose even faster (from 1.47 to 1.69, data from CBS Statline 2006). Similarly, in Flanders the period TFR of women with Belgian nationality has been rising more rapidly than the TFR of women with foreign nationality. Only a part of this trend could be attributed to the naturalisation of foreigners (Van Bavel and Bastiaenssen 2007).

5.2. Replacement migration: can migration substitute 'missing' births?

The previous section has shown that immigrants have a small, but non-negligible positive influence on fertility rates in many parts of Europe. Can immigration also serve as a substitution of births 'missing' due to low fertility? This question lies at the heart of many debates concerning future trends in population size, labour force and population ageing. In 2000, a UN report titled *Replacement migration: Is it a solution to declining and ageing population?* sparked media frenzy about the future of European populations. The remarkably diverse interpretations of its major findings in the media reflect considerable confusion about the role of migration for population change in Europe[5]. Practically all the studies show that any realistic level of migration cannot stop population ageing and can only have a relatively modest impact on slowing down this process. However, migration is likely to have considerable (positive) effect on the size of the labour force (Feld 2000; Bijak et al. 2007) as well as on the total population size (UN 2000; Lutz and Scherbov 2003a). Higher immigration combined with higher

---

5   Teitelbaum (2004: 32) reviews the unexpected media attention to the UN report that had started already before its publication date.

economic activity can partly offset negative economic consequences of population ageing (Bijak et al. 2007).

Do many European countries experience migration levels that can be seen as constituting 'replacement migration'? Although some evidence suggests this may be the case[6], no clear definition of replacement migration exists (see Saczuk 2003 for a critical assessment). One possible conceptualisation of replacement migration assesses whether immigration makes up for the difference between the observed number of births and the hypothetical number of births that would have been achieved if fertility reached replacement level. A long-term combination of sub-replacement fertility and replacement migration should eventually lead to a stationary population, i.e., a population with constant size and fixed age structure (under the assumption that mortality remains constant as well). Such a concept of replacement migration is not easily analysed because migration widely fluctuates over time: hence it is problematic to use migration rates for any particular year to estimate long-term population replacement.

The importance of immigration for childbearing trends and population change in many European countries implies the need to rethink the traditional concepts of replacement-level fertility (Smallwood and Chamberlain 2005). Calot and Sardon (2001) suggest that the 'net replacement rates' which reflect both mortality and migration are preferable to the widely used 'net reproduction rates' and their inclusion may change the evaluation of future population prospects. This is well illustrated by Daguet (2002) who computed different measures of generation replacement for France. A different approach has been proposed by Ortega and del Rey (2007) who compute 'Birth Replacement Ratios' (BRE) relating period numbers of births to the mean size of the mothers' generation at birth.

In order to analyse to what extent migration acts as a substitution for births I propose a simple and intuitively understandable indicator, labelled Gross Replacement Rate (GRE) which combines the readily available period indicator of the Gross Reproduction Rate (GRR)[7] with the subsequent (cohort) changes in the total population of women

---

6 Projection scenarios by Lutz and Scherbov (2003a) for the EU-15 assuming various combinations of fertility and migration provide a strong evidence for the importance of migration for 'substituting' births in the European Union. Their original report published by the IIASA (Lutz and Scherbov 2003b: 11-12) suggests that in the EU-15 "the effect of 100,000 additional immigrants per year corresponds to that of an increase in the TFR of 0.1."

7 Gross Reproduction Rate shows the average number of daughters that would be born to a woman experiencing over her reproductive life the fertility rates observed in a given year, assuming zero mortality until the end of her reproductive period. It is computed by multiplying the period total fertility rate with the proportion of female live-born children.

born in a year for which both GRR and GRE are measured. Unlike in Ortega and del Rey's BRE approach, the GRE does not estimate the impact of migration on birth rates: it shows to what extent immigration itself acts as a substitution for births. Different age categories for computing the GRE may be used; they are defined by the duration since the year for which the GRE is computed. For instance, the GRE for the year 1975 and duration (age) 20 is computed as a ratio of the total number of resident women aged 20 in the year 1995 (1975 + 20) to the original number of live born female children in the year 1975 multiplied by the Gross Reproduction Rate for 1975:

$$GRE(t=1975, a=20) = GRR(t=1975) \cdot PF(t=1995) / BF(t=1975) = TFR(t) \cdot BF(t) / B(t) \cdot PF(t+a) / BF(t),$$

where t is the year for which the GRE is computed, a represents selected duration (age) since the year t, P stands for population, B denotes live births, and the index F stands for females. For age 0, i.e., for the time of birth, the GRE equals the GRR. Subsequently, the total size of any female cohort changes not only through immigration and emigration but also due to mortality. In parallel with the commonly used net and gross reproduction rates, which estimate the number of female children surviving until the usual age at reproduction, the GRE computations may be limited to capturing population change occurring until the typical age at childbearing. For convenience, age 30 may be used as a 'terminal age' for computing the 'final' GRE, labelled GRE-F[8]. The indicator proposed here suffers one obvious disadvantage typical of the cohort data: For any year of interest it reveals the importance of migration only after a sufficient number of years passes during which migration transforms the size of the original birth cohort. GRE-F can be computed only 30 years after the year for which the gross replacement rates are analysed. But this index has also a number of advantages. First of all, by summarising the impact of migration on the original population of each birth cohort over longer periods of time it eliminates the effects of short-term swings in migration streams that would strongly influence the indicators based solely on the period data. The GRE can also be used to trace the impact of migration on each birth-year cohort over time.

I illustrate the use of the GRE using an example of Switzerland, which constitutes an ideal setting for analysing 'replacement migration' as it records long-term low fertility combined with sizeable immigration. The period TFR dropped below 1.6 since 1976

8   For an illustration, consider a computation of the GRE-F for Switzerland for 1975. The Gross reproduction rate (GRR) for that year reached 0.783. By age 30, the total number of resident women born in 1975 reached 48,974 (on 1 January 2006) and increased by a factor of 1.287 when compared with the number of live-born women in 1975 (38,055). A multiplication of this index with the GRR for 1975 yields 1.007, which is the GRE-F for 1975 (i.e., the GRE for 1975 computed for the duration of 30 years). In this particular case, the GRE-F suggests that the potentially negative effect of sub-replacement fertility in 1975 on long-term size of population at prime childbearing ages was fully offset by immigration during the subsequent 30 years.

and remained below this level ever since. Figure 9 shows how the GRE for various years (1970-1994) changes over time as the cohorts of women born in those years are modified through migration. Although the Gross Reproduction Rate reached only 0.72-0-77 in 1975-2000, the Gross Replacement Rate rises strongly due to immigration, especially at ages 18 through 30. For instance the GRR in 1978 reached only 0.73, but subsequently the GRE has risen substantially, reaching 0.98 when the 1978 cohort reached age 27. Whereas the GRR signals that the period fertility rates were 27 per cent below replacement level (ignoring mortality), accounting for migration below age 28 changes the sub-replacement 'deficit' to 2 per cent only and it is very likely that by age 30 the GRE for 1978 will surpass 1, as it did for the years (cohorts) of 1970 to 1975. In sum, Switzerland can be considered a textbook example of a replacement migration country: low fertility rates combined with substantial immigration imply that the final Gross Replacement Rate, measured at age 30, reaches values close to 1 or even higher.

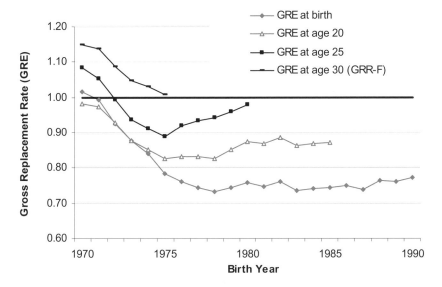

↑

Figure 9: Gross Replacement Rate (GRE) in Switzerland in 1970-1990 in selected age (year) intervals

To see whether Switzerland constitutes an exception or a relatively common pattern Figure 10 looks at the GRE by duration (age) for 1978 in 5 countries with different migration patterns: Austria, the Netherlands, Norway, Spain and Switzerland (for Spain, the GRE for 1984 is analysed). The impact of migration on the GRE is widely different between countries and over time. Overall, the graph shows rather convincingly that when the migration balance is included in the replacement rates computations, the huge deficit depicted by the gross and net reproduction rates may markedly decline or disappear altogether, even in some countries with very low fertility levels. The GRE ratios above 0.9, recorded in most western, northern and southern European countries, convey a less dramatic impression of long-term population trends in Europe than the conventional fertility and replacement indicators.

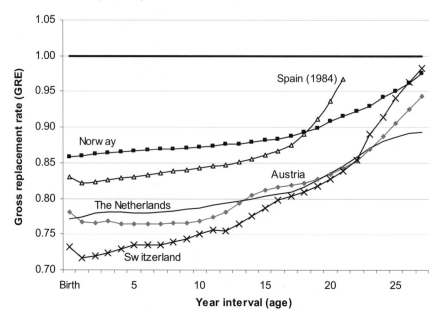

Figure 10: Gross Replacement Rate (GRE) in Austria, the Netherlands, Norway and Switzerland in 1978 and in Spain in 1984 by the number of years elapsed from the year for which the GRE is measured

6. Past and future fertility and migration trends in Europe and their broader implications

Much of the presented evidence lends support to the introductory hypotheses. Lowest-low fertility rates are tightly linked to fertility postponement and so far there is no larger country in Europe that appears likely to experience lowest-low cohort fertility rates as well. Some of the most important features of the second demographic transition such as the intensive fertility postponement, the rising instability of partnerships and unions, and the eroding importance of marriage for childbearing, do not appear to have the expected strong negative impact on fertility, at least when analysed in a cross-country perspective. The aggregate index measuring the demographic and the values components of the SDT shows a positive association with the period TFR, even when the tempo effect is controlled for. Men seem to be less enthusiastic about parenthood than women and their lower fertility desires may exert a slightly negative effect on fertility. Migration has a slightly positive impact on the period fertility rates and a strong and rising influence on the overall number of births. Yet its most important role is in 'substituting' some of the births 'missing' due to low fertility. Immigrants typically come at younger ages and if their numerical impact on the total number of women below the typical age at reproduction is taken into account, population replacement rates in northern, southern and western Europe are close to or even above the threshold necessary to maintain a stable population size.

Although almost all European countries record low period fertility and declining cohort fertility, there are consistent regional differences in low fertility which have crystallised since the 1980s. Anton Kuijsten (1996: 141) argued persuasively that in the course of the second demographic transition "the European family map has grown more diversified rather than more uniform." In analogy, there are signs that fertility trends may become more diverse both between and within countries, with a rising heterogeneity in childbearing behaviour closely linked to social status. Together with unfolding migration trends, contemporary fertility has widely different consequences for long-term population prospects in Europe (see also section 6.3 below). While the European Union may have a relatively stable or slightly rising population and stagnating labour force size, different European regions may be set on widely diverging pathways. If contemporary fertility and migration differences in Europe prevail into the future, the outlook for population trends in different regions could be summarised in a stylised fashion as follows:

- the relatively high fertility and moderate to high migration in most countries of western and northern Europe imply long-term population increase and slower population ageing;
- the rather low fertility of German-speaking countries combined with moderate (Germany) or high (Austria and Switzerland) migration rates implies slow or stagnating population growth;
- the low fertility in southern Europe combined with high immigration (except in Portugal) implies further population growth and less severe population ageing than would be recorded in the absence of migration
- low fertility, spread of one-child families and negative migration balance in the European countries of the former Soviet Union and in some of the Balkan countries (Bulgaria, Romania, Serbia) will lead to a long-lasting depopulation
- in central European post-communist countries, this negative trend is being moderated by a gradual shift in migration trends, turning most of these countries into 'receiving' countries. In contrast with eastern Europe, the rising immigration is likely to prevent a rapid population decline

This simplified summary ignores some specifics of individual countries and regions. Nevertheless it reiterates the message voiced in the introductory part: low fertility, when seen in conjunction with immigration, is not an important threat for Europe as such and especially not for the richer parts of the continent, including most of the EU countries. Rather, it is a regional problem that has most serious consequences in parts of Europe recording a troubling mix of low fertility, emigration and, in some countries, also a relatively high mortality.[9] For these regions, particularly in eastern and south-eastern Europe, but also in eastern Germany, an extended period of low fertility and high emigration will have a long-lasting impact that will probably imply a marked population decline in the decades to come.

A final discussion on fertility, migration and long-term population prospects of Europe focuses on three interrelated issues. First, I speculate why the second demographic transition is positively linked to fertility on a cross-sectional basis. Second, I outline broader social, institutional and economic changes that may positively affect fertility developments in the near future. Third, I emphasise the importance of migration and argue that given contemporary fertility and migration trends, the envisioned population decline in Europe may be avoided or postponed for many decades. In conclusion, I suggest that the fears of European demographic marginalisation are ill-formulated and exaggerated.

6.1. Second demographic transition and very low fertility rates

The positive association between the second demographic transition and fertility as well as the findings on stable fertility in western and northern Europe merit further discussion. Two different, although not mutually exclusive, interpretations may be pursued. First, it is possible that a number of interrelated factors transform societies in a way that is potentially conducive to somewhat higher fertility. This could happen despite the broadening number of competing choices to parenthood. If supported, this possibility might change our perspective about the future of European fertility. Second, a more humble interpretation of the presented results implies that the second demographic transition does not necessarily lead to a permanent decline in period and cohort fertility and fertility intentions below the replacement level. In this respect, the US may not be an exceptional case among industrialised countries after all. France,

---

9   Emigration has another potentially harmful and rather neglected effect on fertility. In addition to affecting younger people most strongly, it is often sex-selective. Societies with an asymmetric sex distribution of emigrants may see a shift in the sex ratio of their resident population that will strain the 'partnership market' and eventually contribute to a lower number of births in the 'residual population'. Such shifts in the sex ratios among younger cohorts (1974-1984) have been documented by Weiss (2006) in the case of the Mecklenburg-Vorpommern region in Eastern Germany, where an intensive emigration of women after 1990 has led to the 'deficit' of about 15% of women in 2003.

with the period TFR reaching 2.0 in 2006 and the completed TFR of women born in 1973 projected at the same level (trend projection in Prioux 2006: 351, T. 5) is the most obvious European example of such a pattern. Under this interpretation, the SDT is not closely connected to fertility level and the 'advanced SDT' countries would continue having different levels of low fertility, with some of them possibly retaining stable fertility close to the replacement level.

The first possibility, on the other hand, suggests that very low fertility may be a temporary result of a combination of fertility postponement (causing a negative tempo effect) and institutional framework (societal norms, gender relations, family policies, welfare system) that has not yet adjusted to the SDT behaviour. Thus the stage of very low fertility would be a temporary by-product of the second demographic transition. Eventually, fertility would rise when societal norms and institutions become more compatible with the new diversity of family forms and living arrangements. On the surface, this argument is problematic. It might be more reasonable to expect a shift towards a one-child family norm in the course of the SDT. As Jan Van Bavel pointed out[10], a one-child family could be considered as an ideal solution compatible with individualistic ideology of self-fulfilment, typical of the second demographic transition. One child enables men and women to achieve parenthood status, give meaning to their lives and, in a broader sense, achieve a "kind of immortality and establish a link to both past and future" (Hagewen and Morgan 2005: 514) without losing too much on other enjoyments life has to offer. However, surveys on fertility intentions lend support to the 'higher fertility' reasoning: even in those countries that score highest in the SDT dimension, such as France, the Netherlands and Sweden, fertility desires remain relatively high and above or around the replacement-level threshold (Testa 2006, see also Figure 9c above). Similarly to the US, a two-child family norm prevails in most of Europe. As Morgan and Hagewen (2005: 12) pointed out, "there is a remarkably pervasive desire (and supporting norms, structure and biological predispositions) for *two children when and if one can afford them and care for them*" (italics by the authors). This conditional wording is important. In advanced societies people highly value many alternatives to parenthood, they postpone binding decisions, pursue high education and job careers, enter intimate partnerships for their own sake and consider leisure and consumption as important factors potentially conflicting with their childbearing decisions. It is possible that the countries scoring high on the SDT dimension have certain features that reduce some obstacles to childbearing and make it easier for individuals to realise their childbearing desires. Consequently, the 'advanced' SDT societies would be characterised not by an overall higher level of desired fertility, but by a smaller gap between desired and eventually realised fertility.

---

10 Comment at the colloquium on "Demographic challenges for the 21st century," Brussels, February 15-16, 2007.

If this reasoning is correct, it is important to ask which conditions are conducive to higher levels of realised fertility and at the same time typical of advanced SDT societies. A search for these factors should encompass cultural and political as well as economic characteristics of these societies, since economic prosperity, affluence and modern welfare state are important preconditions of the SDT. Economic prosperity fuels rising aspirations and formulation of new needs (Lesthaeghe and Surkyn 1998). Particular welfare and family policies may support or hinder the realisation of childbearing desires (Esping-Andersen 1999; McDonald 2002). This is not a unidirectional pattern: change in values and behaviour may also lead to a change in broader institutional conditions, making laws and policies more compatible with the new behaviour. Furthermore, although most behavioural and value shifts are shared across countries, considerable differences are likely to prevail.

6.2. Social, institutional and economic factors that may lead to higher fertility: towards more time and lifestyle flexibility

This section outlines social, political, and economic changes that may be conducive to higher fertility in the countries that have reached very low fertility levels. Many of these characteristics are typical of societies that progressed furthest on the SDT dimension. This selection is rather subjective; a number of other factors that may lead to higher or lower fertility in the future can be outlined (e.g., Lutz 2006).

• Individualised and comprehensive welfare system

Many higher-fertility countries have a comprehensive benefit system based on individualised entitlements. Rather broad welfare coverage reduces the risk of falling into poverty, especially for women and young adults, and gives them more flexibility in making important life decisions. The principle of individualised benefits, which Esping-Andersen (1999) refers to as 'defamilization,' relaxes households' welfare and caring responsibilities and diminishes thus the dependence on kinship. This is in contrast with welfare arrangements centred on 'traditional' family model, especially the 'male breadwinner' family. Esping-Andersen (1999: 49) notes that such model creates a welfare deficit as it is based on a post-war family model that is becoming extinct.[11] Such welfare systems may penalise individuals that do not behave in conformity with the traditional norms and thus have a negative effect on fertility (Rindfuss, Guzzo and Morgan 2003).

---

11 Baizán, Michielin, and Billari (2002) have shown that younger cohorts in Spain provide strong support to gender equality and display tolerance towards individualistic forms of households. However, the less traditional living arrangements are penalised by the 'powerful internationalization of welfare within the family' (Baizán, Michielin, and Billari 2002: 199). This leads to a slower spread of cohabitation, divorce and non-marital childbearing, but also to later home leaving, delayed union formation, delayed childbearing and, consequently, lower fertility.

- Strong support for work-family combination

Support of women's employment and policies that facilitate easy re-entry of mothers into the labour market, typical of northern Europe, appear to be conducive to higher fertility. Such policies, including various child care arrangements and support for part-time and flexible jobs, are responsive to a profound change in women's roles and identity that shifted from a family-centred world to a wider world, whose main components are career and economic independence (Goldin 2006)[12]. For well-educated women who perceive their labour participation as a self-understandable and important part of their lives, the limited possibilities to combine childrearing and employment impinge heavily on their childbearing decisions. A number of countries that provide rather generous family benefits score poorly on this dimension. Austria and Germany are prime examples of such pattern: rather generous parental leave benefits supporting full-time home care of one parent seem to have little impact on fertility as the existing family policies are ineffective in supporting child care and employment for women with small children (for Austria, see OECD 2003). As a result, for a majority of women parenthood implies a prolonged interruption of their work career with potentially damaging effects on their income and career progression—a situation many of them avoid by 'abstaining' from parenthood altogether. High childlessness in the German-speaking countries of Europe, concentrated among highly educated women (Duschek and Wirth 2005, Spielauer 2005), seems to be a consequence of this situation.[13]

- High levels of gender equality in the public and in the private sphere

In almost all countries of Europe, women and men have equal opportunities in education and labour participation. Statistics on the average years of schooling show that younger women (aged 25-34) in most OECD countries have received longer years of schooling than men (OECD 2006). In the public sphere, women's inequality has taken more subtle forms than in the past, in the form of gender pay gaps or low levels of employment security for women who temporarily withdraw from work during their parental leave period. Nordic countries, which are most 'advanced' in the SDT, are also known for their strong support of gender equality in the society at large (e.g., Oláh and Bernhardt 2008). More important gender differences prevail in the private sphere. McDonald (2000) has argued that the lack of gender equity in the family, with

---

12 Goldin (2006: 9) documents a massive shift in the expectations of young women about their future employment that occurred in the United States between the late 1960s and the late 1970s. Whereas only one third of young women interviewed in 1968 expected to be in paid labour force by age 35, this figure increased to about 75% by the late 1970s. In agreement with the SDT concept, Goldin links this massive change in women's identity to the spread of the contraceptive pill, extended education, and the postponement of marriage.

13 Note, however, that the analysis of time trends in selected variables of work-childbearing compatibility has not revealed any association with the time trends in the TFR (Engelhardt and Prskawetz 2004).

traditional norms and expectations about gender roles and almost all the burden of child care, cooking and cleaning falling upon women, may be responsible for low fertility once gender equality in the public sphere reaches high levels. This argument suggests that a combination of state support for work-family combination and greater involvement of men in child care and household tasks, reduce the price of having children for women. Dalla Zuanna's (2001: 150) study on how Italian 'familistic' culture contributes to low fertility gives a similar reasoning: the society is organised according to the 'male breadwinner model', with limited child care facilities, low government support for families, little men's help in the household and high expectations placed on women with respect to the amount of time they should spend with their children (see also Esping-Andersen 1999). Norms prescribing that mothers should stay at home when their children are young increase the (cultural) role incompatibility between motherhood and fertility (Brewster and Rindfuss 2000).[14] Also many post-communist societies experience a persistence of traditional gender norms on employment and the division of household tasks, which preserve asymmetries between partners and which contribute to lower fertility (see Stankuniene and Jasilioniene 2008 for Lithuania). On a micro level, there is some evidence that greater involvement of fathers in the child care is positively linked to subsequent fertility (for second births see Cook 2004; Mencarini and Tanturri 2004).

• Low 'familism' and high levels of 'secular individualism'

Secularisation and individualisation are perceived as important factors fostering low fertility during and after the first demographic transition (Lesthaeghe 1983). Paradoxically, the rise of 'secular individualism' may eventually pave the way to higher fertility in countries with very low fertility levels, where prevailing social norms and institutional arrangements discourage behaviour that may have a positive impact on fertility, such as early leaving of parental home, cohabiting or having a non-marital child (e.g., Dalla Zuanna 2001). Secularisation is weakening traditional cultural norms, making people more tolerant of divorce, cohabitation, abortion, homosexuality and cultural change in general (Lesthaeghe 1983; Norris and Inglehart 2004). In countries where 'secular individualism' is strongly established, and where non-marital fertility is widely accepted, women "can more fully realize their fertility desires without being constrained by men's preferences" (Presser 2005).

---

14 A more extreme version of such gender-stratified norms, including strict expectations about women's domestic role after marriage, is frequently used to explain the low marriage rate and very low fertility in Japan (e.g., Retherford, Ogawa, and Matsukura 2001).

- Fostering low unemployment, high female employment and flexible work arrangements

Many studies, especially those focusing on southern and central-eastern Europe, link very low fertility to high unemployment and employment insecurity among young adults. The rapid rise in unemployment in these regions—during the 1980s in southern Europe and the 1990s in central-eastern Europe—coincided with the fall in the period TFR and an intensive fertility postponement. Young people in Spain have a particularly precarious position in the labour market due to legislation providing a strong protection to the long-term employees and creating barriers for new entrants to the labour market (e.g., Baizán, Michielin and Billari 2002). This regulation has the perverse effect of fostering an expansion of temporary employment. Adsera (2005) gives evidence that both high unemployment rates and a high gender gap in unemployment have a strong negative effect on fertility rates across Europe. On the other hand, high proportions of government jobs, a flexible labour legislation and high proportions of part-time employment all have a positive effect on fertility, which under these conditions may approach the replacement level (Adsera 2004). As unemployment has been falling in most parts of Europe since the early 2000s and labour market reforms will stimulate labour flexibility, more part-time work and a higher participation of women, the negative effects of employment insecurity on fertility are likely to diminish in the countries that have been most affected.

- The brave new world of assisted reproduction

The use and the possibilities of assisted reproduction technology (ART) have expanded massively since 1978, when the first baby resulting from in-vitro fertilisation was born in the United Kingdom. At present, new modes of assisted reproduction are rapidly developed and tested, with methods like freezing ovaries or gathering and using donor eggs moving from the realm of science fiction to common use (e.g., special issue of *New Scientist* on 'Reproductive revolution', 21 October 2006). In most countries of Europe, 1 to 4 per cent of children born in 2002 were conceived through ART methods (Nyboe Andersen et al. 2006). ART use has greatly contributed to some peculiar trends in fertility, especially to a rapid increase in the number and proportion of multiple births (Stephen 2000), occurring due to a common practice of transferring two or more embryos into a woman's uterus. The spread of ART has also resulted in a rising number of women having children at extreme late childbearing ages, including women past menopause, and has repeatedly led to reaching new record-high childbearing ages (Sobotka, Kohler and Billari 2007). There are many reasons to expect that the importance of ART will further increase in the future: improvements in the technology, the continuing postponement of childbearing to ages when more women will face infertility and, possibly, also a general increase in male-factor infertility. However, at present, most common ART methods suffer very low success rates at later childbearing ages, especially at age 40 and above.[15] Any future rise in the importance of ART for fertility will in part depend on the improvements of its success rates among late mothers-to-be.

In sum, besides the ending of tempo distortions, there are numerous reasons why fertility may increase somewhat in the lowest-fertility countries of Europe. Very low fertility is not inevitable in Europe. The arguments summarised above suggest that the institutional framework most conducive to reaching relatively high level of realised fertility is that of the Nordic welfare state (see also Esping-Andersen 1999; Liefbroer and Fokkema, this volume). It does not mean that different parts of Europe are likely to adopt the full package of the Nordic welfare regime. But it is likely that the existing social policies in different parts of Europe will adopt some features of this regime, such as increased provision of child care, more emphasis on work-family combination, support for gender equality and fathers' involvement in child care. This may happen gradually as a lagged adaptation to the vastly changed norms and behaviours related to family and gender roles, but in part also due to specific EU policies promoting gender equality and family-friendly policies. In parallel, secularisation and individualisation are likely to continue in the more 'familistic' and 'traditional' regions, decreasing the social pressure to follow traditional pathways and increasing the likelihood that more people will enter non-traditional families and living arrangements (Thornton 1989). Recent evidence for southern Europe shows that this change is already well under way there.

An alternative scenario involves a shift towards liberal welfare regimes, typical of Anglo-Saxon nations, which provide less generous protection against various risks individuals may face. Especially some countries of central-eastern Europe, with lower economic affluence and tight budget constraints, seem to be moving in this direction. This may lead towards a more polarised version of the SDT and, generally, to more socially stratified societies with higher poverty rates, large social status disparities in living arrangements, family size and in the timing of union formation and childbearing. However, similarly to the Nordic countries of Europe, this shift may also be compatible with an overall higher fertility. The United States and the United Kingdom achieve fertility rates similar to those in northern European countries or France due to their social status heterogeneity in parity distribution and the existence of sizeable minorities having relatively large families.

Various factors that may potentially reduce the observed gap between intended and realised fertility have one thing in common: by reducing the objective as well as

---

15 In the US only 11% of ART cycles using non-donor eggs or embryos resulted in a live birth when performed at age 41-42 in 2004; the success rate was much higher (37%,) among women using ART below age 35 (CDC 2006).

perceived obstacles to childbearing they broaden the life-course flexibility with respect to decisions on the timing of childbearing, the number of children, and also the choice of living arrangement preferred for childbearing. Note that none of these factors are explicitly pronatalist: they constitute a mix of changes that are likely to progress spontaneously and policies designed to improve the economic performance or the well-being of individuals and families. More such factors may be listed. For instance, Hakim's (2003) argument that a significant fraction of women remains home-centered and displays strong family and child-orientation implies that specific family policies may be designed to support these women and, as a by-product, also to encourage fertility. In a broader perspective, the argument on the potentially positive effects of rising life-course flexibility on fertility also relates to the argument pursued by Avramov and Cliquet (2003) who posited that policies should aim to spread "more innovatively paid and unpaid duty-free time over the entire life course."

6.3. Migration and fertility combined: can the European population implosion be avoided?

At present the European Union attracts more migrants than the United States, a classical country of immigration and a symbol of endless opportunities for the new 'settlers'. Immigration has become the main engine of the EU population growth already since the early 1990s and many countries record population growth only due to substantial migration streams. An interaction between the rising number of immigrants, their relatively young age structure and their higher fertility implies that migration has a strong and long-lasting impact on population growth and structure. Sizeable migration streams are radically and permanently transforming European populations in ways unforeseen until recently by demographers and social scientists. Coleman (2006b: 402) proposes that low fertility combined with high immigration is "changing the composition of national populations and thereby the culture, physical appearance, social experiences, and self-perceived identity of the inhabitants of European nations".

Migration is also the most unstable and the least predictable component of population change. Spain provides a telling example of the unexpected effects of migration on population trends: between 1999 and 2006 the total population of Spain has risen by 4.0 million persons, i.e., by one tenth, of which 3.7 million constituted a net increase due to migration (Eurostat 2006b; Council of Europe 2006). This trend has rendered even the relatively recent population projections obsolete.[16] Yet until 1990 Spain was a country of

---

16 For instance, the Eurostat projection published in 1996 envisioned in its baseline scenario that the Spanish population, which reached 43.8 million in 2006, would peak soon after 2010, when it would reach 40.4 million. Even the high variant, which expected considerably higher fertility than is actually being recorded, projected that the population size recorded in 2006 would not be reached until after 2020 (Eurostat 1996 and Shaw et al. 1997).

emigration, recording a negative migration balance each year. Surprisingly, only limited attention has been paid to the evaluation of migration assumptions in national and regional population projections for Europe. Moreover, there is a growing gap between the booming field of migration theories and the projection practice, which remains disconnected from these theories and usually continue to "rely on ad-hoc assumptions based on little theory and virtually no definable methodology" (Howe and Jackson 2005: 1).

Typically, as in the case of Spain, past projections in many European countries tended to underestimate future immigration. This has occasionally led to projecting an early onset of population decline which eventually has not materialised in the expected time frame. However, the opposite trend may occur as well. David Coleman (2006b) points out the examples of Denmark and the Netherlands, where the tightening of the migration legislation after 2002 has markedly reduced immigration and led to net migration decline below the projected levels. The substantial uncertainty related even to migration trends in the near future should be taken into account in the evaluation of the link between migration, fertility and population trends.

Having this limitation in mind, it seems safe to conclude that in many parts of Europe immigration taking place at lower ages (childhood and young adulthood) serves as a substitution for most of the births 'missing' due to sub-replacement fertility, even when very low fertility persists for long periods of time. Switzerland constitutes a model example of such development.[17] Section 5 suggests that more European countries follow a similar pattern. Dalla Zuanna (2006), focusing on the industrial triangle of north-west Italy and including both the effects of international and internal (south to north) migration, shows that significant and continuous waves of immigration may slow population ageing and prevent population decline even in a region experiencing half a century of very low fertility. The study hypothesises that there is a cyclical generational process, where high aspirations for the social mobility of their children lead couples to limit their fertility. Their children subsequently achieve high levels of education and cannot fill the demand for low-paid and low-skilled jobs. This demand is met by immigrants who, upon their arrival, soon reduce their fertility in order to achieve a better socio-economic position for their children. Dalla Zuanna (2006: 201) asserts that during the last two decades of the 20th century "the most developed and economically dynamic regions [in the EU] were those with the strongest positive migratory balances".

---

17 Wanner (2002) projected a hypothetical population change in Switzerland that would have occurred in the absence of international migration after 1945. By the year 2000, Swiss population would be declining and would reach only 5.2 million persons as compared with the currently registered value of 7.2 million, almost 40 percent above the zero migration scenario.

If this reasoning holds[18] the new members of the EU, especially the former state-socialist societies of central Europe whose economy has been rapidly expanding, will soon experience increasing immigration streams, comparable to trends recorded two or three decades ago in southern Europe[19]. More generally, the envisioned slight increase in period fertility rates combined with a continuation of sizeable immigration implies that the frequently projected population decline of Europe and the European Union in particular may not occur in the foreseeable future, at least not until 2050[20]. This possibility finds support in a recent projection for the EU-15 countries, Norway, Iceland and Switzerland by Alho et al. (2006), which assumes a higher life expectancy and higher immigration levels than the past projections by the United Nations and Eurostat. However, as this and other studies show, population ageing is certain to continue and governments should pursue a mix of strategies for reducing its expected negative influences (Bongaarts 2004).

6.4. European Union vs. the United States: The exaggerated fears of European decline

When speculating about the future of European population, van de Kaa (1999: 35) proposed that the second demographic transition was likely to become 'permanent'. This suggestion remains at least as plausible now as it was almost a decade ago. If the arguments pursued in this article are correct, a further progression of the SDT should not have a negative impact on fertility rates. On the contrary, in some countries with very low fertility, further advancement of the SDT might indeed have a beneficial effect on fertility rates as it will broaden the choice of generally accepted pathways to have children and lift some obstacles to childbearing. This effect may be partly counterbalanced by declining fertility preferences in countries that have experienced a prolonged period of very low fertility (Lutz, Skirbekk and Testa 2006). European regions will almost certainly continue to experience divergent pathways in their fertility, migration and population trends.

The fears of a European demographic decline and marginalisation may be exaggerated. Paul Demeny (2003: 14) proposed that "European demographic marginalization is fait accompli, one that is bound to be further accentuated during the present century." This statement is valid on a continent-wide perspective, but Europe has never been a unified

---

18 A comparative study by Jennissen (2004) concluded that GDP per capita and unemployment are important determinants of migration levels in Europe.

19 This increase in immigration has already been recorded in some countries of Central Europe. The Czech Republic has seen a steady rise in registered net migration from around 10 thousand in the mid-1990s (0.10%) to 35 thousand in 2006 (0.34%, CZSO 2007).

20 The baseline scenario of the most recent Eurostat projection published in 2006—EUROPOP2004 (Eurostat 2006c)—anticipates that the EU will experience a population decline by 2025.

entity with coherent social or political organisation. It is only in the last half century that an unprecedented economic and political integration has been taking place across Europe, symbolised by the rise of the European Union. Despite its heavy bureaucracy and profound disagreement between its members even on the basic facets of its status and purpose (also embodied in the recent disputes about the EU constitution), the successful extensions of the EU, the creation of the common monetary union and the establishment of the common border agreement are not suggestive of a civilisation in decline (van de Kaa 1999). When compared with the United States—the usual and the most meaningful unit of reference—the continuing expansion has given European Union a sizeable lead in population size as well as the ability to 'catch up' with the US in the overall economic power (Figures AP1 and AP2 in Appendix).

In contrast to the commonly accepted view that an extensive welfare system with high taxation may be too obtrusive for economic prosperity and competitiveness, recent analysis by Aiginger (2005) found that three Nordic countries of Europe, Denmark, Finland, and Sweden, can be ranked as the three best economic performers (as measured by output growth, productivity growth, and employment rate) in the EU-15 in 1993-2002. He suggests that "there may be a new kind of reformed European model, which combines welfare and sustainability on the one hand with efficiency and economic incentives on the other" (Aiginger 2005: 113). This finding adds another layer to my speculations about the future of Europe's populations: the social welfare model which embodies many values that are at the heart of European distinctiveness (individualised and rather broad welfare coverage, gender equality, high value of the quality of life and environmental protection) appears effective and sustainable. This model is compatible with the second demographic transition, and, at the same time, conducive to higher fertility. Thus the renewed fears of a European low fertility crisis, a population slump and the demise of the European welfare state remain largely unsubstantiated.

7. Acknowledgements

Modified parts of sections 2 and 5 will be published in a comparative study on "Childbearing trends and policies in Europe." I am thankful for the permission of the book's co-editors, especially Tomas Frejka, to use selected materials in this study. I gratefully acknowledge many comments and suggestions provided by Jan Van Bavel, Dirk van de Kaa and Johan Surkyn on the previous drafts of this study. Richard Gisser, Wolfgang Lutz, Dimiter Philipov, Alexia Prskawetz, Vegard Skirbekk, and Arland Thornton supplied useful suggestions when this manuscript was presented at the Vienna Institute of Demography in July 2007. Werner Richter carefully edited the manuscript. Finally, my acknowledgements also extend to Ron Lesthaeghe, whose publications on various topics related to European fertility and the second demographic transition have provided a great inspiration for this article. Without his work this article would look very different.

8. References

Adsera, A. 2004. "Changing fertility rates in developed countries. The impact of labour market institutions." *Journal of Population Economics* 17(1): 1-27.

Adsera, A. 2005. "Vanishing children: From high unemployment to low fertility in developed countries." *American Economic Review, Papers and Proceedings*, 95(2): 189-193.

Aiginger, K. 2005. "Towards a new European model of a reformed welfare state: An alternative to the United States model." Chapter 7 in *Economic Survey of Europe* 2005/I, United Nations Economic Commission for Europe, Geneva, pp. 105-114.

Alho, J., M. Alders, H. Cruijsen, N. Keilman, T. Nikander, and D. Q. Pham. 2006. "New forecast: Population decline postponed in Europe." *Statistical Journal of the United Nations ECE* 23: 1-10.

Avramov, D. and R. Cliquet. 2003. "Economy of time and population policy. Rethinking the 20th Century life course paradigm." *Zeitschrift für Bevölkerungswissenschaft* 28(2-4): 369-402.

Baizán, P., F. Michielin, and F. C. Billari. 2002. "Political economy and life course patterns: The heterogeneity of occupational, family, and household trajectories of young Spaniards". *Demographic Research* 6, Article 8: 191-240. [www.demographic-research.org].

Berrington, A. 2004. "Perpetual postponers? Women's, men's and couples fertility intentions and subsequent fertility behaviour." *Population Trends* 117 (Autumn 2004): 9-19.

Bijak, J., D. Kupiszewska, M. Kupiszewski, K. Saczuk, and A. Kicinger. 2007. "Population and labour force projections for 27 countries, 2002-2052: impact of international migration on population ageing." *European Journal of Population* 23(1): 1-31.

Billari, F. C. 2005. "Partnership, childbearing and parenting trends of the 1990s." Chapter 5 in.: M. Macura, A. L. MacDonald, and W. Haug (eds.) *The new demographic regime. Population challenges and policy responses.* New York and Geneva: United nations, pp. 63-89.

Billari, F. C. and R. Borgoni. 2005. "Assessing the use of sample selection models in the estimation of fertility postponement effects." *Statistical Methods and Applications* 14(3): 389-402.

Billari, F. C. and H.-P. Kohler. 2004. "Patterns of low and very low fertility in Europe". *Population Studies* 58 (2): 161-176.

Billari, F. C. and C. Wilson. 2001. "Convergence towards diversity? Cohort dynamics in the transition to adulthood in contemporary Western Europe". MPIDR Working paper WP 2001-39, Max Planck Institute for Demographic Research, Rostock; [www.demogr.mpg.de/Papers/Working/WP-2001-039.pdf].

Bongaarts, J. 2002. "The end of the fertility transition in the developed world". *Population and Development Review* 28(3): 419-443.

Bongaarts, J. 2004. "Population aging and the rising cost of public pensions." *Population and Development Review* 30(1): 1-23.

Bongaarts, J. and G. Feeney. 1998. "On the quantum and tempo of fertility". *Population and Development Review* 24(2): 271-291.

Brewster, K. L. and R. R. Rindfuss. 2000. "Fertility and women's employment in industrialized nations". *Annual Review of Sociology* 26: 271-296.

Buber, I. and A. Prskawetz. 2000. Fertility in second unions in Austria. Findings from the Austrian FFS. *Demographic Research*, Vol. 3, Article 2. [www.demographic-research.org].

Caldwell, J. C. and T. Schindlmayr. 2003. "Explanations of the fertility crisis in modern societies: A search for commonalities". *Population Studies* 57(3): 241-263.

Calot, G. and J.-P. Sardon. "Fécondité, reproduction et replacement." *Population* 56(3): 337-396.

CBS Statline. 2006. CBS Statline. Internet database of the Centraal Bureau voor de Statistiek [Statistics Netherlands], Voorburg. Accessed at [http://statline.cbs.nl].

CDC. 2006. *Assisted reproductive technology success rates 2004*. U.S. Department of Health and Human Services, Centers for Disease Control and Prevention, Atlanta. Accessed at
[http://www.cdc.gov/ART/ART2004/download.htm].

Chesnais, J.-C. 1992. *The demographic transition. Stages, patterns, and the economic implications*. Oxford: Oxford University Press.

Chesnais, J.-C. 2001. "Comment: A march toward population recession". In.: R. A. Bulatao and J. B. Casterline (eds.) *Global Fertility Transition, supplement to Population and Development Review* 27: 255-259.

Coleman, D. 2004. "Why we don't have to believe without doubting in the "Second demographic transition"—some agnostic comments." *Vienna Yearbook of Population Research* 2004: 11-24.

Coleman, D. 2006a. "Europe's demographic future: Determinants, dimensions, and challenges." In.: P. Demeny and G. McNicoll (eds.) *The political economy of global population change, 1950-2050.*, supplement to *Population and Development Review* 32: 52-95.

Coleman, D. 2006b. "Immigration and ethnic change in low-fertility countries: A third demographic transition." *Population and Development Review* 32(3): 401-446.

Coleman, D., P. Compton, and J. Salt. 2002. "Demography of migrant populations: the case of the United Kingdom." In.: Haug, W., P. Compton, P. and Y. Courbage (eds.) *The demographic characteristics of immigrant populations*. Population Studies, No. 38, Strasbourg: Council of Europe Publishing, pp. 497-552.

Compton, P. and Y. Courbage. 2002. "Synthesis report." In.: Haug, W., P. Compton, P. and Y. Courbage (eds.) *The demographic characteristics of immigrant populations*. Population Studies, No. 38, Strasbourg: Council of Europe Publishing, pp. 553-592.

Cook. L. P. 2004. "The gendered division of labor and family outcomes in Germany." *Journal of Marriage and Family* 66(5): 1246-1259.

Corijn, M. and E. Klijzing (eds.). 2001. *Transitions to adulthood in Europe.* European Studies of Population, Vol. 10, Dordrecht: Kluwer Academic Publishers

Corijn, M., A. C. Liefbroer, and J. de Jong Gierveld. 1996. "It takes two to tango, doesn't it? The influence of couple characteristics on the timing of the birth of the firs child." *Journal of Marriage and the Family* 58: 117-126.

Council of Europe. 2006. *Recent demographic developments in Europe 2005.* Strasbourg: Council of Europe Publishing.

CZSO. 2007. Population data published by the Czech Statistical Office, Prague. Accessed at [http://www.czso.cz].

Dalla Zuanna, G. 2001. "The banquet of Aeolus: A familistic interpretation of Italy's lowest-low fertility". *Demographic Research* 4, Article 5: 133-161. [www.demographic-research.org].

Dalla Zuanna, G. 2006. "Population replacement, social mobility and development in Italy in the twentieth century." *Journal of Modern Italian Studies* 11(2): 188-208.

Daguet, F. 2002. "Le remplacement des générations." Chapter 12 in.: *Un siècle de fécondité française: Caractéristiques et évolution de la fécondité de 1901 á 1999.* Paris: INSEE, pp. 235-252.

Debré, R. and A. Sauvy. 1946. *Des Français pour la France (Le problème de la population).* Paris: Gallimard.

Delgado, M., Meil G., and F. Zamora López. 2008. "Spain: Short on children and short on family policies." Forthcoming in.: Frejka, J. Hoem, T. Sobotka, and L. Toulemon (eds.) *Childbearing trends and policies in Europe.*

Demeny, P. 2003. "Population policy dilemmas in Europe at the dawn of the twenty-first century." *Population and Development Review* 29(1): 1-28.

Duschek, K.-J. and H. Wirth. 2005. "Kinderlosigkeit von Frauen im Spiegel des Mikrozensus. Eine Kohortenanalyse der Mikrozensen 1987 bis 2003." *Wirtschaft und Statistik* 8/2005, Statistisches Bundesamt, Wiesbaden. Accessed at [http://www.destatis.de/]

Eckhard, J. 2006. "Kinderlosigkeit durch Partnerschaflosigkeit. Der Wandel der Partnerschaftbiographien und Zusammenhänge mit der Geburtenentwicklung" *Zeitschrift für Bevölkerungswissenschaft* 31(1): 105-126.

Engelhardt, H. and A. Prskawetz. 2004. "On the changing correlation between fertility and female employment over space and time." *European Journal of Population* 20(1): 35-52.

Engstler, H. and S. Menning. 2003. *Die Familie im Spiegel der amtlichen Statistik.* Berlin: Bundesministerium für Familie, Senioren, Frauen und Jugend. Accessed at [http://www.bmfsfj.de/Kategorien/Publikationen/Publikationen,did=3122.html].

Esping-Andersen, G. 1999. *Social foundations of postindustrial economies.* Oxford University Press, Oxford.

European Commission. 2005. Green Paper "Confronting demographic change: a new solidarity between the generations." Brussels, Commission of the European Communities. [http://ec.europa.eu/employment_social/news/2005/mar/comm2005-94_en.pdf].

Eurostat. 1996. *Population statistics 1996.* Brussels and Luxembourg: Office for official Publications of the European Communities.

Eurostat. 2006a. *Population statistics. 2006 edition.* Luxembourg: Office for official Publications of the European Communities.

Eurostat. 2006b. "Population in Europe 2005. First results." *Statistics in Focus,* Population and Social Conditions, 16/2006, Luxembourg: European Communities.

Eurostat. 2006c. "Long-term population projections at national level." *Statistics in Focus,* Population and Social Conditions, 3/2006, Luxembourg: European Communities.

Eurostat. 2007. *Population and Social Conditions.* Online database accessed at [http://epp.eurostat.ec.europa.eu].

Feld, S. 2000. "Active population growth and immigration hypotheses in Western Europe." *European Journal of Population* 16(1): 3-40.

Festy, P. 1979. *La fécondité des pays occidentaux de 1870 à 1970.* Travaux et Documents No. 85. Paris: INED – PUF.

Foster, C. 2000. "The limits to low fertility: A biosocial approach". *Population and Development Review* 26(2): 209-234.

Frejka, T. and J.-P. Sardon. 2004. *Childbearing trends and prospects in low-fertility countries.* Volume 13, European Studies of Population, Kluwer Academic Publishers, Dordrecht.

Giddens, A. 1992. *The transformation of intimacy. Sexuality, love & eroticism in modern societies.* Polity Press, Cambridge.

Goldin, C. 2006. "The quiet revolution that transformed women's employment, education, and family." *American Economic Review* 96(2): 1-21.

Goldscheider, F. K. and G. Kaufman. 1996. "Fertility and commitment. Bringing men back in". In.: J. B. Casterline, R. D. Lee, and K. A. Foote (eds.) *Fertility in the United States. New patterns, new theories.* Supplement to *Population and Development Review* 22, Population Council, New York, pp. 87-99.

Goldstein, J. R. 2006. "How late can first births be postponed? Some illustrative population-level calculations." *Vienna Yearbook of Population Research* 2006: 153-165.

Gonzáles, M. 2005. "The determinants of the prevalence of single mothers: A cross-country analysis." *Discussion Paper Series,* IZA DP-1677, Institute for the Study of Labor, Bonn. Accessed at [ftp://repec.iza.org/RePEc/Discussionpaper/dp1677.pdf].

Griffith, J. D., H. P. Koo, and C. M. Suchindran. 1985. "Childbearing and family in remarriage". *Demography* 22: 73-88.

Grünheid, E. 2006. "Die demographische Lage in Deutschland 2005." *Zeitschrift für Bevölkerungswissenschaft,* 31(1): 3-104.

Halman, L. 2001. *The European Values Study. A third wave.* Source book of the 1999/2000 European Values Study surveys. WORC, Tilburg University.

Hagewen, K. and S. P. Morgan. 2005. "Intended and ideal family size in the United States." *Population and Development Review* 31(3): 507-527.

Hakim, C. 2003. "Preference theory: A new approach to explaining fertility patterns". *Population and Development Review* 29(3): 349-374.

Howe, N. and R. Jackson. 2005. *Projecting immigration. A survey of the current state of practice and theory.* A report of the CSIS Global Aging Initiative. Washington: CSIS. [http://www.csis.org/media/csis/pubs/0504_howe_jacksonprojimmigration.pdf]

Heuveline, P. and J. M. Timberlake. 2004. "The role of cohabitation in family formation: The United States in comparative perspective." *Journal of Marriage and Family* 66: 1214-1230.

Heuveline, P., J. M. Timberlake, and F. F. Furstenberg, Jr. 2003. "Shifting childrearing to single mothers: Results from 17 Western countries". *Population and Development Review* 29 (1): 47-71.

INE. 2006. "Vital Statistics 2005. Definitive data." Madrid: Instituto National de Estadística. Accessed at [http://www.ine.es/inebase/cgi/um?M=%2Ft20%2Fe301&O=inebase&N=&L=1]

INSEE. 2007. Data on completed fertility of French women born in 1885-1954 accessed at: [http://www.insee.fr/fr/ppp/ir/accueil.asp?page=SD2004/dd/SD2004_FECONDITE.htm]

Jennissen, R. 2004. *Macro-economic determinants of international migration in Europe.* Doctoral thesis, Amsterdam: Dutch University Press.

Jensen, A.-M. 1995. "Partners and parents in Europe: A gender divide". *Comparative Social Research* 18: 1-29.

Johansson, L. and F. Finnäs. 1983. *Fertility of Swedish Women Born 1927-60.* Urval Nr. 14, Stockholm: Statistics Sweden.

Kiernan, K. 2004. "Unmarried cohabitation and parenthood in Britain and Europe". *Law & Policy* 26(1): 33-55.

Kohler, H.-P., F. C. Billari, and J. A. Ortega. 2002. "The emergence of lowest-low fertility in Europe during the 1990s". *Population and Development Review* 28 (4): 641-680.

Konietzka, D. and M. Kreyenfeld. 2002. "Women's employment and non-marital childbearing: A comparison between East and West Germany in the 1990s". *Population-E* 57(2): 331-358.

Kravdal, Ø. 1997. "Wanting a child without a firm commitment to the partner: Interpretations and implications of a common behaviour pattern among Norwegian cohabitants." *European Journal of Population* 13: 269-298.

Kuijsten, A. C. 1996. "Changing family patterns in Europe: A case of divergence?" *European Journal of Population* 12(2): 115-143.

Kytir, J. 2006. "Demographische Strukturen und Trends 2005". *Statistische Nachrichten* 2006(9): 777-790.

Lesthaeghe, R. 1983. "A century of demographic and cultural change in Western Europe: An exploration of underlying dimensions". *Population and Development Review* 9(3): 411-435.

Lesthaeghe, R. 1995. "The second demographic transition in Western countries: An interpretation". In.: K. O. Mason and A.-M. Jensen (eds.) *Gender and family change in industrialized countries.* Oxford, Clarendon Press, pp. 17-62.

Lesthaeghe, R and G. Moors. 2000. "Recent trends in fertility and household formation in the industrialized world". *Review of Population and Social Policy* 9: 121-170.

Lesthaeghe, R. and K. Neels. 2002. "From the first to the second demographic transition: An interpretation of the spatial continuity of demographic innovation in France, Belgium and Switzerland". *European Journal of Population* 18(4): 325-360.

Lesthaeghe, R. and L. Neidert. 2006. "The second demographic transition in the United States: Exception or textbook example?" *Population and Development Review* 32(4): 669-698.

Lesthaeghe R. and J. Surkyn. 1988. "Cultural dynamics and economic theories of fertility change."*Population and Development Review* 14(1): 1-45.

Lesthaeghe, R. and P. Willems. 1999. "Is low fertility a temporary phenomenon in the European Union?" *Population and Development Review* 25(2): 211-228.

Liefbroer, A. C. 2005. "The impact of perceived costs and rewards of childbearing on entry into parenthood: Evidence from a panel study." *European Journal of Population* 21(4): 367-391.

Longman, P. 2004. *The empty cradle. How falling birthrates threaten world prosperity [and what to do about it].* Basic Books, New York.

Lutz, W. 2006. "Alternative paths for future European fertility: Will the birth rate recover or continue to decline?" In.: W. Lutz, R. Richter, and C. Wilson (eds.) *The new generations of Europeans. Demography and families in the enlarged European Union.* IIASA and Earthscan, London and Sterling, pp. 83-100.

Lutz, W. and S. Scherbov. 2003a. "Can immigration compensate for Europe's low fertility?" *European Demographic Research Papers 2003*, No. 1, Vienna Institute of Demography.

Lutz, W. and S. Scherbov. 2003b. "Future demographic change in Europe: The contribution of migration." *Interim Report* IR-03-66, international Institute for Applied Systems Analysis, Laxenburg. [http://www.iiasa.ac.at/Admin/PUB/Documents/IR-03-066.pdf]

Lutz, W., B. C. O'Neill, and S. Scherbov. 2003. "Europe's population at a turning point". *Science* 299: 1991-1992.

Lutz, W., V. Skirbekk, and M. R. Testa. 2006. "The low fertility trap hypothesis. Forces that may lead to further postponement and fewer births in Europe." *Vienna Yearbook of Population Research* 2006: 167-192.

McDonald, P. 2000. "Gender equity, social institutions and the future of fertility". *Journal of Population Research* 17(1): 1-15.

McDonald, P. 2002. "Sustaining fertility through public policy: The range of options". *Population-E* 57(3): 417-446.

McDonald, P. 2006. "Low fertility and the state: The efficacy of policy." *Population and Development Review* 32(3): 485-510.

McLanahan, S. 2004. "Diverging destinies: How children are faring under the second demographic transition?" *Demography* 41(4): 607-627.

Mencarini, L. and M. L. Tanturri. 2004. "Time use, family role set and childbearing among Italian working women." *Genus* 60(1): 111-137.

Menken, J. 1985. "Age and fertility. How late can you wait?" *Demography* 22 (4): 469-483.

Morgan, S. P. 2003. "Is low fertility a twenty-first century demographic crisis?" *Demography* 40(4): 589-603.

Morgan, S. P. and K. Hagewen. 2005. "Is very low fertility inevitable in America? Insights and forecasts from an integrative model of fertility." Chapter 1 in.: A. Boot and A. C. Crouter (eds.) *The new population problem. Why families in developed world are shrinking and what it means.* Lawrence Erlbaum Associates, Mahwah, New Jersey, pp. 3-28.

Morgan, S. P. and M. G. Taylor. 2006. "Low fertility at the turn of the twenty-first century." *Annual Review of Sociology* 2006, 32: 375-399.

Munoz-Perez, F. and F. Prioux. 2000. "Children born outside marriage in France and their parents: Recognitions and legitimations since 1965." *Population: An English Selection,* 12(2000): 139-195.

Nazio, T. and H.-P. Blossfeld. 2003. "The diffusion of cohabitation among young women in West Germany, East Germany and Italy." *European Journal of Population* 19(1): 47-82.

Norris, P. and R. Inglehart. 2004. *Sacred and secular. Religion and politics worldwide.* Cambridge University Press, Cambridge.

Nyboe Andersen, A., L. Gianaroli, R. Felberbaum, J. de Mouzon, and K. G. Nygren. 2006. "Assisted reproductive technology in Europe, 2002. Results generated from European registers by ESHRE." *Human Reproduction* 21(7): 1680-97.

OECD. 2003. *Babies and bosses. Reconciling work and family life.* Vol. 2: Austria, Ireland and Japan. Organisation for Economic Co-operation and Development, Paris.

OECD. 2006. *Education at a glance 2006.* Organisation for Economic Co-operation and Development, Paris. Tables accessed at [http://www.oecd.org/document/6/0,3343,en_2825_495609_37344774_1_1_1_1,00.html]

OECD. 2007. *OECD Factbook 2007* – Economic, environmental and social statistics. Organisation for Economic Co-operation and Development, Paris. Data accessed at [http://miranda.sourceoecd.org/vl=16335786/cl=42/nw=1/rpsv/factbook/].

Oláh, L. and E. Bernhardt. 2008. "Sweden: Combining childbearing and gender equality." Forthcoming in.: Frejka, J. Hoem, T. Sobotka, and L. Toulemon (eds.) *Childbearing trends and policies in Europe.*

ONS. 2006. Birth statistics. Review of the Registrar General on births and patterns of family building England and Wales, 2005. Series FM1, No. 34, Office of National Statistics, London. Accessed at [http://www.statistics.gov.uk/downloads/theme_population/FM1_34/FM1_no34_2005.pdf]

Oppenheimer, V. K. 1994. "Women's rising employment and the future of the family in industrialized societies." *Population and Development Review* 20: 293-342.

Ortega, J. A. and L. A. del Rey. 2007. "Birth replacement ratios in Europe: A new look at period replacement." Paper presented at the 2007 Annual Meeting of the Population Association of America, New York, 29-31 March 2007.

PDR. 1984. "The European Parliament on the need for promoting population growth." *Population and Development Review* 10(3): 569-570.

Population Trends. 2006. Table 3.2 in *Population Trends* 125 (Autumn 2006), accessed at: [http://www.statistics.gov.uk/downloads/theme_population/PT125_main_part3.pdf].

Philipov, D. 2005. "Portrait of the family in Europe." Chapter 2 in.: L. Hantrais, D. Philipov, and F. C. Billari (eds.) *Policy implications of changing family formation.* Population Studies, No. 49, Strasbourg: Council of Europe Publishing.

Presser, H. B. 2005. "The importance of gender relations for understanding low fertility and single motherhood." Chapter 11 in.: A. Boot and A. C. Crouter (eds.) *The new population problem. Why families in developed world are shrinking and what it means.* Lawrence Erlbaum Associates, Mahwah, New Jersey, pp. 161-169.

Prinz, C. 1995. *Cohabiting, married, or single: Portraying, analyzing, and modelling new living arrangements in the changing societies of Europe.* Aldershot: Avebury.

Prioux, F. 2006. "Recent demographic developments in France." *Population-E* 61(4): 323-364.

Prskawetz, A., T. Sobotka, I. Buber, R. Gisser, and H. Engelhardt. 2008. "Austria: persistent low fertility since the mid-1980s." Forthcoming in.: Frejka, J. Hoem, T. Sobotka, and L. Toulemon (eds.) *Childbearing trends and policies in Europe.*

Prskawetz, A, E. Thomson, M. Spielauer, and M. W. Dworak. 2007. "Union instability as an engine of fertility? A micro-simulation model for France." Paper presented at the 2007 Annual Meeting of the Population Association of America, New York, 29-31 March 2007.

Prskawetz, A., A. Vikat, D. Philipov, and H. Engelhardt. 2003. "Pathways to stepfamily formation in Europe: Results from the FFS." *Demographic Research* 8, Article 5: 107-149.

Ravanera, Z. R. and F. Rajulton. 2004. "Social status polarization in the timing and trajectories to motherhood." Discussion Paper 04-06, Population Studies Centre, University of Western Ontario, London. Accessed at [http://sociology.uwo.ca/popstudies/dp/dp04-06.pdf].

Reher, S. D. 1998. "Family ties in Western Europe: Persistent contrasts". *Population and Development Review* 24(2): 203-234.

Retherford, R. R., N. Ogawa, R. Matsukura. 2001. "Late marriage and less marriage in Japan." *Population and Development Review* 27(1): 65-102.

Rindfuss, R. R., K. B. Guzzo, and S. P. Morgan. 2003. "The changing institutional context of low fertility." *Population Research and Policy Review* 22: 411-438.

Rindfuss, R. R., S. P. Morgan, and G. Swicegood. 1988. *First Births in America. Changes in the Timing of Parenthood*, University of California Press, Berkeley, California.

Roig Vila, M. and T. Castro Martín. 2005. "Immigrant women, Spanish babies: Longing for a baby-boom in a lowest-low fertility society." Paper presented at session 66 of the IUSSP Population Conference, Tours, France, 18-23 July 2005.

Saczuk, K. 2003. "A development and critique of the concept of replacement migration." CEFMR Working Paper 4/2003, Central European Forum for Migration Research, Warsaw. [http://www.cefmr.pan.pl/docs/cefmr_wp_2003-04.pdf].

Sardon, J.-P. 1991. "Generation replacement in Europe since 1900." *Population: An English selection* 3(1990): 15-32.

SFSO. 2006. "Statistique du mouvement naturel de la population. Résultats définitifs 2005." Neuchâtel: Swiss Federal Statistical Office. Accessed at [http://www.bfs.admin.ch/].

Shaw, C., H. Cruijsen, J. de Beer, and A. de Jong. 1997. "Latest population projections for the European Union." *Population Trends* 90 (Winter 1997): 18-30.

Shkolnikov, V., E. M. Andreev, R. Houle, and J. W. Vaupel. 2007. "The concentration of reproduction in cohorts of women in Europe and the United States." *Population and Development Review* 33(1): 67-99.

Smallwood, S. 2002b. "New estimates of trends in births by birth order in England and Wales". *Population Trends*, No. 108: 32-48. Accessed at [www.statistics.gov.uk/statbase/Product.asp?vlnk=6303].

Smallwood, S. and J. Chamberlain. 2005. "Replacement fertility, what has it been and what does it mean?" *Population Trends* 119 (Spring 2005): 16-27.

Sobotka, T. 2004a. *Postponement of childbearing and low fertility in Europe*. PhD Thesis, University of Groningen. Amsterdam: Dutch University Press.

Sobotka, T. 2004b. "Is lowest-low fertility explained by the postponement of childbearing?" *Population and Development Review* 30(2): 195-220.

Sobotka, T. 2005. "Childless societies? Trends and projections of childlessness in Europe and the Unites States" Paper presented at the 2005 PAA Annual Meeting Meeting, Philadelphia, 31 March-2 April 2005.

Sobotka, T. 2008. "The rising importance of migrants for childbearing in Europe." Forthcoming in.: T. Frejka, J. Hoem, T. Sobotka, and L. Toulemon (eds.) *Childbearing trends and policies in Europe*.

Sobotka, T., H.-P. Kohler, and F. C. Billari. 2007. "The increase in late childbearing in Europe, Japan and the United States." Paper presented at the 2007 Annual Meeting of the Population Association of America, New York, 29-31 March 2007.

Sobotka, T. and M. R. Testa. 2008. "Childlessness attitudes and intentions in Europe." In.: Ch. Höhn, D. Avramov and I. Kotowska (Eds.) *People, Population Change and Policies: Lessons from the Population Policy Acceptance Study* (Vol. 1). European Studies of Population 16/1, Springer-Verlag.

Spielauer, M. 2005. "Concentration of reproduction in Austria: General trends and differentials by educational attainment and urban-rural setting." *Vienna Yearbook of Population Research* 2005: 171-195.

Stankuniene, V and A. Jasilioniene. 2008. "Lithuania: Fertility decline and its determinants." Forthcoming in.: T. Frejka, J. Hoem, T. Sobotka, and L. Toulemon (eds.) *Childbearing trends and policies in Europe.*

Statistics Denmark. 2004. Befolkningens bevægelser 2003. Vital statistics 2003. Copenhagen: Danmarks Statistik.

Statistics Sweden. 2006. Tabeller över Sveriges befolkning 2005. Statistiska centralbyrån (Statistics Sweden), Stockholm.

Stephen, E. H. 2000. "Demographic implications of assisted reproductive technologies." *Population research and Policy Review* 19(4): 301-315.

Surkyn, J. and R. Lesthaeghe. 2004. "Value orientations and the Second Demographic Transition (SDT) in Northern, Western and Southern Europe: An update", *Demographic Research*, Special Collection 3, Article 3: 45-86. [www.demographic-research.org].

Teitelbaum, M. S. 2004. "Western experiences with international migration in the context of population decline." *The Japanese Journal of Population* 2(1): 29-40. [http://www.ipss.go.jp/webj-ad/WebJournal.files/population/2004_3/michael2004mar.pdf]

Teitelbaum, M. S. and J. M. Winter. 1985. *The fear of population decline.* London: Academic Press.

Testa, M. R. 2006. "Childbearing preferences and family issues in Europe." Special Eurobarometer 253/Wave 65.1 – TNS Opinion & Social, European Commission.

Thornton, A. 1989. "Changing attitudes toward family issues in the United States." *Journal of Marriage and the Family* 51(4): 873-893.

Thomson, E. 2004. "Stepfamilies and childbearing desires in Europe." *Demographic Research*, Special collection 3, Article 5: 117-134. [www.demographic-research.org].

Thomson, E. and J. M. Hoem. 1998. "Couple childbearing plans and births in Sweden." *Demography*, 35(3): 315-322.

Thomson, E., J. M. Hoem, A. Vikat, A. Prskawetz, I. Bubber, L. Toulemon, U. Henz, A. L. Goldecker, and V. Kantorová. 2002. "Childbearing in stepfamilies: How parity matters." Chapter 6 in.: E. Klijzing and M. Corijn (eds.) *Dynamics of fertility and partnerships in Europe*, Vol. II. New York and Geneva: United Nations, pp. 87-99.

Toulemon, L. 2004a. "Le fécondité est-elle encore naturelle ? Application au retard des naissances et à son influence sur la descendance finale." In.: *Chaire Quetelet 2002*, Academia Bruylant/L'Harmattan, pp. 1-28.

Toulemon, L. 2004b. "Fertility among immigrant women: new data, new approach." *Population & Societies* 400 (April 2004). [http://www.ined.fr/en/resources_documentation/publications/pop_soc/bdd/publication/540/].

Toulemon, L. and M. Mazuy. 2001. "Les naissances sont retardées mais la fécondité est stable". *Population* 56(4): 611-644.

UN. 2000. *Replacement migration. Is it a solution to declining and aging populations?* Population Division, United Nations, New York.

US Census Bureau. 2007. Historical statistics on population 1900-2002. Downloaded at: [http://www.census.gov/statab/hist/HS-01.pdf].

Van Bavel, J. 2007. "Subreplacement fertility in the West before the baby boom (1900-1940): Current and contemporary perspectives." Paper presented at the 32nd Annual Meeting of the Social Science History Association, Chicago IL, November 18, 2007.

Van Bavel, J. and V. Bastiaenssen. 2006. "De evolutie van de vruchtbaarheid in het Vlaamse Gewest tussen 2001 en 2005." Interface Demography Working Paper 2006-1, Vrije Universiteit Brussel, Brussels.

Van de Kaa, D. J. 1987. "Europe's second demographic transition". *Population Bulletin* 42(1).

Van de Kaa, D. J. 1999. "Europe and its population: The long view". In.: D. J. van de Kaa, H. Leridon, G. Gesano, and M. Okólski (eds.) *European Populations: Unity in Diversity.* Dordrecht: Kluwer Academic, pp. 1-49.

Van de Kaa, D. J. 2001. "Postmodern fertility preferences: From changing value orientation to new behavior". In.: R. A. Bulatao, J. B. Casterline (eds.) *Global fertility transition.* Supplement to *Population and Development Review* 27, New York, Population Council, pp. 290-338.

Van de Kaa, D. J. 2002. "The idea of a Second Demographic Transition in industrialized countries." Paper presented at the Sixth Welfare Policy Seminar of the National Institute of Population and Social Security, Tokyo, Japan, 29 January 2002. [http://www.ipss.go.jp/webj-ad/WebJournal.files/population/2003_4/Kaa.pdf].

Van de Kaa, D. J. 2004. "The true commonality: In reflexive societies fertility is a derivative". *Population Studies* 58(1): 77-80.

Van Imhoff, E. 2001. "On the impossibility of inferring cohort fertility measures from period fertility measures". *Demographic Research* 5, Article 2: 23-64. [www.demographic-research.org].

Vatican. 2006. "Address of His Holiness Benedict XVI to the Roman Curia offering them his Christmas greetings." Accessed at [http://www.vatican.va/holy_father/benedict_xvi/speeches/2006/december/documents/hf_ben_xvi_spe_20061222_curia-romana_en.html]

VID. 2006. *European demographic data sheet 2006.* Vienna Institute of demography, IIASA, Population Reference Bureau. [http://www.oeaw.ac.at/vid/popeurope/index.html].

Vikat, A., E. Thomson, and J. M. Hoem. 1999. "Stepfamily fertility in contemporary Sweden: The impact of childbearing before the current union." *Population Studies* 53(2): 211-225.

Vishnevski, A. (ed.) 2006. *Demograficheskaya modernizatsia Rossii 1900-2000* [Demographic Modernization of Russia 1900-2000]. Novoe Izdatelstvo, Moscow.

VAZG. 2007. Tables on births in Flanders provided by the Flemish Healthcare Agency (Vlaams Agentschap Zorg en Gezondheit); [http://www.zorg-en-gezondheid.be/topPage.aspx?id=684].

Voas, D. 2003. "Conflicting preferences: A reason fertility tends to be too high or too low." *Population and Development Review* 29(4): 627-646.

Wanner, P. 2002. "The demographic characteristics of immigrant populations in Switzerland." In.: Haug, W., P. Compton, P. and Y. Courbage (eds.) *The demographic characteristics of immigrant populations.* Population Studies, No. 38, Strasbourg: Council of Europe Publishing, pp. 419-496.

Weiss, W. 2006. "Zur Entwicklung einer Residualbevölkerung infolge lang anhaltender Abwanderung in Mecklenburg-Vorpommern." *Zeitschrift für Bevölkerungswissenschaft* 31(3-4): 469-506.

9. Appendix

Construction of the SDT indexes used in the analysis in Section 4

• SDT1 index (demographic dimension)

This index, composed for 34 countries, is based on the following indicators for 2004 (or the latest year available):

1) Mean age of mother at birth of first child (MAFB);
2) Sum of age-specific fertility rates below age 20, per 1000 women (TEENFERT);
3) Percentage of non-marital births (NONMAR);
4) Total first marriage rate (TFMR);
5) Mean age at first marriage (MAFM);
6) Total divorce rate (TDR).

Finally, the index is adjusted upwards by 0.5 if more than 10 per cent of coresidential unions were made up by cohabiting couples (data for 2001 based on Philipov 2005 and national data sources). Maximum, minimum and mean values of these indicators and the assigned SDT scores are displayed in Table AP-2.

• SDT2 index (attitudes and values dimension)

This index is based on the 1999/2000 results of the European Values Study, published in Halman (2001). It is based on the responses in 29 countries to the following questions and statements.:

1) "...how important it is in your life: leisure time" (LEISURE, % "very important")
2) "How often do you spend time in church, mosque, or synagogue" (CHURCH, % "every week");
3) "Please use the scale to indicate how much freedom of choice and control you feel you have over the way your life turns out?" (CONTROL, mean value on the scale of 1 (=none control at all) to 10 (= a great deal of control));
4) "Do you think that a woman has to have children in order to be fulfilled or is this not necessary?" (NEED_KIDS, % responses "not necessary");
5) "Marriage is an outdated institution" (MARRIAGE, % "agree");
6) "A job is alright, but what women really want is a home and children" (F_HOME, % "agree strongly");
7) "One does not have the duty to respect and love parents who have not earned it by their behaviour and attitudes" (PAR_RESPECT, % "agree");
8) "Do you approve or disapprove abortion (...) where a married couple does not want to have any more children?" (ABORTION, % "approve").

Several questions were not asked in all the participating countries; the SDT2 index for these countries was based on the mean score of the responses to the remaining items. Maximum, minimum and mean values of these indicators and the assigned SDT scores are displayed in Table AP-2.

Table AP-1: SDT indexes and demographic indicators used in the regression analysis in section 4
↓

	SDT indexes			Demographic indicators			
	SDT1 (2004)	SDT2 (2000)	SDT-C (2000, 2004)	TFR (2004)	TFRadj (2002)	MAFB (2004)	Intended TFR[1] (2006)
WESTERN EUROPE							
Austria	6.9	6.5	6.7	1.42	1.63	27.04	1.54
France	7.6	5.9	6.8	1.91	2.02	28.5 [2]	2.36
Germany	6.6	6.3	6.5	1.36	1.51	28.5 [2]	1.91
Ireland	5.0	5.4	5.2	1.93	2.22	28.53	2.76
Luxembourg	7.0	6.6	6.8	1.69	1.83	28.65	2.18
Netherlands	7.4	7.8	7.6	1.73	1.82	28.88	2.30
Switzerland	6.4	...	...	1.41	1.69	29.0 [2]	...
United Kingdom	6.4	7.4	6.9	1.77	1.85	27.0 [2]	2.38
NORTHERN EUROPE							
Denmark	7.5	8.4	7.9	1.78	2.00	28.37	2.24
Finland	7.2	7.1	7.1	1.80	1.88	28.0 [2]	2.62
Norway	8.0	...	...	1.83	2.07	27.60	...
Sweden	8.8	8.3	8.6	1.75	1.91	28.64	2.27
Iceland	7.1	6.5	6.8	2.04	2.33	26.17	...
SOUTHERN EUROPE							
Greece	3.9	4.3	4.1	1.29	1.49	28.2 [2]	2.09
Italy	5.1	4.2	4.6	1.33	1.41	29.0 [2]	1.76
Portugal	4.9	3.7	4.3	1.40	1.80	27.15	2.06
Spain	5.4	5.1	5.2	1.32	1.33	29.3	1.73
CENTRAL-EASTERN EUROPE							
Croatia	3.1	4.7	3.9	1.35	1.64	26.3 [2]	2.13
Czech Republic	6.0	5.6	5.8	1.23	1.67	26.31	1.98
Hungary	5.5	4.0	4.8	1.28	1.76	26.27	2.42
Poland	3.7	2.4	3.1	1.23	1.64	25.55	2.12
Slovak Republic	4.0	4.4	4.2	1.24	1.60	25.34	1.88
Slovenia	7.2	6.4	6.8	1.25	1.63	27.46	2.08

	SDT indexes			Demographic indicators			
	SDT1 (2004)	SDT2 (2000)	SDT-C (2000, 2004)	TFR (2004)	TFRadj (2002)	MAFB (2004)	Intended TFR[1] (2006)
SOUTH-EASTERN EUROPE							
Bulgaria	3.8	4.4	4.1	1.29	1.53	24.38	2.17
Romania	1.7	3.3	2.5	1.29	1.58	24.4 [2]	1.71
BALTIC REPUBLICS							
Estonia	6.5	4.2	5.3	1.47	1.70 [2]	25.0 [2]	2.20
Latvia	4.8	3.0	3.9	1.24	1.56	24.71	2.14
Lithuania	4.2	4.5	4.3	1.26	1.66	24.82	2.11
EASTERN EUROPE							
Belarus	3.2	3.2	3.2	1.20	1.44	23.97	...
Moldova	3.3	...	...	1.25	1.65	23.29	...
Russia	3.6	4.1	3.8	1.33	1.47	23.98	...
Ukraine	2.8	3.3	3.0	1.22	1.36	23.53	...
MIN	1.7	2.4	2.5	1.20	1.33	23.29	1.54
MAX	8.8	8.4	8.6	2.04	2.33	29.30	2.76
MEAN	5.3	5.2	5.3	1.46	1.70	26.69	2.13

Notes: 1) Mean intended family size among women aged 25-39, Eurobarometer survey 2006 (Testa 2006: 63, Table 12); 2) Estimated values

Sources: Council of Europe (2006); Eurostat (2006a and 2006b), Eurostat (2007), Halman (2001), Philipov (2005), Testa (2006), and national statistical offices.

Table AP-2: Variables used for computing the SDT indexes: Mean, maximum, minimum and threshold values for selected SDT scores (0, 5, and 10)

↓

Variable	Values of SDT scores			Observed values			Mean SDT score
	SDT score=0	SDT score=5	SDT score=10	MIN	MAX	MEAN	
Index SDT1							
MAFB	<24	27	>30	23.29	29.30	26.60	4.3
TEENFERT	>180	90	0	26.0	209.3	84.4	5.3
NONMAR	0	30	>60	4.9	63.7	32.0	5.3
TFMR	>0.80	0.60	<0.40	0.405	0.826	0.577	5.6
MAFM	<23	27	>31	22.91	30.90	26.72	4.6
TDR	<0.15	0.35	>0.55	0.11	0.55	0.36	5.2
LEISURE	<16	32	>48	15.5	54.2	31.5	4.8
CHURCH	>30	15	0	3.1	34.2	14.8	5.2
CONTROL	<5.3	6.4	>7.5	5.4	7.6	6.7	6.2
NEED_KIDS	<5	45	>85	5.9	92.9	45.9	5.1
MARRIAGE	<6	20	>34	8.3	36.3	18.7	4.5
F_HOME	>35	20	<5	3.0	34.1	17.4	5.8
PAR_RESPECT	0	30	>60	13.5	67.3	29.6	4.9
ABORTION	<20	55	>90	15.2	85.1	56.9	5.3

Source: Halman (2001)

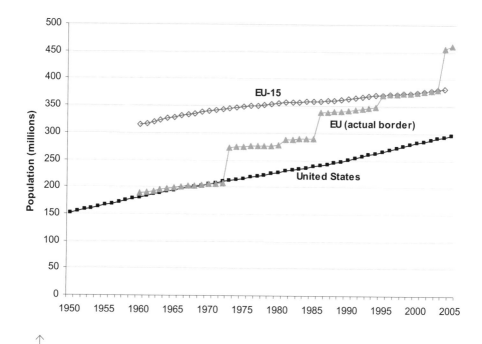

↑

Figure AP1: Population size of the European Union and the United States, 1950 (1960)-2005
<u>Sources</u>: Council of Europe (2006), Eurostat (2006a and 2007), US Census Bureau (2007)

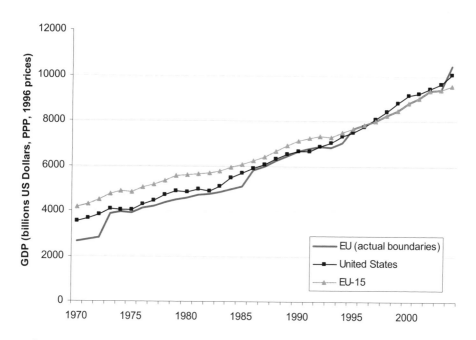

↑

Figure AP2: GDP in purchasing power parity (billion US dollars) in the European Union and the
United States, 1970-2004 (prices computed in the 1996 levels)

- 89

–

03 Education and Permanent Childlessness:
Austria vs. Sweden. A Research Note

Gerda Neyer and Jan M. Hoem[*]

–

[*]   Acknowledgement: We are grateful to Adelheid Bauer and Josef Kytir of Statistics Austria for preparing
      the data for us, to Kathrin Teschner for programming support, and to Gunnar Andersson for insightful
      comments.

1. Introduction and descriptive summary

In all European countries fertility levels have declined in recent decades, often to well below the replacement level. Low fertility levels and the rising share of women among individuals with a higher education have generated a lot of interest in the relationship between education and permanent childlessness. In the German-speaking countries this interest has been further nurtured by estimates of forty or more percent childlessness among highly educated women (Dorbritz 2003). Even if subsequent studies find somewhat lower levels than this (e.g. Schmitt and Winkelmann 2005, Duschek and Wirth 2005, Scharein and Unger 2005), they confirm the observation that in Germany permanent childlessness is considerably higher among women with an academic education than among other women.[1]

In a recent paper based on Swedish data, Hoem, Neyer, and Andersson (2006) demonstrated that the association between educational attainment and childlessness can be much less straightforward than this. They found that while childlessness largely does increase with educational level, the increase is not very strong in their data. Moreover, the differences in childlessness by educational level diminish over the life-course so that in the case of Sweden, highly educated women in their forties have the same level of childlessness as less highly educated women of the same age (Neyer, Hoem, and Andersson 2007). There are, however, pronounced differentials in childlessness by educational field. Hoem, Neyer, and Andersson (2006) find that in Sweden the field of education is more important than the educational level. Swedish women educated for jobs in teaching and health care have much lower permanent childlessness at each educational level than any other major educational grouping. By contrast, women educated in arts and humanities or for religious occupations have unusually high percentages permanently childless. The pattern seems to be similar in Norway (Lappegård and Rønsen 2005).

Hoem, Neyer, and Andersson (2006) point out several features which could produce the pattern they find: the structure and flexibility of the educational system, the differences in the labor-market and employment conditions for different educational groups, the gender patterns in education and in the labor market, and social norms and preferences linked to education and childbearing. An obvious question is whether these patterns of childlessness are unique to the Scandinavian type of society or whether they extend to countries with different educational systems, different labor-market structures, and different welfare-state setups. Comparing the patterns of different countries would allow us to better assess the interlinkages between institutional, cultural, and individual factors in shaping childbearing behaviour.

---

1   Due to the lack of reliable statistics in Germany the level of permanent childlessness can only be approximated (Kreyenfeld 2004).

In the present paper we focus on childlessness in Austria, a country that shares some features with Sweden, but differs markedly in others. As in our Swedish study, we make use of individual-level data of women born between 1955 and 1959, grouped into some sixty educational categories defined by field and level of education. We observe the share of childless among these women at an age when most of them have completed childbearing, namely at age 41 to 46.

Our main findings are twofold: First, the Austrian pattern of childlessness by educational field is very similar to the one found for Sweden, with women educated for teaching and health having lower levels of childlessness than most others on each educational level. Second, Austria differs markedly from Sweden with regard to the differentials in childlessness by educational level. Contrary to Sweden, Austrian women with a secondary or tertiary education have much higher childlessness than women with lower educational attainment. These differences and similarities between the two countries seem to underline the importance of institutional factors in shaping childbearing decisions. It seems that such factors influence individual and cultural factors, such as preferences and social norms, and thus set the frame for the different patterns of childbearing behaviour across Europe.

In the following Section 2 we outline some of the institutional and cultural features of Austria that may be relevant for childbearing, and we present the main characteristics of the educational system in Section 3. We describe our data and present the core results of our exploration in Section 4. In the final section of our paper we sum up our explanations for the Austrian pattern of childlessness and its differences from the Swedish pattern.

2. Austria – a country of educational and social conservatism

Austria and Sweden share a sufficient number of features to make them interesting cases for comparison. Both countries are small welfare states of approximately the same population size (8 to 9 million people). Both countries have coordinated market economies. They are considered to offer a high degree of employment protection and of skill protection due to the dominant role of organizations like trade unions and employers' associations in labor-market policies, social policy, and vocational-training policies (Hall and Soskice 2001; Soskice 2005; Estévez-Abe, Iversen, and Soskice 2001; Estévez-Abe 2005; Pontusson 2000). During the 1970s Sweden served as a model for the Austrian government in its endeavor to modernize Austrian society and the Austrian welfare state (Hoem, Prskawetz, and Neyer 2001, 250).

However, and despite this endeavor, Austria and Sweden have taken markedly different paths regarding their educational systems, their welfare-state setups, their parental-leave and childcare policies, and their gender- and social-equality policies. Sweden is commonly regarded as the prototype of a universal welfare state with a commitment to enabling mothers to participate in the labor market and to enhancing gender and social equality; Austria on the other hand represents a conservative, gendering welfare state which supports mothers' absence from the labor market and which does not strive actively to reduce gender and social inequality. (For an overview over the policies of both countries covering the decades relevant for our cohort, see Hoem, Prskawetz, and Neyer 2001.)

Austrian welfare-state policies have maintained class- and gender-related social differences (Esping-Andersen 1990; 2002). Parental-leave policies, introduced in the late 1950s, have supported mothers' absence from the labor market through comparatively long, rather inflexible parental leaves of one to three years duration[2], which, until 1990, were exclusively reserved for mothers, i.e., fathers were not entitled to parental leave. Childcare facilities for children under age three and after-school arrangements for school children are rare. Labor-market policies have given priority to protecting the rights of employees rather than to increasing female employment and to reducing the gender gaps in employment, job positions, pay, or care (Biffl 1997). Gender-equality policies have not been institutionalized consistently, and Austria is still a less (gender) egalitarian society than Sweden.

3. The Austrian educational system and its differences from the Swedish system

The class- and gender-differentiating orientation of Austrian society is also mirrored in its educational system. Like Sweden[3], Austria started to reform its educational system in the early 1960s. Until then, it was characterized by three features: (i) the influence of the Catholic Church in educational matters, (ii) gender segregation in education (no co-educational classes wherever possible), and (iii) the dual system of vocational education, with vocational schools mainly organized through the general educational system and apprenticeships dominated by the social partnership (corporatist) institutions.[4] A reform of the school system in 1962 and subsequent amendments aimed at increasing the general level of education in the population and making it easier to change between educational tracks. However, Austria did not develop a comprehensive school system as Sweden did, but maintained early separation of pupils into different

---

2 In our description we focus on the period relevant to our cohort (between the 1960s and 2000). Details of the policies can be found in Hoem, Prskawetz, and Neyer 2001.

3 See Hoem, Neyer, and Andersson 2006 for a description of the Swedish system.

4 For a history of the Austrian educational system after 1945 and in particular during the period relevant for our cohort, see Engelbrecht 1988, 485ff.

tracks of education. It continued to offer the dual system of vocational schools and apprenticeships; and it stuck to women-specific lines of education or curricula well into the 1980s.

The Austrian educational system is split into an array of different types of schools, which may themselves be subdivided into a number of lines of education. Despite attempts to coordinate the various curricula, there exist strong differences in teaching requirements and achievement expectations, and these differences hamper moves between the various types of schools or educational lines. The following description provides an overview over the Austrian educational system during the years in which our five-year cohort passed through education, see Figure 1. We only sketch the main educational tracks relevant for our study of childlessness, and we present the tracks in their hierarchical order.

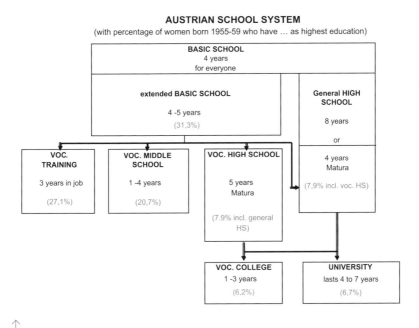

Figure 1: Austrian educational system

Primary school (Level 1). In Austria, all children go to basic school ("Volksschule") for four years. After four years (at age 10), pupils are separated into those who continue in basic school ("Hauptschule") and those who prepare for entry into general high school ("Allgemeinbildende höhere Schule") (Level 4).

Pupils who continue in basic school ("Hauptschule") go on for another four years. Subsequently (at age 14) they can transfer to another type of school (see below: Level

3, Level 4) or move to apprenticeships in vocational training (Level 2). If they do not continue schooling in another type of school or in an apprenticeship, they must take a fifth year of basic schooling ("Polytechnischer Lehrgang") to complete nine years of compulsory education. In our cohort, some 31% of the women left the school system through this route.

Vocational training (Level 2) usually lasts for three years (from age 14 to 17 or so). The training is given through apprenticeships and is provided on the job. Pupils go to school ("Berufsschule") only one or two days a week. More than three hundred professions are taught in this way, but women are usually concentrated in education for a narrow range of professions (sales, textile production, hair-dressing, or work in hotels and restaurants). Some 27% of the women of our cohort ended their education at this level.

Vocational middle school (Level 3) lasts for one to four years. This type of school offers professional training in office work, technical drawing, nursing, social work, home economics, household administration, hotel- and restaurant activities, farming, and so on. In our cohort, almost 21% of the women left school at this level.

General high school (Level 4) has two levels, namely the lower general high school (for pupils aged 10 to 14) and the upper general high school (for pupils aged 15 to 18). The lower-level part offers a general curriculum during the first two years. Thereafter (i.e., at the age of 12) pupils must select an orientation (streaming). The main differentiation lies between (i) a line more oriented toward languages, (ii) a line more oriented toward mathematics and natural sciences, and (iii) a line oriented toward (home-) economics. The latter line has been particularly aimed at women.

Vocational high school (also Level 4) usually lasts for five years (from age 14 to 19) and thus is one year longer than (upper) general high school. In addition to the theoretical education of general high schools, vocational high schools provide educations for specific occupations, such as any technical profession (including technicians below the tertiary level), industrial professions (e.g., for the textile industry), work in business and administration, and so on. In our grouping of educational attainment we have combined vocational high school with general high school on Level 4, but we have maintained the educational orientation ("general" for "general high school" and the respective fields for women who completed a vocational high school). In our cohorts, almost 8% ended up with high school (general or vocational taken together) as their highest level of education.

All high schools end with the "maturation examination" (called "Matura").[5] It confers the right to enter institutions of higher education and opens up higher-echelon career tracks in the civil service that are not available to persons who have not taken the

---

5   This corresponds to the German "Abitur", the French "baccalauréat", or the Swedish "student-examen" and corresponding examinations in the other Nordic countries ("examen artium" and so on).

Matura. The Matura is the watershed that divides educational groups into people with and people without the possibility for higher education. It is the entrance to higher social status.

Vocational college (Level 5) can be entered by women and men who have completed high school (i.e., who have the Matura). It usually lasts for one or two years (sometimes for three years) and offers professional training in specific fields, e.g. to become a teacher for schools below high school, a medical technician, a social worker, a professional in commerce and trade, in tourism, in advertising activities, and so on. In our cohorts, some 6% ended up with vocational college.

University (Level 6) studies[6] were supposed to last mostly for four years for a degree (Magisterium[7]; Diploma; Doctorate). On average, students have needed longer than this, however, and getting a university degree usually has taken seven to eight years of study (Dell'Mour and Landler 2001).[8] In our cohorts, almost 7% of the women completed a university-level education.

There are some striking general differences between the Austrian and Swedish educational systems. First, Austria separates its pupils into different streams at a much earlier age than Sweden does. While in Sweden all pupils pass through a nine-year comprehensive school up to the age of 16 and most pupils continue further to lower- or upper-secondary (two- and three-years) high school[9], Austria separates its pupils into different educational tracks after 4 years of school already (at age 10) and again after four further years (at age 14).

Second, the Austrian system of vocational apprenticeship is segregated from the general school system, while in Sweden vocational training is largely offered within the general high-school system (in our case, mostly as two-year tracks). The Austrian training system via apprenticeships offers much less general education than the Swedish system does (Lassnigg 2006; Culpepper 2007). It thus provides less "portable" skills, and this is assumed to make job changes more difficult (Estévez-Abe et al 2001).

Third, the Swedish system of comprehensive and integrated education at the primary and secondary level facilitates changes in educational fields as pupils pass through their studies. It is furthermore set up to offer all women and men the opportunity to enter higher education and/or to make up for missed education later in life. By

---

6   We count institutions called "Universitäten" and "Hochschulen" to institutions at this level.

7   This is the Austrian designation for a degree on the master level.

8   During the time when most women of our cohort went through academic education, bachelor's degrees did not exist. Furthermore, one did not necessarily need a Magisterium to take a doctorate. Some lines (such as law and medicine) did not offer separate master and doctorate studies, but everyone who completed these lines was awarded a doctorate. In cases where a magisterium/diploma was a pre-requisite for a doctorate, students needed another two to four years of study on average.

9   Two- and three-year lines of upper secondary education existed when the cohort of women born between 1955 and 1959 went to school. The two-year lines have later been extended to three-year lines.

contrast, the organization of the Austrian school and apprenticeship system makes changes in educational choices rather difficult. During the time when most women of our cohort received their education, changes between different types of schools or lines of education (below college and university level) were hampered by differences in curricula, grade requirements, or age limits. Access to higher (academic) education has been restricted mainly to those who have passed the Matura. At all levels of education (below college and university) the possibilities to make up for missed education or training are limited, not least due to age restrictions regarding participation in public education and training.

Fourth, the Swedish system of education provides substantial opportunities to re-enter, re-train, upgrade, or complement educational attainment throughout the life course. The Austrian system, by contrast, is much more closed. Opportunities to interrupt and subsequently re-enter the educational system are rare (and almost impossible below university level), and possibilities to re-train or refresh previous training are not readily available. Active labor-market policies which support (re)training in case of job loss or employment interruption have also been much more developed and widely available in Sweden than in Austria, narrowing Austrian women's possibilities to maintain their "educational capital" or adjust their education to their child caring needs.

Finally, the Swedish school system has as a goal to support gender and social equality in education and training (Erikson and Jonsson 1996). Austria, even though it shares the same goals in principle, nevertheless adhered to women-specific educational lines and programs well through the period when our cohort went to school (Engelbrecht 1988, 479ff.; Brehmer and Simon 1997, 318-324; Mikula 1997) and the organization of its school system has made it even more difficult than in Sweden to reduce social-class differences in educational participation and educational attainment. In summary the Austrian educational system is much more prone to channel pupils into specific educational tracks; it is much more rigid regarding educational participation and educational careers; and it offers much fewer possibilities to re-arrange one's education according to one's changing interests and family needs. Such features cannot fail to influence childbearing.

4. Data and main results

Our empirical analysis is based on individual-level data from the Austrian census of 2001. The cohort of 1955-1959 comprises about 297.000 women. This matches the size of the cohort of our Swedish study (about 250.000 women). It contains the highest education attained by each census member, coded into about 650 educational groups. Using the international standard classification of education (ISCED classification of 1997) we have re-coded these groups into some sixty more comprehensive educational lines, further summarized into seven main educational fields. The educational lines and fields correspond largely to the educational groups which we used in our Swedish study.[10] The classification of the educational levels follows the structure of the Austrian school system described above. Due to the differences between the Austrian and the Swedish educational system, the Austrian levels of education do not correspond entirely to the levels which we used in our Swedish study. In particular, the Austrian separation between vocational training as apprenticeship and vocational middle school does not exist as such in the Swedish system, where, as we mentioned above, vocational training is provided in the comprehensive school. Furthermore, the Austrian data do not allow us to differentiate between women who have an education at the master's level and women who have a doctorate as their highest degree, as was possible in our Swedish study (Hoem, Neyer and Andersson 2006). These differences in organization need to be taken into account when we compare childlessness by education of Austrian and Swedish women.

4.1. Educational field and childlessness

As we mentioned in our introduction, two results of our investigation are striking. First, Austria and Sweden display a largely similar pattern of childlessness by educational field (see Figure 2 and Figure 2a below). In both countries, women trained to be teachers or for a health occupation have lower childlessness than most others at each educational level. They often have lower childlessness than women educated in other fields at a lower educational level. For example, Austrian[11] primary school teachers (16.5% childless), who have passed through a vocational college, have lower childlessness than women with an apprenticeship as beautician (17.8%), as sales personnel in insurance, banking and travel (18.7%), as book sellers (25.7%), or women who have finished general high school (22.9%) or a vocational high school for tourism (24.2%) or for textile, chemistry, computer work, and the like (22.9%). Likewise, "only" a quarter of female physicians are permanently childless in our study of Austria, which is about the same as women with a much briefer training for professions in tourism or as booksellers (Figure 2 below and Table 1 on page 104).

At the other end of the spectrum, Austrian women trained in the social sciences, journalism, art, theology, and humanities have very high percentages childless (about one-third). Women trained as teachers in art, theology, or humanities have lower childlessness than those who have completed the same field of study, but without teaching qualifications. This is similar to the situation in Sweden. In both countries,

—

10 Some educations are provided in Sweden but not in Austria (such as the education of librarians and police personnel) and vice versa (like the education in tourism in Austria). We have included specifically Austrian educations here if they are noteworthy for the understanding of childlessness and if they comprise a sufficiently large number of women.

11 We report mainly the Austrian findings here and use selected findings for Sweden for comparison only. For further details on Sweden, see Hoem, Neyer, and Andersson 2006.

it seems that teachers who specialize in humanities, arts, or music remain childless more often than those who specialize in, say, the natural sciences or economics. Childlessness is also higher among women who have an education close to humanities and arts, such as booksellers (Austria) or librarians (Sweden). In Austria there are some groups of women with a university degree in the arts or humanities who display exceptionally high levels of childlessness, like art historians (45.6%), women who studied theatre production or theatre as a science (47%), women with a degree in painting, graphics, and design (39.8%) and historians (40,0%).[12] The childlessness among these women reaches levels that signal that a life without children is a common life-pattern for them.

–

12 We do not display them separately in our diagram, where we only show the field of education, not the subject
    a woman specialized in. However, there are sufficient numbers of women with the specific specialization
    mentioned to consider them in the text.

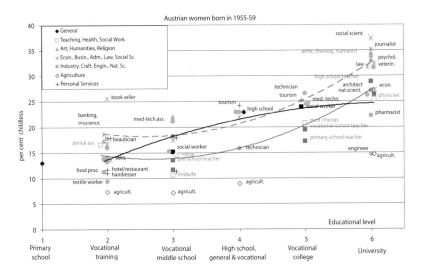

↑

Figure 2: Percent permanently childless, by educational group;

Note: The curvilinear descriptive trendlines in the diagram are intended to facilitate spotting its patterns. We have restricted ourselves to trendlines for the most extensive types of education. The trendline in light blue relates to educations in health and teaching; the black trendline to education for professions in industry, craft, engineering, natural and technical science; the stippled trendline to economics, business, administration, law and the social sciences.

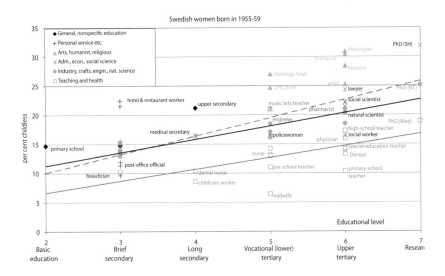

↑

Figure 2A: Per cent permanently childless, by educational group;

Source: Hoem, Neyer, and Andersson 2006

4.2. Educational level and childlessness

Our second main finding concerns childlessness by educational level in Sweden and in Austria. Two results are remarkable: Both countries have the same level of overall childlessness, namely 15.7%. But Austria and Sweden differ markedly with regard to the childlessness of highly educated women: In each group Austrian women with an upper-secondary or higher education have much the higher childlessness than Swedish women do (Figure 3).

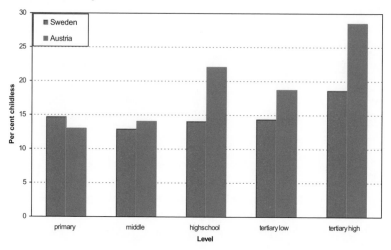

↑

Figure 3: Childlessness by level of education

Note:

          Austria: primary: basic school (up to age 15)

                      middle: apprenticeship; vocational middle school

                      high school: general or vocational high school

                      tertiary low: vocational college

                      tertiary high: university

          Sweden: primary: comprehensive school (up to age 16)

                      middle: two-year secondary school

                      high-school: three-year secondary school

                      tertiary low: vocational college

                      tertiary high: upper tertiary education and research degrees

In Sweden, there is no real difference in childlessness levels between women with a comprehensive education, a two-year secondary school, a three-year secondary school, and a vocational college or a lower-tertiary education (Figure 3). Only women with an upper-tertiary education (that is a degree at the master's level) or a research degree (doctorate) remain more often childless than others.[13] In Austria, by contrast, it is already women with an upper-secondary education ("Matura") who display noticeably higher childlessness than do women with a lower education. Moreover, at each educational level, the discrepancy in childlessness between highly educated women and those with less education is much more pronounced in Austria than in Sweden. Unlike in Sweden, there seems to be a clear division in fertility behaviour by educational status in Austria, with the main difference being between those who have finished at least high-school ("Matura") and those who have not.

The difference in childlessness by educational status in Austria is also visible if we compare childlessness among women in the same field but at different levels of education. As an example, Table 1 lists the percent childless among women with an education in teaching and health. In Sweden, women with an education in these fields have notably lower childlessness than women in any other field of education, as we have mentioned already. Austrian women with such educations have higher childlessness than the Swedes at all educational levels, but the really strong difference lies between those who have a university degree and those who do not. Compared to Swedish women, but also compared to Austrian women with the same field of education attained at an institution below the university level, Austrian women with a university education in teaching or health have some ten percentage points higher childlessness (see Table 1, Figure 2, and Figure 2a).

—

13 The Swedish data allow us to distinguish between women with a master's level education (upper-tertiary education) and women with a research degree (doctorate). The latter group has much higher childlessness (24.5%) than women on the master's level (18.5%). However, the level of childlessness among women with a Ph.D. is still lower than the level of childlessness among Austrian women with a university degree (28.6%). Since we cannot differentiate between these upper levels in our Austrian data, we only present the share of childlessness among women with a university degree in Figure 3.

Table 1: Per cent childless, by educational level and orientation.
Austrian and Swedish women born in 1955-59

	Austria	Sweden
Teachers		
pre-school teacher	13.5	11.0
primary-school teacher	16.5	10.3
high-school teacher	29.1	17.3
Health personnel		
midwife	10.6	6.4
nurse	14.5	13.0
physician	25.4	15.9
Below "Matura"		
beautician, hairdresser	12.7	9.6
textile worker	10.6	13.9
apprenticeship	9.3	
vocational school	15.2	
hotel and restaurant worker	12.7	22.4
apprenticeship	11.7	
vocational school	17.9	
agricultural work	7.4	15.5
University-level outliers		
journalist	35.0	22.2
social scientist[14]	37.3	32.9
theologian	33.9	30.9
artist (university level)	34.5	25.3
humanist (non-teach.)	33.1	30.4
psychologist	32.5	32.7
veterinary	31.6	22.0[15]
Engineers and natural scientists (university level)		
engineer	14.6	19.0
natural scientist	26.2	22.0

–

14 Sociologist, political scientist, anthropologist.

15 Agronomists and veterinaries taken together.

Similar differences in childlessness by educational level can be found for other fields of education, such as textile, leather, and fashion production, hotel work and tourism, and social work. In all these educations childlessness increases from about 10% for educations taken as apprenticeship to about 15% to 18% if the woman went to a middle school, and to about 25% for those who took the education in a vocational high-school or a vocational college (see Figure 2).

4.3. Childlessness among women without "Matura"
At the basic and lower secondary levels the two national systems are sufficiently different to make it difficult to compare educational groups directly. For most groups, rather low levels of education are mostly associated with low levels of childlessness in both countries. For Austria, we furthermore find that childlessness increases somewhat with the educational level. On average, women who learned their profession through training in an apprenticeship have lower childlessness than women who received their training in the same profession in a vocational middle school (see examples above). This result, as well as a comparison between different professions, suggests that childlessness increases with the social status of the education or of the profession it leads to.

Compared to Sweden, some results are surprising: Austrian women educated to be hotel and restaurant workers have much lower childlessness (11.7% for an apprentice; 17.9% for vocational school) than their Swedish counterparts (22.4%). In Sweden, this group is taken as typical of educations that lead to occupations with long and odd working hours and high employment mobility, for which reasons one would expect much childlessness (Hoem, Neyer, and Andersson, 2006, Section 5.2.2). The Austrian counterexample seems to show that such explanations need not be sufficient. The fact that there are about fourteen times as many women with an apprenticeship or vocational training for the hotel, restaurant and tourist sector in Austria than in Sweden, that the vast majority of employees in this sector work in (their own) family businesses, and that the hotel, restaurant and tourist sector has a high share of seasonal workers, may provide elements of a further explanation. It may be that the structure of the business (small/large; seasonal/non-seasonal; family business/non-relative employer) has a bearing on childbearing behaviour. If so, the differences in business structure between Austria and Sweden (Katzenstein 1988; Culpepper 2007) may account for some of the differences in childlessness we find for specific educational fields. However, viewed across all educational fields the findings are not conclusive.

Swedish women with an education for the agricultural sector have much higher childlessness (15.5%) than women with a similar education in Austria (about 7% for both apprenticeship and vocational agricultural school). The same applies to women with an agricultural education at higher educational levels. Compared to childlessness among women in general, Austrian women with an education for the agricultural sector have unusually low percentages permanently childless (Figure 2). We suspect that there may be a strong component of tradition in this finding, in that educations of this nature are more likely to be taken by women with an agricultural background, many of whom will eventually enter or take over their family business. Moreover, vocational agricultural schools are often located in agricultural regions and may provide the only further education available in the region. These schools also offer a broad spectrum of education covering all areas necessary for running an agricultural business, including areas considered useful for women, such as housekeeping, food processing, and nutrition. These factors may explain why among our cohorts there are almost three times as many Austrian women who finished an education in agriculture (through apprenticeship or vocational school) than there are Swedish women with such an education.

4.4. University-level outliers

The fourth panel in Table 1 lists a number of educations that have unusually high percentages childless in both countries, but particularly in Austria, where these educational groups almost invariably have higher childlessness than corresponding groups in Sweden.

In Austria, women educated as engineers constitute a group that deviate in the opposite direction (see the fifth panel in Table 1). Their childlessness (15%) is lower than that of all other academic groups (except female agronomists) and below that of many groups with much less education. Women who went to a vocational high-school with a focus on technical engineering or construction also have lower childlessness than women with an education from a general high-school or a vocational high school with a different focus (Figure 2). We would have expected both groups of women with an engineering degree to have childlessness on the level of natural scientists. However, there are much fewer women who take a technical education than women who take an education in the natural sciences, at all levels of education. Women with a technical education are trained to work in highly masculine professions. It may be that women find the working conditions and the career options in such occupations so unfavorable that they turn to other pursuits than engineering and that they are less inclined to forgo motherhood for a career than women with an education that leads to less unfavorable working conditions.[16] Studies also indicate that women who choose a technical education more often have highly educated parents (Fischer-Kowalski 1985). It is possible that highly educated women who come from a highly educated family background may have less difficulty than other women in combining work and childbearing.

Veterinaries, who are often coded as having an agricultural education, similarly deviate from the general pattern of childlessness among women with an agricultural

---

16 Studies of the 1980s showed that many women who chose technical (and male) dominated professions left these more often than women in other professions (Pelz, Spitzy, and Wagner 1983).

education. They have much higher childlessness than women with an academic degree in agriculture, and they even range among the academically trained women with particularly high levels of childlessness (such as women trained in law or psychology; see Figure 2 and Table 1). Almost one-third of female veterinaries remain childless. Why veterinaries should be so different, is open to speculation. As a brief review of the current specialization of female veterinaries shows, their professional activity is not so often connected to farm animals but rather to domestic pets in an urban environment. The vast majority of veterinary are self-employed, and this may lead to a higher share of childlessness.

5. Reflections

As we have outlined in the introduction and in our previous paper (Hoem, Neyer, and Andersson, 2006), patterns of childlessness are bound to reflect several institutional, cultural, and individual factors: the structure and organization of the educational system, the conditions on the labor marked that women encounter when they have completed their education, the gender patterns in education and occupation, the gendering or de-gendering of the welfare state and of public policies, as well as social norms and preferences. Correspondingly, the patterns of childlessness in Austria and Sweden may reflect similarities and differences between the systems and thus in the opportunities and constraints for women regarding education, work, and childrearing in the two countries. Since our data do not allow us to investigate childbearing behaviour in detail, we restrict ourselves to sketching some of the differentials that might produce the patterns we have found.

As we spelled out above, Austria has an educational system that is much more segregated by gender and by social class, and that is relatively inflexible, while Sweden has a comprehensive, more egalitarian, and flexible system. Though both countries have aimed at increasing the share of women (and men) in higher education, in our cohort Austrian women who get a higher education are still a select group. The differences to Sweden are striking: Only 13% of the Austrian women in our cohort got a tertiary education (vocational college or university); the figure for Sweden is 33%. The share of women with the highest (university level) educational attainment was twice as large in Sweden (12.1 %) as in Austria (6.7%). Among Austrian women 79% did not complete an education with high-school level ("Matura"), which compares with 53% in Sweden. Almost twice as many Austrian women (31%) as Swedish women (16%) had no more than basic education. The fact that Austrian women with a high school ("Matura") or a higher degree constitute such a small minority in our cohort may contribute to the high share of childlessness among women with higher education in Austria. Having a high education offers employment possibilities which are not accessible to others, and it may well be that women with such opportunities do not want to endanger them through childbearing. This may also explain the increase in childlessness by educational level below high school and the higher childlessness among women with an education in a field that offers access to occupations with higher social status (e.g.: white-collar rather than blue-collar jobs). In both cases, childlessness may be due both to the scarce opportunities to re-enter the educational system once one has left it, and to the problems of interrupting employment for childbearing and childrearing. The latter issue may lead to a depreciation of educational capital and the risk of having to subsequently accept employment below one's educational and thus social status.

Contrary to Sweden, Austrian educational, labor-market, welfare-state, and family policies do not counter such depreciation sufficiently. Parental-leave and childcare policies in Austria support mothers' absence from the labor market rather than their employment, while Sweden does the opposite (Hoem and Hoem 1997, Hoem at al. 2001). The attitude that mothers should primarily devote their lives to their children is still common in Austria, where three-quarters of the people hold the view that a pre-school child is likely to suffer if his or her mother works (Halman 2001, 141). By comparison, only half as many Swedes (38%) share this opinion.

In addition to centering family policies on motherhood, Austria has also policies less firmly oriented toward gender equality than Sweden has. When our Austrian cohort passed through the educational system, even co-education was not fully established. Almost a third of all women in high school and more than half of all women in vocational middle schools or in apprenticeships were in a predominantly[17] female school or line of education and had curricula with a gendered content. In particular, programs specifically addressing women as mothers and housewives were still in place (Fischer-Kowalski et al. 1985; Lassnigg and Paseka 1997). Such education may have been out of step with the orientation of (many) women and may have aroused resistance to motherhood, particularly during the 1970s and 1980s, when feminist debates about motherhood as a gate to discrimination of women were part of the public and political discourse in Austria.

Women in Austria concentrate on a rather narrow range of educational fields, and the fraction of women is high in particular employment areas and jobs. The pattern is similar in Sweden, but this country has managed to reduce gender differentials in employment and in care much more than Austria has. Researchers assume that gender inequality in the workplace (and also in the household) may account for low fertility and may produce high childlessness (McDonald 2000; Neyer 2003). As regards the workplace the high childlessness among Austrian women with a tertiary education that leads to employment in the public sector (teaching in high school; law) may reflect such features.

Regulations protecting parenthood for public-sector employees are in place in both countries, and, as is the case among Swedish women, one would expect to find lower

17 A line with at least 95% females.

childlessness among Austrian women with an education that leads to employment in the public sector. In Austria, too, the public sector offers tenure and much better employment protection than the private sector does; it has a more egalitarian wage structure than the private sector, and it used to offer longer parental leaves than the private sector did. However, tenure was usually dependent on continual employment (seniority) and full-time employment, both of which may be forfeited in the case of childbearing. A study from 1993 revealed that 60% of the female employees in the Austrian public sector lacked tenure, while only 20% of the men were in such a situation (Seidl 1993, cit. by Hofmeister 1995). It may well be that inequalities of this character affect childbearing decisions and lead to a higher share of childlessness among women with specific educations. Conversely, the fact of higher childlessness in an educational group may in turn influence attitudes towards childlessness and childbearing in general in a self-reinforcing spiral that may lead to the group-specific patterns of childlessness indicated in Figure 1.[18]

In summary, our Swedish-Austrian comparison of the patterns of childlessness among women with different educational fields and levels underlines the delicate balance between institutional contexts and individual childbearing decisions. Although some similarities in the level of childlessness among women with similar educations in Sweden and Austria suggest that preferences regarding education and childbearing determine fertility behaviour (as in the case of women with an education in humanities and art), other results do not support such an interpretation (as in the case of women who opt for a technical education). It seems that the structure of the educational system, the labor market, the welfare state, and the social and gender system are important determinants of fertility patterns, and that they constitute much more than the factual conditions for education and childbearing. They also set the realm for the ideational orientation of a society, an element central to the individual, to whom this article is dedicated.

---

18   See also Hoem, Neyer, and Andersson 2006.

6. References

Biffl, G. (1997). Schule – Wirtschaft – Frauen. In L. Lassnigg, and A. Paseka, (Eds.), Zum Geschlechterverhältnis im Bildungswesen (pp. 234-249). Innsbruck: Studien-Verlag.

Brehmer, I. and Simon, G. (Eds.) (1997). Geschichte der Frauenbildung und Mädchenerziehung in Österreich. Graz: Leykam.

Culpepper, P. D. (2007). Small States and Skill Specificity. Austria, Switzerland, and Interemployer Cleavages in Coordinated Capitalism. Comparative Political Studies, 40, 611-637.

Dell'Mour, R., and Landler F. (2001). Determinanten des Studienerfolgs. Projektbericht des Bundesministeriums für Bildung, Wissenschaft und Kultur. Wien.

Dobritz, J. (2003). Polarisierung versus Vielfalt - Lebensformen und Kinderlosigkeit in Deutschland - eine Auswertung des Mikrozensus. Zeitschrift für Bevölkerungswissenschaft, 28(2-4), 403-421.

Duschek, K.-J., and Wirth H. (2005). Kinderlosigkeit von Frauen im Spiegel des Mikrozensus. Eine Kohortenanalyse der Mikrozensen 1987-2003. Wirtschaft und Statistik, 2005(8), 800-820.

Engelbrecht, H. (1988). Geschichte des österreichischen Bildungswesens. Bd. 5: Von 1918 bis zur Gegenwart. Wien: Österreichischer Bundesverlag.

Erikson, R. and Jonsson, J. O. (Eds.) (1996). Can Education Be Equalized? The Swedish Case in Comparative Perspective. Boulder: Westview Press.

Esping-Andersen, G. (1990). The Three Worlds of Welfare Capitalism. Princeton: Princeton University Press.

Esping-Andersen, G. (2002). A New Gender Contract. In: G. Esping-Andersen with D. Gallie, A. Hemerijck, and J. Myles: Why We Need a New Welfare State (pp. 68-95). Oxford: Oxford University Press.

Estévez-Abe, M., Iversen T., and Soskice D. (2001). Social Protection and the Formation of Skills. A Reinterpretation of the Welfare State. In: P. Hall, and D. Soskice (Eds.): Varieties of Capitalism: The Institutional Foundation of Comparative Advantage (pp. 143-183). Oxford: Oxford University Press.

Estévez-Abe, M. (2005). Gender Bias in Skills and Social Policies: The Varieties of Capitalism Perspective on Sex Segregation. Social Politics 12(2), 180-215.

Fischer-Kowalski, M. et al (1985). Bildung. Bericht über die Situation der Frau in Österreich. Frauenbericht 1985(2). Wien: Bundeskanzleramt.

Hall, P. and Soskice D. (Eds) (2001). Varieties of Capitalism: The Institutional Foundation of Comparative Advantage. Oxford: Oxford University Press.

Halman, L. (2001). The European Values Study: A Third Wave. Source Book of the 1999/2000 European Values Study Survey. Tilburg University: WORC.

Hoem, B., and Hoem J. M. (1997). Sweden's family policies and roller-coaster fertility. Journal of Population Problems (Tokyo), 52(3-4), 1-22.

Hoem, J. M., Prskawetz, A, and Neyer, G. (2001). Autonomy or conservative adjustment? The effect of public policies and educational attainment on third births in Austria. Population Studies, 55(3), 249-261. Reprinted in the Vienna Yearbook of Population Research, 2003, 101-119.

Hoem, J. M., Neyer, G., and Andersson, G. (2006). Education and childlessness: The relationship between educational field, educational level, and childlessness among Swedish women born in 1955-59. Demographic Research, 14(15), 331-380. Available: http://www.demographic-research.org/Volumes/ Vol14/15/14-15.pdf .

Hofmeister, L. (1995). Der männliche Geschlechtsvorzug im österreichischen Bundesdienst. In: U. Floßmann (Ed.), Feministische Jurisprudenz: Blicke und Skizzen (pp. 69-90). Linz: Universitätsverlag R. Trauner.

Kreyenfeld, M. (2004). Politikdiskussion fehlt verlässliche statistische Grundlage. Demografische Forschung aus Erster Hand, 1(3), 4.

Lappegård, T., and Rønsen, M. (2005). The multifaceted impact of education on entry into motherhood. European Journal of Population, 21, 31-49.

Lassnigg, L. (2006). Forschungsfragen zur Zukunft der dualen Ausbildung in Österreich. Vienna: Institute for Advanced Studies.

Lassnigg, L. and Paseka A. (1997) (Eds.). Zum Geschlechterverhältnis im Bildungswesen. Innsbruck: Studien-Verlag.

McDonald, P. (2000). Gender equity, social institutions and the future of fertility. Journal of Population Research 17(1), 1-16.

Mikula, R. (1997). "Die Verweiblichung der Buben und eine Vermännlichung der Mädchen". Die Koedukationsdebatte im 20. Jahrhundert. In: I. Brehmer, and G. Simon (Eds.): Geschichte der Frauenbildung und Mädchenerziehung in Österreich (pp. 235-260). Graz: Leykam.

Neyer, G. (2003). Family policies and low fertility in Western Europe. MPIDR working paper WP 21. Rostock. Max Planck Institute for Demographic Research. Available: http://www.demogr.mpg.de/papers/working/wp-2003-021.pdf

Neyer, G., Hoem, J. M., and Andersson, G. (2007). Kinderlosigkeit, Bildungsrichtung und Bildungsniveau. Ergebnisse einer Untersuchung schwedischer Frauen der Geburtenjahrgänge 1955-59. In: D. Konietzka, and M. Kreyenfeld (Eds.): Ein Leben ohne Kinder. Kinderlosigkeit in Deutschland (pp. 105-134). Wiesbaden: Verlag für Sozialwissenschaften.

OECD (1999). Classifying Educational Programmes. Manual for ISCED-97; Implementation in OECD Countries. Paris: OECD Publishing.

Pelz, M., Spitzy Ch., and Wagner I. (1983). Mit technischem Verstand. Mädchen in nicht-traditionellen Berufen. Forschungsbericht aus Arbeitsmarkt und Sozialpolitik 4. Wien: Bundesministerium für soziale Verwaltung.

Pontusson, J. (2000). Labor Market Institutions and Wage Distribution. In: T. Iversen, J. Pontusson and D. Soskice, (Eds.), Employment and Central Banks. Macroeconomic Coordination and Institutional Change in Social Market Economies (pp. 292-330). Cambridge: Cambridge University Press.

Scharein, M., and Unger, R. (2005). Kinderlosigkeit bei Akademikerinnen? Die Aussagekraft empirischer Daten zur Kinderlosigkeit bei Akademikerinnen. BiB-Mitteilungen, 26(2), 6-13.

Schmitt, C., and Winkelmann, U. (2005). Wer bleibt kinderlos? Was sozialstrukturelle Daten über Kinderlosigkeit bei Frauen und Männern verraten. Feministische Studien, 23(1), 9-23.

Seidl, M. (1993). Einkommensunterschiede zwischen Männern und Frauen im Bundesdienst. Diploma thesis. Vienna: Economics University.

Soskice, D. (2005). Varieties of capitalism and cross-national gender differences. Social Politics, 12(2), 170-179.

Statistics Sweden (1996). Svensk utbildningsnomenklatur, Del 1. Systematisk version. Meddelanden i samordningsfrågor 1996, 1.

—

04 Recent Trends in Demographic Attitudes and Behaviour: Is the Second Demographic Transition Moving to Southern and Eastern Europe?

Aart C. Liefbroer and Tineke Fokkema[*]

—

[*] This chapter has partly been written within the project 'Households in Transition – A Policy Oriented Analysis', funded by a grant (SI2.425788) from the Unit on Social and Demography Analysis of DG Employment, Social Affairs and Equal Opportunities of the European Commission. The authors would like to thank Francesco Billari and Bruno Schoumaker for their stimulating comments on an earlier version of this chapter.

1. Introduction

Ron Lesthaeghe's name is inseparably linked to the concept of the 'Second Demographic Transition', a term he coined together with Dirk van de Kaa in a Dutch language article in the journal 'Mens en Maatschappij' back in 1986 (Lesthaeghe and Van de Kaa 1986). The title of that article was 'Two demographic transitions?' The question mark at the end of the title suggests that, at least at that time, the authors were not completely convinced that a second demographic transition was underway. In the course of the last twenty years, however, the concept of the Second Demographic Transition (abbreviated to SDT) has become one of the key concepts used to understand the changes in demographic behaviour that have occurred in many modern societies from the 1960s onwards. The wide-reaching impact of the SDT concept is to a large extent due to Ron's own inspiring publications on the topic (e.g. Lesthaeghe 1995; Lesthaeghe and Moors 2002; Lesthaeghe and Neidert 2006; Lesthaeghe and Surkyn 1988; Surkyn and Lesthaeghe 2004).

The SDT concept has contributed at least two innovative elements to our thinking about demographic change in the second half of the 20th century. Firstly, it was innovative in suggesting that a seemingly diverse set of demographic changes – postponement of parenthood and marriage, decrease in family size, increase in divorce, unmarried cohabitation and extra-marital childbearing – were actually closely entwined. Secondly, it was innovative in suggesting that these changes were the expression of large-scale changes in value orientations in Western societies. As Lesthaeghe and Neidert (2006) recently reiterated, these changes have included a shift from materialist to post-materialist values (Inglehart 1977; Inglehart and Baker 2000), and a shift from 'lower' to 'higher order' needs (Maslow 1954). In their original publication, Lesthaeghe and Van de Kaa (1986) summarized this value change by stating that, whereas the first demographic transition was driven by an altruistic motive – in this case giving central stage to the needs of the child – the second demographic transition was driven by egoistic motives: giving central stage to the individual's own needs. Although Lesthaeghe and Van de Kaa pointed out, both in their original publication and in subsequent ones (e.g. Lesthaeghe 1995; Van de Kaa 1987), that value change was not the sole factor driving demographic change – economic changes and changes in institutional arrangements were also deemed influential – it was the connection between value change and demographic change that received most emphasis. In his most recent work, Lesthaeghe (Lesthaeghe and Neidert 2006; Lesthaeghe and Surkyn 2006) forcefully stresses this connection once again.

Unsurprisingly, the SDT thesis has generated extensive discussion, including fierce criticism (e.g. Cliquet 1991; Coleman 2004). These criticisms notwithstanding, considerable knowledge has been accumulated to support the basic tenets of the

SDT. At the individual level, the causal link between attitudes and values on the one hand and demographic behaviour on the other has been well established, in particular as a result of panel studies showing that current attitudes and values influence subsequent demographic outcomes (e.g. Axinn and Thornton 1992, 1993; Barber, Axinn and Thornton 2002; Jansen and Kalmijn 2002; Moors 2002). At the country or state level, it has been shown that a high correlation exists between value indicators and demographic indicators, and that parallel changes can be observed in both types of indicators (Lesthaeghe and Neidert 2006; Lesthaeghe and Surkyn 1988, 2006). Nonetheless, a number of issues are still far from clear. A major issue is whether the SDT has not only spread across Northern and Western Europe, but also to Southern (Billari et al. 2002; Fernandez Cordon 1997; Reher 1998) and Eastern Europe (Macura, Mochizuki-Sternberg and Garcia 2002; Sobotka, Zeman and Kantorova 2003). Statistics on fertility behaviour suggest that the SDT has indeed crossed the Alps, the Pyrenees and the former Iron Curtain (Kohler, Billari and Ortega 2002; Sobotka 2004). However, much less information is available as to whether the same applies to other basic elements of the SDT, such as the expected increase in the popularity of unmarried cohabitation. Another issue is the macro-factors driving these changes in Southern and Eastern European countries. With regard to these changes, it has been suggested that the factors of crucial importance are economic and institutional rather than cultural (e.g. Dalla Zuanna 2001; Kohler and Kohler 2002; Macura et al. 2002). If this is true, the existence of the link between values and behaviour as implied by the SDT is at stake.

The aim of this chapter is to contribute to the debate on the spread of the SDT to Southern and Eastern Europe. We will do so by presenting fresh evidence on changes to SDT-related attitudes and behaviour across Europe. In particular, we will focus on three interrelated questions:

1. How do attitudes regarding cohabitation, divorce and parenthood differ across Western societies, and have these attitudes changed during the last decade?
2. How popular is unmarried cohabitation across Europe, and has its popularity increased during the last decade?
3. To what extent are attitudes regarding cohabitation, divorce and parenthood on the one hand, and family-formation behaviour on the other, related at the macro level?

In order to answer these questions, we will use data from the International Social Survey Program (ISSP), conducted in over 35 countries around the globe, and the Labour Force Survey (LFS), conducted in a number of member states of the European Union.

2. Attitudes to cohabitation, divorce and parenthood

Comparative information on the demographic attitudes – and the changes in these attitudes – of the population of Western societies is relatively scarce. Few repeated surveys exist that cover a large number of countries, and those that do exist often have surprisingly little information on demographically relevant attitudes. This is particularly true of opinions on cohabitation. The International Social Survey Program (ISSP) constitutes an exception to this rule. The ISSP is a collaboration between scientific institutes in over 35 countries. Every year, a kind of general social survey is held in all these countries. However, the focus of the survey changes every year, and some topics are repeated after a number of years. The 1994 and 2002 waves of the ISSP survey on 'Family and Changing Gender Roles' included a number of questions on cohabitation, divorce and parenthood. In 1994, 22 countries participated in the ISSP, and in 2002 35 countries participated (ISSP 1994, 2002). From these participating countries, we selected all the European countries plus the English-speaking former colonies: – the United States of America, Australia, and New Zealand. In both 1994 and 2002, five items of clear demographic interest were included: – two on cohabitation, one on divorce, and two on parenthood. The wording of these items was:

- It is all right for a couple to live together without intending to get married ('Non-marital cohabitation acceptable').
- It is a good idea for a couple who intends to get married to live together first ('Premarital cohabitation good idea').
- Divorce is usually the best solution when a couple can't seem to work out their marriage problems ('Divorce sometimes best solution').
- Watching children grow up is life's greatest joy ('Children greatest joy').
- People who have never had children lead empty lives ('Childless lead empty lives').

A drawback of this set of items is that agreement with the items on cohabitation and divorce indicates that people favour non-traditional family attitudes, whereas agreement with the items on fertility indicates being in favour of traditional family attitudes. In addition, the items on fertility are formulated in a rather extreme manner, leading to a relatively low percentage of people endorsing them. Finally, it has to be kept in mind that people in countries where strong social norms exist may feel a stronger need to give socially desirable answers than people in countries with weak norms, thus exaggerating the real differences between these countries in the attitudes of the population.

Because the SDT is often assumed to start among young people (but see De Jong Gierveld, De Valk and Blommesteijn [2002] for evidence of the SDT among older adults), our focus is on the attitudes of people between the ages of 18 and 35. In Table 1, the proportion of this age group that 'agrees' or 'strongly agrees' with each of the five opinions stated above is presented for each country. The countries are grouped into five clusters, namely 'Social Democratic', 'Liberal', 'Conservative', 'Southern European' and 'Eastern European,', largely based on Esping-Andersen's welfare state typology (Esping-Andersen 1999)[1]. For 19 countries, information on attitudes in 1994 and 2002 is available. For 9 additional countries information is only available for 2002, and for 1 country – Italy – information is only available for 1994.

The most striking finding with regard to attitudes towards non-marital cohabitation is that even in 1994, a majority of 18 to 35 year olds in all the participating countries agreed or strongly agreed that it is acceptable for a couple to live together without intending to get married. The percentage of people who agreed or strongly agreed with this statement varied from 58 percent in the United States to 88 percent in Sweden, Norway and the Netherlands. On average, the percentage who agreed was highest in Social-Democratic countries (88), followed by Conservative countries (84). Percentages were lower, but still over 70, in Liberal (73), Southern European (74) and Eastern European countries (73). Between 1994 and 2002 the percentage of young people who believe that non-marital cohabitation is acceptable increased in most – though not all – countries. Of the new countries participating in 2002, the percentage who agreed with the statement was by far the lowest in Slovakia. In fact, Slovakia is the only country where only a minority believe that non-marital cohabitation is acceptable. On average, the proportion of people who agreed with the statement was slightly higher in 2002 than in 1994.

---

1   Esping-Andersen (1990) proposed a typology of welfare state regimes, mainly based on whether the State, the family or the market bears prime responsibility for providing care to citizens in need. In social-democratic welfare state regimes, individuals rely predominantly on the State for welfare benefits. In liberal welfare state regimes the market is the dominant provider of such benefits, whereas the family is viewed as the main provider of social benefits in conservative regimes. In later work, a Mediterranean welfare state regime, characterized by a rudimentary welfare system and a very strong reliance on the family, has been distinguished as well (Esping-Andersen, 1999). Esping-Andersen does not include the Eastern European countries in his typology. We include them as a separate category, mainly because they share a Communist background. Whether these countries are relatively close to each other with regard to their demographic attitudes is viewed as an empirical issue.

Table 1: Proportion of 18-35 year olds (strongly) agreeing with specified statements
↓

Country	Year	Non-marital cohabitation acceptable	Premarital cohabitation good idea	Divorce sometimes best solution	Children greatest joy	Childless lead empty lives
Norway	1994	0.88	0.87	0.42	0.76	0.14
	2002	0.84	0.81	0.44	0.72	0.13
Sweden	1994	0.88	0.90	0.43	0.76	0.12
	2002	0.91	0.91	0.44	0.68	0.06
Finland	2002	0.87	0.84	0.51	0.53	0.32
Denmark	2002	0.96	0.89	0.59	0.75	0.08
Great-Britain	1994	0.83	0.72	0.43	0.73	0.12
	2002	0.85	0.77	0.50	0.70	0.11
Northern Ireland	1994	0.68	0.60	0.48	0.80	0.20
	2002	0.83	0.76	0.58	0.58	0.08
Ireland	1994	0.76	0.74	0.62	0.78	0.14
	2002	0.79	0.78	0.46	0.69	0.10
United States	1994	0.58	0.50	0.36	0.80	0.14
	2002	0.60	0.64	0.31	0.83	0.13
Australia	1994	0.74	0.60	0.41	0.76	0.19
	2002	0.79	0.66	0.39	0.77	0.15
New Zealand	1994	0.76	0.64	0.34	0.72	0.09
	2002	0.76	0.70	0.38	0.67	0.11
The Netherlands	1994	0.88	0.61	0.64	0.61	0.08
	2002	0.90	0.74	0.67	0.59	0.10
West Germany	1994	0.84	0.79	0.64	0.76	0.34
	2002	0.81	0.82	0.69	0.82	0.27
Austria	1994	0.81	0.83	0.65	0.85	0.43
	2002	0.85	0.85	0.77	0.77	0.25
France	2002	0.86	0.90	0.50	0.86	0.21
Flanders	2002	0.93	0.74	0.53	0.73	0.09
Switzerland	2002	0.91	0.83	0.52	0.71	0.11
Italy	1994	0.67	0.54	0.56	0.87	0.32
Spain	1994	0.80	0.72	0.75	0.80	0.27
	2002	0.90	0.83	0.80	0.76	0.18
Portugal	2002	0.89	0.65	0.69	0.86	0.43
Cyprus	2002	0.69	0.87	0.82	0.90	0.29

East Germany	1994	0.82	0.73	0.65	0.87	0.50
	2002	0.93	0.85	0.68	0.83	0.35
Hungary	1994	0.85	0.64	0.47	0.93	0.71
	2002	0.86	0.80	0.52	0.91	0.59
Poland	1994	0.57	0.47	0.41	0.85	0.28
	2002	0.70	0.61	0.47	0.86	0.22
Czech Republic	1994	0.68	0.82	0.49	0.78	0.34
	2002	0.71	0.83	0.57	0.79	0.42
Slovenia	1994	0.67	0.83	0.56	0.87	0.55
	2002	0.80	0.86	0.53	0.89	0.43
Bulgaria	1994	0.70	0.82	0.53	0.80	0.51
	2002	0.70	0.79	0.65	0.82	0.48
Russia	1994	0.83	0.81	0.44	0.88	0.45
	2002	0.70	0.79	0.43	0.93	0.49
Latvia	2002	0.67	0.85	0.56	0.75	0.28
Slovakia	2002	0.40	0.58	0.58	0.82	0.29

Source: ISSP 1994, 2002

The first item on cohabitation indicates whether people are tolerant towards couples who live together without planning to marry. It does not imply that people would contemplate doing so themselves as well. The second item on cohabitation is different, because people have to indicate here whether they themselves think that it is a good idea to cohabit prior to marriage. Agreement with this statement is therefore a stronger indication that young people would be willing to contemplate cohabitation as a serious option in their own lives. As can be observed from Table 1, the majority of young people in most countries agree with this statement as well. Indeed, on average the proportions of people who agree with this statement do not differ too much from those agreeing with the other statement on cohabitation. What is – once again – particularly striking is the fact that the majority of young people in all Southern European countries and in most Eastern European countries agree that premarital cohabitation is a good idea. In Italy, 54 percent of young people thought so in 1994, and as many as 83 percent agreed in Spain in 2002.

The third item asks whether divorce is the best solution if there seems to be no other way for couples to solve their problems. The results show that the opinion on divorce is generally much less favourable than that on cohabitation. On average, about half of the 18 to 35 year olds in these countries agree or strongly agree that divorce is usually the best solution if a couple can not seem to work out their marital problems, but there is considerable variation. In liberal welfare states, and particularly in the

United States, Australia and New Zealand, agreement with this statement is lowest, with only about one in every three young people agreeing. In some conservative welfare states – the Netherlands, West Germany and Austria – and in Southern European countries, the level of agreement is much higher, with about two in every three young people agreeing with the statement. Again this is striking, given that the behavioural evidence on divorce suggests that divorce rates are much higher in a country like the United States than in Southern Europe. Between 1994 and 2002, a slight increase in the percentage of young people who endorse the statement on divorce can be observed. In 2002, the average percentage of young people agreeing that divorce is usually the right solution if it seems that marital problems can not be worked out varies from 77 in Southern European countries through 61 in Conservative countries, 55 in Eastern European countries and 50 in Social-Democratic countries to 44 in Liberal countries.

The last two items in Table 1 focus on young people's opinions concerning the importance of parenthood. The first of these emphasizes the joy children bring. In all countries, a majority of young people agree or strongly agree that watching children grow up is life's greatest joy, thus effectively stating that parenthood is at the top of the list of life's priorities. This view is most strongly endorsed in Southern and Eastern European countries, with usually 80 to 90 percent of young people agreeing with this statement. Agreement is somewhat lower, but still substantial in the other groups of countries. In general, between 1994 and 2002, a slight decrease in the centrality of parenthood can be observed. At the same time, in some countries – the United States, West Germany and Russia – an increase in agreement with this statement can be observed.

The final item in Table 1 focuses on how people feel about not having children. In most countries only small minorities (strongly) agree that people who have never had children live empty lives. Combined with the much higher proportion endorsing the other statement on parenthood, this suggests that most people feel that having children is at the top of their priority list, but that it is still possible to live a worthwhile life if this goal remains unfulfilled. At the same time, it can be noted that agreement with this statement is generally much higher in Eastern and Southern European countries than in the other groups of countries. However, agreement is also relatively high in Finland, West Germany and Austria. In most countries, the percentage of respondents who agree with this statement decreased between 1994 and 2002, but an increase could be observed for the Czech Republic and Russia.

The questions on attitudes discussed so far tap into important aspects of the SDT – cohabitation, divorce and parenthood. It is unclear, however, to what extent attitudes concerning these different aspects of the SDT are related to each other. Do they form one underlying attitudinal dimension, or multiple ones? To investigate this issue, we performed a factor analysis on the five items. It resulted in a two-factor solution. The factor loadings of the five items, based on a principal components analysis, followed by a Varimax rotation, are presented in Table 2.[2]

Table 2: Results of a factor analysis on five attitudinal items, ISSP 1994-2002

	Factor 1 Alternative living arrangements	Factor 2 Parenthood
Non-marital cohabitation acceptable	0.83	-0.15
Premarital cohabitation good idea	0.83	0.00
Divorce sometimes best solution	0.55	0.09
Children greatest joy	-0.06	0.79
Childless lead empty lives	-0.07	0.81
Explained variance	33.8	25.7

Source: ISSP 1994, 2002

The three items on cohabitation and divorce have high factor loadings on the first factor and negligible ones on the second factor, whereas the opposite pattern can be observed for the two items on parenthood. Therefore, the first factor can be interpreted as an 'alternative living arrangements' factor. People with a high score for this factor attach relatively little importance to marriage and are in favour of cohabitation, and approve of divorce when marital problems are insurmountable. People scoring low for this factor are strongly opposed to cohabitation and divorce. The second factor can be interpreted as a 'parenthood' factor. People scoring high for this factor attach high value to parenthood, whereas people scoring low for this factor attach relatively little value to it.[3]

---

2   A factor analysis allowing for oblique factors led to almost identical results.

3   We pointed out above that agreement with the items on cohabitation and divorce indicates that people favour non-traditional family attitudes, whereas agreement with the items on fertility indicates being in favour of traditional family attitudes. The pattern of factor loadings observed could partly mirror this difference in the wording of the questions. It would be interesting to have data in which all the items were formulated in the same direction, to test whether the same two-factor solution would emerge. The data on life-course norms that were collected in the 2006 wave of the European Social Survey will offer an opportunity to do so.

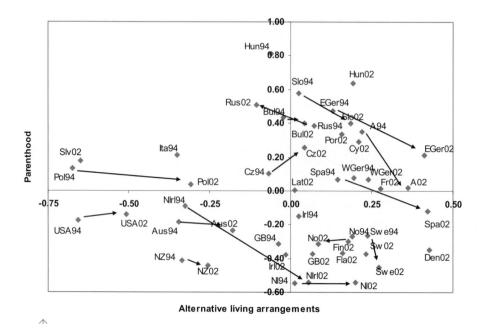

Figure 1: Location of countries on two attitudinal dimensions, based on ISSP data
Source: ISSP 1994, 2002

For each of the countries, mean factor scores for people aged 18 to 35 can be calculated. These mean factor scores are presented in Figure 1, plotted in two-dimensional space. Scores for the 'alternative living arrangements' factor are plotted along the x-axis. The further a country is located to the right, the more importance is attached to this factor within this country. The further to the left, the lower the score for the 'alternative living arrangements' factor. Factor scores for the 'parenthood' dimension are plotted on the y-axis. The higher the score for this dimension, the more central parenthood is considered to be in a country.

A number of conclusions can be drawn from Figure 1. First of all, the fact that almost all the European countries are located on the right-hand side of the figure suggests that only relatively small differences exist across Europe in the valuation of alternative living arrangements. This can be illustrated by looking at the three countries at the far right of Figure 1. In 2002, the strongest endorsements of alternative living arrangements were found in Denmark, Spain and East Germany, countries widely spread across the continent. Nonetheless, a few European countries have relatively low scores for this dimension. These countries are Italy in 1994, Slovakia in 2002 and Poland in both 1994 and 2002. The other countries with relatively low scores for the 'alternative living arrangements' factor are the United States, Australia and New Zealand, implying that traditional views on marriage still have a relatively strong hold in these countries. This suggests that the diffusion of attitudes towards core elements of the SDT has been slower in Western societies outside of Europe than inside Europe.

A second conclusion that can be drawn from Figure 1 is that parenthood is less central in Liberal and Social Democratic countries than in Conservative, Southern European and Eastern European countries. The second group of countries are in the top half of Figure 1, whereas the first group of countries are in the bottom half. In the bottom half, the Netherlands is an exception in the sense that it is the only country in the Conservative welfare states group that has a relatively low score for the parenthood dimension. This mirrors results from other surveys such as the Population and Policy Acceptance (PPA) surveys (e.g. Fokkema and Esveldt 2006).

Viewed in conjunction, three main clusters of countries emerge. In the bottom right quadrant of Figure 1, Social Democratic welfare states, the Netherlands, and some European Liberal welfare states emerge as countries with a relatively low value for the parenthood dimension and a relatively high value for the alternative living arrangement dimension. These countries appear to be classic cases – at least at the attitudinal level – of countries that have more or less completed the SDT. In the top right quadrant are countries with high scores for both the parenthood and alternative living arrangement dimensions, suggesting that views on cohabitation are relatively favourable but that high importance is attached to parenthood as well. This combination of characteristics is found mainly among Conservative welfare states as well as among most Eastern and Southern European countries. In the bottom left quadrant of Figure 1 are countries with the opposite set of characteristics: a relatively weak importance attached to parenthood but a strong attachment to marriage. This set of characteristics is mainly found in Liberal welfare states outside of Europe. Finally, there is also a small group of countries with a low score for the alternative living arrangements dimension and a high score for the parenthood dimension are located in the upper left hand quadrant of Figure 1, suggesting that – at an attitudinal level at least – the SDT had not yet been internalized to a large extent by 1994 in Italy and by 2002 in Slovakia and Poland.

An interesting aspect of Figure 1 is that for a number of countries, changes in factor scores can be traced between 1994 and 2002. For these countries, shifts in location are presented by pointed arrows showing the shift from 1994 to 2002. Of these 16 arrows, all but two point to the right, suggesting that the attitude towards alternative living arrangements has become more favourable between 1994 and 2002. Particularly strong shifts can be detected for Spain, East Germany, Northern Ireland and Poland. Shifts along the parenthood dimension are somewhat less spectacular: the largest shifts are for East Germany, Austria, Sweden, Ireland and Northern Ireland. In all these countries, the importance attached to parenthood decreased between 1994 and 2002.

Taken as a whole, this data from the ISSP supports the hypothesis that attitudes towards central dimensions of the SDT, in particular concerning unmarried cohabitation and divorce, are relatively positive across Western societies. What is particular striking is that a majority of young people in most Eastern and Southern European countries agreed that premarital cohabitation is a good idea as early as 1994. This suggests that the minds of young people in those parts of Europe should have been ready for a change in behaviour by the middle of the 1990s. What is unclear however, is whether such a behavioural change actually occurred. It is to that question that we now turn our attention.

3. Changes in the incidence of unmarried cohabitation and parenthood among young people

Whereas we know a great deal about changes in fertility behaviour across Europe in the last two decades (e.g. Sobotka 2004), we know much less about changes in living arrangements. What is clear is that marriage is declining in popularity (Kiernan 2001, 2002), but in many countries we do not know whether this is due to postponement of union formation, the substitution of unmarried cohabitation for marriage, or to both of these processes at the same time. The most significant reason for this is that information on trends in unmarried cohabitation across Europe is relatively scarce, in particular as far as Southern and Eastern Europe are concerned. The most useful tool would be data on the proportion of people who have ever cohabited without being married, but such data is hard to come by. Instead, we have charted the development in the percentage of women aged 20 to 34 who are living with a partner without being married. We have done so for a number of countries belonging to the European Union using data from the EU Labour Force Survey (LFS). The LFS is a survey of households in the European Union that has been carried out annually and quarterly[4] since 1983 in ten Member States of the European Union: Belgium, Denmark, France, Germany, Greece, Ireland, Italy, Luxembourg, the Netherlands (with the exception of 1984 and 1986), and the United Kingdom. Portugal and Spain joined in 1986, Austria, Finland, Iceland, Norway, Sweden and Switzerland in 1995, Hungary and Slovenia in 1996, Estonia, the Czech Republic, Poland and Romania in 1997, Latvia, Lithuania and Slovakia in 1998, Cyprus in 1999 and Bulgaria and Malta in 2000. Croatia was the most recent country to join in 2002.

---

4 From 1983 to 1997, the LFS was conducted only in spring. The data for the additional quarters has become progressively available from 1998 onwards.

The LFS contains nationally representative samples of private households; it does not cover those living in communal or collective households. It provides detailed information on employment, unemployment and other socio-economic indicators for each household member aged 15 and over. In addition, data is collected on demographic characteristics such as age, sex and marital status. The LFS is unique in terms of its sample size and the length of the time series it offers for a large number of European countries. Moreover, the degree of comparability between LFS outcomes across countries is relatively high due to the use of the same questionnaire and definitions for all countries, the use of common classifications and a single set method of recording, as well as the fact that the data is centrally processed by Eurostat. Despite close coordination between the national statistical institutes and Eurostat, some differences in the survey inevitably remain from country to country (e.g. different order of their questionnaires and difference in sample designs). In most countries, information is available on whether partners are present in the household, and if so, whether the partners are married or not. However, this information is not equally reliable in every country or for all years within a country. Therefore, we have restricted ourselves to countries (and years) where the data appears to be reasonably reliable (see Fokkema and Liefbroer [2006] for additional information on the quality of LFS data in this respect).

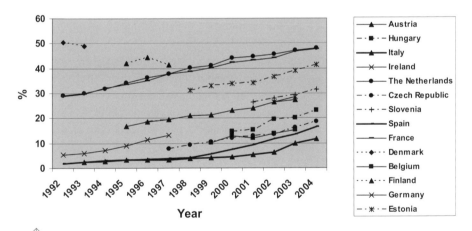

Figure 2: Percentage of all partnered women aged 20 to 34 living with a partner outside marriage
Source: LFS 1992-2004

For each year in which reliable data is available, we have calculated the percentage of women between 20 and 34 years of age living with a partner without being married, then divided this by the percentage of all women who were living with a partner. This results in the proportion of 'partnered' women who were cohabiting outside marriage. This percentage is presented in Figure 2 for all countries with relevant data. We will discuss the results starting with the Scandinavian countries, then move on to Western Europe, Eastern Europe and Southern Europe.

The information on the incidence of unmarried cohabitation among partnered women in Denmark and Finland is restricted to the 1990s. At that time, these two countries had the highest cohabitation rates of all the countries included in our data. In Denmark, about half of all partnered women aged 20 to 34 were cohabiting outside marriage in 1992 and 1993. In Finland, the percentage varied between 40 and 45 % in the period 1995-1997. These percentages are very high, particularly if one considers that these figures only include current cohabitation.

Information on cohabitation is available for a number of Western European countries, most of which – Belgium, the Netherlands, France, Germany, and Austria – can be classified as belonging to the Conservative cluster within Esping-Andersen's classification. Only Ireland belongs to the Liberal welfare state cluster as defined by Esping-Andersen. The highest percentages of partnered women who live in a consensual union can be found in France and the Netherlands. In both countries, about 30 percent of all partnered women cohabited without being married during the early 1990s, and this percentage has risen steadily to about 48 percent in 2004. Evidently, unmarried cohabitation is a very popular living arrangement in these countries. The percentage of couples who cohabit without being married is much lower in other Western European countries, but seems to be rising everywhere. In Austria, the percentage of partnered women who cohabit outside marriage rose from 17 percent in 1995 to 27 percent in 2002, to almost the same level as Germany (29 percent in 2003). Although a more modest proportion, the percentage of unmarried, partnered women in Belgium rose from 10 percent in 1999 to 15 percent in 2003. Unfortunately, the data for Ireland dates back to the 1990s, but there, too, an increase could be observed from 6 percent in 1992 to 13 percent in 1997. As this data makes clear, the level of current cohabitation varies widely in Western Europe, but the trend is upward in all countries for which data is available.

Information on the occurrence of unmarried cohabitation is available for four Eastern European countries: Estonia, Slovenia, Hungary and the Czech Republic. An upward trend in the occurrence of unmarried cohabitation is visible in each of these countries. In Estonia, the percentage of 20 to 34 year old partnered women who cohabit without being married increased from 31 in 1998 to 41 in 2002. In Slovenia, it increased from 19 percent in 1996 to 32 percent in 2003. In Hungary, this proportion grew from 15 percent in 2000 to 23 in 2004. In the Czech Republic, finally, it rose from eight percent in 1997 to 19 percent in 2004. As in Western Europe, the level of cohabitation varies substantially across countries, but the trend is upwards in all of them.

Finally, information is available for two Southern European countries: Italy and Spain. This is very fortunate as it offers the opportunity to examine whether this aspect of the SDT has stopped at the Alps and the Pyrenees or diffused across them. Until the end of the 1990s, the percentages of partnered women who cohabited outside marriage in these two countries were by far the lowest of all the countries where data is available. During the 1990s it rose slowly from 1.5 to about 4 percent in Spain, and in Italy it hovered between 3 and 5 percent between 1995 and 2000. But from the start of the new millennium onwards, things seem to be changing in both countries. In Italy, the percentage of partnered women aged 20 to 34 who are cohabiting outside marriage more than doubled from 5 percent in 2000 to 12 percent in 2004. In Spain, a fourfold increase from 4 percent in 1998 to 17 percent in 2004 can be observed. These figures suggest that the SDT might not have crossed the Alps and Pyrenees during the 1990s, but has passed them since the beginning of the new millennium.

In addition to data on the incidence of unmarried cohabitation, the LFS also offers information on the percentage of women aged 20 to 34 who live in a household with one or more of their own children. Although this information is less specific than the data on unmarried cohabitation, it still warrants a brief discussion. In Figure 3, the trend in the percentage of women aged 20 to 34 who live with a child or children is presented for those countries which have data for a number of consecutive years.

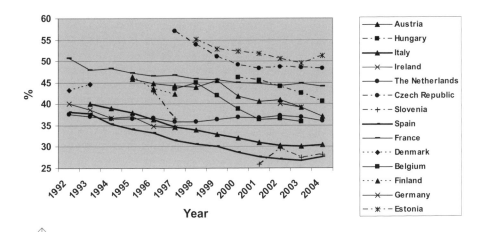

↑
Figure 3: Percentage of all women aged 20 to 34 living with a child (or children) of their own
Source: LFS 1992-2004

A few things are worth mentioning in Figure 3. Firstly, the percentage of women who live with one or more children varies widely across Europe. It is highest in Estonia and the Czech Republic, and lowest in Italy and Spain. A second important observation is that almost all countries – with the exception of the Netherlands – show a decrease in the proportion of women who live with one or more children, suggesting that family formation is being postponed. Finally, signs of stabilisation are visible in a number of countries. In Spain, Italy, Belgium, France, Estonia and the Czech Republic the negative gradient in the curve has recently disappeared.

Taken as a whole, this data shows a wide variability in demographic behaviour among young adults in Europe. However, some common patterns can be observed as well. An increase in unmarried cohabitation is visible across Europe, as is a postponement of family formation. These are both important aspects of the demographic changes entailed by the SDT. At the same time, the SDT suggests that these changes are related to changes in values and attitudes. It is to this 'missing link' that we now turn our attention.

4. Interplay between demographic attitudes and behaviour at the country level

The SDT implies that country-level differences and changes in demographic behaviour are connected to country-level differences and changes in the values and attitudes that co-determine demographic choices. We dealt separately above with attitudes and behaviour with regard to cohabitation and parenthood. In this section, we will link the attitudinal and behavioural dimensions by focussing on the correlations between the two dimensions at the country level. To begin with, attention will be paid to the issue of cohabitation, and then we will discuss the relationship between parenthood attitudes and behaviour.

The data presented in the previous section shows a marked increase in the incidence of unmarried cohabitation between the mid-1990s and the early 2000s in all European countries for which data were available. It is interesting to link these changes to the changes in attitudes towards alternative living arrangements discussed earlier. The problem, however, is that we only have data for a very limited number of countries. Therefore, our analysis can only be tentative. In Figure 4 the location of countries is plotted in a two-dimensional space consisting of country-level scores for the alternative living arrangement factor and for the incidence of unmarried cohabitation.

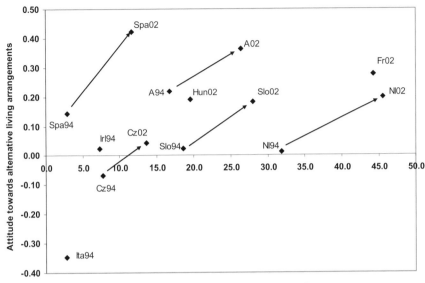

↑

Figure 4: Location of countries by alternative living arrangement factor score and incidence of unmarried cohabitation among partnered women aged 20 to 34
Source: ISSP / LFS 1994, 2002

An initial observation from Figure 4 is that the data points suggest a positive relationship between the country score on the attitude towards alternative living arrangements and the incidence of unmarried cohabitation in that country (r = 0.44). However, given the small number of observations, this correlation is not statistically significant (p = 0.11). Still, this pattern corresponds to expectations based on the SDT. What is even more indicative, however, are the changes in the time points for countries for which data from 1994 and 2002 is available. As the arrows in Figure 4 show, all these changes are in the same direction. Within countries, a change towards more favourable attitudes towards alternative living arrangements coincides with an increase in the incidence of unmarried cohabitation. Therefore, although we have too little information to perform a rigorous test, this data suggests that attitudes and behaviour concerning unmarried cohabitation co-vary according to expected patterns, and that changes in attitudes and changes in behaviour also co-vary as predicted by the SDT thesis.

Now we will turn our attention to the relationship between the dimensions of attitudes towards parenthood and fertility behaviour. In this case, we have not compared attitudes from the LFS data to the percentage of 20 to 34 year old women who have children, but to the total fertility rate (TFR) of the countries in question. This choice is mainly based on practical considerations: the TFR is available for almost all of the countries for which ISSP attitudinal data is available, whereas information on the percentage of 20 to 34 year old women with children is only available for a very small number of countries. Evidently, the use of the TFR has drawbacks as well; it does not allow quantum and timing effects to be disentangled (e.g. Bongaarts and Feeney 1998), and the TFR is not just based on women between 20 and 34 years of age. Unfortunately, no better indicator for all these countries and time periods is available. In Figure 5 the country-level association between the factor score for the parenthood dimension and the TFR for the respective countries is plotted.

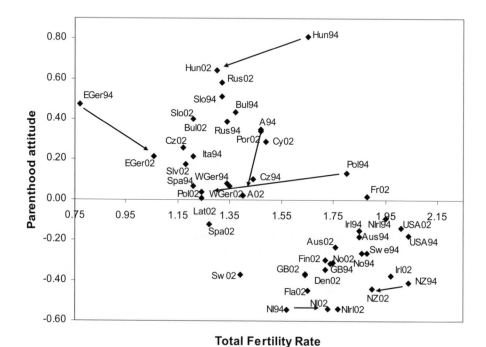

Figure 5: *Location of countries by parenthood factor score and total fertility rate*
<u>Source</u>: ISSP 1994, 2002

Figure 5 shows a very strong correlation between the general attitude towards parenthood among young adults in a country and the TFR in that country. However, the correlation is the complete opposite to what one would expect: the more young adults in a country favour parenthood, the lower the TFR in that country, and vice versa (r = -0.62, p < 0.01). In almost all countries with a TFR above 1.50, the factor score for the parenthood dimension is below average; in almost all countries with a TFR below 1.50, the factor score for the parenthood dimension is above average. Another point to be noted from Figure 5 is that the shift in the location of countries between 1994 and 2002 is rather haphazard. To illustrate this, we have drawn a small number of arrows to accentuate the fact that a downward trend in the TFR sometimes occurs in combination with hardly any change in attitudes towards parenthood (e.g. in Poland and Hungary); a downward trend in attitudes towards parenthood is sometimes accompanied by hardly any change in the TFR (e.g. in Austria); and sometimes an upward trend in the TFR is even accompanied by a downward trend in attitudes towards parenthood (e.g. in East Germany).

To examine the relationship between the TFR and parenthood attitudes in somewhat more detail, a multi-level random effects model was estimated with the TFR score of a country as the dependent variable. This analysis allows one to control for multiple observations per country and to disentangle the influence of attitudes towards parenthood on the differences between countries and the changes within countries. The results of this analysis are presented in Model 1 in Table 3. The statistically significant negative parameter for attitudes towards parenthood confirms the strongly negative effect between TFR and attitudes towards parenthood observed in Figure 5. On average, countries that are half a standard deviation below average for the attitudes towards parenthood dimension have a TFR that is about 0.42 higher than countries that have a score for attitudes towards parenthood that is half a standard deviation above average. This variable explains 42 percent of the variation in the TFR between countries, but only 4 percent of the changes in the TFR within countries. A separate fixed-effect analysis confirms that the effect of the attitudes towards parenthood dimension on changes in the TFR within countries is not statistically significant.

Table 3: Results of a random effects multi-level regression of the total fertility rate
↓

	Model 1	Model 2
Constant	1.54**	1.79**
Attitude towards parenthood	-0.42**	0.09
Liberal welfare state		0.11
Conservative welfare state		-0.25*
Southern European welfare state		-0.46**
Eastern European welfare state		-0.53**
Explained variance within countries	0.04	0.04
Explained variance between countries	0.43	0.73
Number of observations	47	47
Number of countries	28	28

* $p < 0.05$; ** $p < 0.01$

To further explore the relationship between attitudes towards parenthood and the TFR, we have divided the countries into five categories, largely based on the welfare state typology developed by Esping-Andersen, with the Southern European countries and Eastern European countries added as additional categories. Countries belonging to the Social Democratic welfare state type constitute the reference category. The random-effects model was rerun and the results are presented in Model 2 in Table 3. Adding the welfare state typology to the equation considerably changes the results of the model. The statistically significant effect of parenthood disappears, suggesting that the effect observed in Model 1 was spurious rather than real. In addition, the welfare state dummies show a clear pattern of results. The TFR is highest in Social Democratic and Liberal welfare states, considerably lower in Conservative welfare states, and lowest in Eastern and Southern European countries. Together, these variables explain 73 percent of the variation between countries. Because countries do not shift in their class membership between 1994 and 2002, the variance within a country does not change between Models 1 and 2. Based on these results, one would conclude that differences in fertility rates across Europe are not linked to the attitude towards parenthood within those countries, but can be explained to a very large extent by the type of welfare state regime to which countries belong.

To further substantiate this conclusion, we have calculated the correlation between parenthood attitudes and the TFR in Liberal and Social Democratic welfare states and those in the other countries. In Liberal and Social-Democratic welfare states a positive, albeit non-significant correlation occurred ($r = 0.38$, $p = 0.12$), whereas a negative, marginally significant correlation occurred in the other countries (r = -0.33, p = 0.08). If the Netherlands – a country whose welfare state is sometimes classified as Conservative, sometimes as Social Democratic – is classified as Social Democratic, the positive correlation in these countries becomes statistically significant (r = 0.52, p = 0.02), whereas it becomes non-significant in the other group of countries (r = -0.17, p = 0.38). We also performed a multi-level random effects model that included an interaction between attitudes towards parenthood and whether or not countries belonged to the Liberal or Social Democratic welfare regime type. Although the estimated effect parameters were in line with the results based on bivariate correlations, the interaction failed to reach statistical significance. Still, these results suggest an interesting hypothesis that young people might be better able to realize attitudes towards parenthood in countries where relatively good facilities to combine parenthood and employment exist than in countries where these facilities are poor. In Social Democratic countries, the state provides generous childcare facilities, whereas these are provided for by the market in Liberal countries. In the Netherlands, the availability of part-time jobs facilitates the combination of employment and parenthood. For a variety of reasons, arrangements to successfully combine motherhood and a professional career are much less well-developed in most Conservative, Southern and Eastern European countries (Castles 2003; Den Dulk 2001). As a result, in countries where the opportunities for women to combine parenthood and employment are relatively good, fertility rates are relatively high, whereas they are relatively low in countries with relatively poor facilities to combine employment and motherhood. In addition, in the former set of countries, young people might be able to realize their attitudes towards parenthood better than in the latter set of countries.

5. Discussion

Within twenty years, the concept of the 'Second Demographic Transition' has become one of the most influential ideas in demographic research. Its appeal derives from its ability to link seemingly diverse types of demographic behaviour and to connect them to long-term value change in Western societies. As the concept of the SDT has clearly come of age, new questions arise. In this discussion, we want to touch on a number of these issues, based partly on some of the empirical results presented in this chapter, and partly on new developments in Western societies.

In the countries where the SDT was first observed, such as Sweden, Norway and the Netherlands, there are signs that a new standard pathway through young adulthood is emerging (Elzinga and Liefbroer 2007). This new standard includes unmarried cohabitation, a clear postponement of marriage and entry into parenthood, and – during the earlier phase of union formation – a relatively high probability that at least one non-marital union will end in separation. If one takes the idea of the SDT as a transition from one standard to another seriously, this pathway may become the new norm. However, whether a new standard will really emerge is an issue that warrants more attention. There are at least two reasons why this might not occur. Firstly, the SDT is driven by an increasing emphasis on self-actualization. Self-actualization seems to imply the idea of individual decision-making and a reluctance to adopt standard solutions to developmental challenges. If so, a continued high level of de-standardization of family life courses may be expected in countries that have passed through the SDT. Secondly, it remains to be seen whether a new standard has already crystallised in the countries that pioneered the SDT. Will marriage lose all relevance in such societies and be completely replaced by unmarried cohabitation? Is further postponement of fertility possible? One might speculate that the answer to these questions is 'no', given that many cohabitants decide to marry after a number of years (Kiernan 2002) and given that there is a levelling-off of the percentage of young people who postpone entry into parenthood in countries like the Netherlands that are well advanced in the SDT (Sobotka 2004). However, it may still be too early for any degree of certainty.

As the results on unmarried cohabitation presented in this chapter convincingly demonstrate, the SDT has begun in Eastern and Southern Europe. In both parts of Europe, attitudes towards pre-marital cohabitation and non-marital cohabitation in general have become surprisingly positive, and this has been translated into an increased incidence of unmarried cohabitation over the last ten years. Nevertheless, important questions remain. One question is why there was hardly any unmarried cohabitation among young adults in Spain and Italy in 1994, a time when the attitudes towards unmarried cohabitation were already very positive, as the ISSP data clearly shows. An explanation could be that young adults are reluctant to enter into a consensual union because their parents disapprove. A recent study shows that the decisions of young adults in the Netherlands to leave home in order to live with a partner is influenced by their perceptions of their parents' opinions about the appropriate timing of this event (Billari and Liefbroer 2007). If parents influence the union formation choices of their children in a 'leading' SDT country like the Netherlands, it is even more likely that this will be the case in a strongly familistic society like Italy or Spain (Rosina and Fraboni 2004). In any case, it is important to examine why a discrepancy exists in a number of countries between attitudes and behaviour concerning family formation. Normative factors might be one of the key explanations for this discrepancy.

Given that SDT-like behaviour has become very widespread in some countries, a key issue for future research is why it does not seem to be catching on in other countries. In a recent analysis of spatial differences in the United States, Lesthaeghe and Neidert (2006) found a clear division between states where SDT behaviour is very widespread and states where it is not. An important question for future research is how it is possible that the SDT does not seem to be catching on in some countries or states, even in an era in which the ideas that drive the SDT have been diffused widely. The related question, of course, is whether the SDT will take off in these states in the foreseeable future or whether it is possible to 'successfully' resist the SDT.

It has been suggested that the drop in fertility rates that has occurred in Eastern and Southern European countries supports the idea that the SDT has spread to Eastern and Southern Europe (Lesthaeghe and Surkyn 2006). In fact, the TFR is generally much lower in Eastern and Southern European countries than in most of Western Europe and the English-speaking countries. However, it is questionable whether the low level of fertility in Eastern and Southern Europe really supports the SDT thesis. The strongly negative relationship between attitudes towards parenthood and the TFR observed in this chapter suggest that the TFR might be low in these parts of Europe for the 'wrong reasons'. It is clearly not low because it reflects a relatively low value attached to parenthood, as the SDT would predict. It seems more likely that economic insecurity and insufficient facilities for combining parenthood and employment are important factors in explaining low fertility in these parts of Europe (Billari, Liefbroer and Philipov 2006). In any case, these results suggest that future research should focus more strongly on the interplay between cultural, economic and institutional factors. One key question is what circumstances influence the likelihood that values and attitudes are transformed into corresponding behaviour.

The interpretation that differences in fertility behaviour across Europe have little to do with differences in parenthood attitudes, but are more likely to be related to institutional arrangements that facilitate the combination of motherhood and employment, fits in quite well with recent findings on the changing relationship between female labour force participation and fertility. Engelhardt and her colleagues (Engelhardt, Kögel and Prskawetz 2004; Engelhardt and Prskawetz 2004) have argued that the relationship between female labour force participation and fertility has been changing and that it is becoming positive, because women in countries where good facilities for combining employment and parenthood are available are particularly likely to combine the two types of activity in practice. This line of reasoning focuses on the changing role of women in modern societies and its consequences for demographic behaviour. This is a topic which has received relatively little attention within the SDT literature (Bernhardt 2004). In future research and theorizing on value orientations, this shortcoming needs to be redressed. For instance, one should focus more on the relative importance of parenthood and employment in the value hierarchy of women – and men – and on the opportunities to realize both these values than on studying parenthood values in isolation.

6. References

Axinn, W.G., and Thornton, A. (1992). The Relationship Between Cohabitation and Divorce: Selectivity or Causal Influence? *Demography*, 29, 357-374.

Axinn, W.G., and Thornton, A. (1993). Mothers, Children and Cohabitation: The Intergenerational Effects of Attitudes and Behavior. *American Sociological Review*, 58, 233-246.

Barber, J.S., Axinn, W.G., and Thornton, A. (2002), The Influence of Attitudes on Family Formation Processes. In R. Lesthaeghe (Ed.), *Meaning and Choice: Value Orientations and Life Course Decisions* (pp. 45-93). The Hague, the Netherlands: NIDI/CBGS.

Billari, F.C., M. Castiglioni, T. Castro Martin, F. Michielin, and F. Ongaro (2002). Household and Union Formation in a Mediterranean Fashion: Italy and Spain. In E. Klijzing and M. Corijn (Eds.), *Dynamics of Fertility and Partnership in Europe. Insights and Lessons From Comparative Research, Volume 2* (pp. 17-41). New York: United Nations.

Billari, F.C., and Liefbroer, A.C. (2007). Should I Stay or Should I Go? The Impact of Age Norms on Leaving Home. *Demography*, 44, 181-198.

Billari, F.C., Liefbroer, A.C., and Philipov, D. (2006). The Postponement of Childbearing in Europe: Driving Forces and Implications. In Philipov, D., Liefbroer, A.C., and Billari, F.C. (Eds.), Postponement of childbearing in Europe (pp. 1-17). Special issue of the *Vienna Yearbook of Population Research 2006*. Vienna: Austrian Academy of Sciences.

Bernhardt, E. (2004). Is the Second Demographic Transition a Useful Concept for Demography? *Vienna Yearbook of Population Research 2004*, 25-28.

Bongaarts, J., and Feeney, G. (1998). On the Quantum and Tempo of Fertility. *Population and Development Review*, 24, 271-291.

Castles, F. G. (2003). The World Turned Upside Down: Below Replacement Fertility, Changing Preferences and family-Friendly Public Policy in 21 OECD Countries. *Journal of European Social Policy, 13*, 209-227.

Cliquet, R. (1991). *The Second Demographic Transition: Fact or Fiction?* Strasbourg: Council of Europe.

Coleman, D. (2004). Why We Don't Have to Believe Without Doubting in the "Second Demographic Transition" - Some Agnostic Comments. *Vienna Yearbook of Population Research 2006*, 11-24.

Dalla Zuanna, G. (2001). The Banquet of Aeolus: A Familistic Interpretation of Italy's Lowest Low Fertility. *Demographic Research*, 4, 131-162.

De Jong Gierveld, J., De Valk, H., and Blommesteijn, M. (2002). Living Arrangements of Older Persons and Family Support in More Developed Countries. *Population Bulletin of the United Nations*, 42-43, 193-217.

Den Dulk, L. (2001), *Work-Family Arrangements in Organisations. A Cross-National Study in the Netherlands, Italy, the United Kingdom and Sweden.* Amsterdam: Rozenberg Publishers.

Elzinga, C.H., and Liefbroer, A.C. (2007). De-Standardization and Differentiation of Family Life Trajectories of Young Adults: A Cross-National Comparison. *European Journal of Population*, 23, 225-250.

Engelhardt, H., Kögel, T., and Prskawetz, A. (2004). Fertility and Women's Employment Reconsidered: A Macro-Level Time-Series Analysis for Developed Countries, 1960-2000. *Population Studies, 58*, 109-120.

Engelhardt, H., and Prskawetz, A. (2004). On the Changing Correlation Between Fertility and Female Employment over Space and Time. *European Journal of Population*, 20, 35-62.

Esping-Andersen, G. (1990). *Three Worlds of Welfare Capitalism*. Cambridge: Polity Press.

Esping-Andersen, G. (1999). *Social Foundations of Postindustrial Economies*. Oxford: Oxford University Press.

Fernandez Cordon, J.A. (1997). Youth Residential Independence and Autonomy: A Comparative Study. *Journal of Family Issues, 16*, 567-607.

Fokkema, T., and Esveldt, I. (2006), Work Package 7: Child-friendly Policies. Dialog Report No. 7. Wiesbaden: Bundesinstitüt fur Bevölkerungsforschung.

Fokkema, T., and Liefbroer, A.C. (2006). Trends in Living Arrangements in Europe: Convergence or Divergence. Internal Paper. The Hague, the Netherlands: NIDI.

Inglehart, R. (1977), *The Silent Revolution. Changing Values and Political Styles Among Western Publics*. Princeton: Princeton University Press.

Inglehart, R. and Baker, W.E. (2000). Modernization, Cultural Change, and the Persistence of Traditional Values. *American Sociological Review*, 65, 19-51.

ISSP (1994). Family and Changing Gender Roles II. Codebook ZA Study 2620. Köln: Zentral Archive.

ISSP (2002). Family and Changing Gender Roles III. Codebook ZA Study 3880. Köln: Zentral Archive.

Jansen, M., and Kalmijn, M. (2002). Investments in Family Life: The Impact of Value Orientations on Patterns of Consumption, Production and Reproduction in Married and Cohabiting Couples. In R. Lesthaeghe (Ed.), *Meaning and Choice: Value Orientations and Life Course Decisions* (pp. 129-159). The Hague, the Netherlands: NIDI/CBGS.

Kiernan, K. (2001). The Rise of Cohabitation and Childbearing Outside Marriage in Western Europe. *International Journal of Law, Policy and the Family*, 15, 1-21.

Kiernan, K. (2002). The State of European Unions: An Analysis of FFS Data on Partnership Formation and Dissolution. In M. Macura and G. Beets (Eds.), *Dynamics of Fertility and Partnership in Europe: Insights and Lessons from Comparative Research*, Volume 1 (pp. 57-76). New York and Geneva: United Nations.

Kohler, H.P., Billari, F.C., and Ortega, J.A. (2002). The Emergence of Lowest-Low Fertility in Europe During the 1990s. *Population and Development Review*, 28, 641-680.

Kohler, H.-P., and Kohler, I. (2002). Fertility Decline in Russia in the Early and Mid 1990s: The Role of Economic Uncertainty and Labour Market Crises. *European Journal of Population*, 18, 233-262.

Lesthaeghe, R. (1995). The Second Demographic Transition in Western Countries: An Interpretation. In K.O. Mason and A.-M. Jensen (Eds.), *Gender and Family Change in Industrialized Countries* (pp. 17-62). Oxford: Clarendon Press.

Lesthaeghe, R., and Moors, G. (2002). Life Course Transitions and Value Orientations: Selection and Adaptation. In R. Lesthaeghe (Ed.), *Meaning and choice: Value orientations and life course decisions* (pp. 1-44). The Hague, the Netherlands: NIDI/CBGS.

Lesthaeghe, R., and Neidert, L. (2006). The Second Demographic Transition in the United States: Exception or Textbook Example? *Population and Development Review*, 32, 669-698.

Lesthaeghe, R., and Surkyn, J. (1988). Cultural Dynamics and Economic Theories of Fertility Change. *Population and Development Review*, 14, 1-45.

Lesthaeghe, R., and Surkyn, J. (2006). When History Moves on: Foundations and Diffusion of a Second Demographic Transition. In R. Jayakody, A. Thornton and W. Axinn (Eds.), *International Family Change: Ideational Perspectives*. Mahwah, NJ: Lawrence Erlbaum.

Lesthaeghe, R., and Van de Kaa, D.J. (1986). Twee Demografische Transities? In D.J. Van de Kaa and R. Lesthaeghe (Eds.), *Bevolking: groei en krimp* (pp. 9-24). Deventer, the Netherlands: Van Loghum Slaterus.

Macura, M., Mochizuki-Sternberg, Y., and Garcia, J.L. (2002). Eastern and Western Europe's Fertility and Partnership Patterns: Selected Developments From 1987 to 1999. In: M. Macura and G.C.N. Beets (Eds.), *Dynamics of Fertility and Partnership in Europe. Insights and Lessons from Comparative Research. Volume 1* (pp. 27-55). New York: United Nations.

Maslow, A. (1954). *Motivation and Personality*. New York: Harper & Row.

Moors, G. (2002). Reciprocal Relations Between Gender Role Values and Family Formation. In R. Lesthaeghe (ed.), *Meaning and choice: Value orientations and life course decisions* (pp. 217-250). The Hague, the Netherlands: NIDI/CBGS.

Reher, D.S. (1998). Family Ties in Western Europe: Persistent Contrasts. *Population and Development Review*, 24, 203-224.

Rosina, A., and Fraboni, R. (2004). Is Marriage Loosing its Centrality in Italy? *Demographic Research*, 11, 149-172.

Sobotka, T. (2004). *Postponement of Childbearing and Low Fertility in Europe*. Amsterdam: Dutch University Press.

Sobotka, T., Zeman, K., and Kantorova, V. (2003). Demographic Shifts in the Czech Republic after 1989: A Second Demographic Transition View. *European Journal of Population*, 19, 249-277.

Surkyn, J., and Lesthaeghe, R. (2004). Value Orientations and the Second Demographic Transition (SDT) in Northern, Western and Southern Europe: An Update. *Demographic Research*, Special Collection 3, 45-86.

Van de Kaa, D.J. (1987). Europe's Second Demographic Transition. *Population Bulletin*, 42, whole issue.

–

05 Measuring International Migration:
a Challenge for Demographers

Michel Poulain and Nicolas Perrin

Demographers consider international migration to be a topic of increasing importance for their discipline. However, policy-makers dealing with international migration show limited interest in the work of demographers. This paradox is particularly apparent in Europe, a setting where the issue of migration has become a key priority for European policy-makers. Specifically, in order to support the development of a common migration policy, the European Union is faced with an urgent need for better statistics on migration and asylum and the international migration statistics are frequently unreliable, not only in Europe, but in all countries around the world. A recent meeting organised by the UN's Statistical Division in New York[1] concluded firstly: the most recent set of recommendations on international migration statistics is not being followed, secondly: the requested data is often unavailable, and where it is available, is often unreliable and finally: that all the available data considered sufficiently reliable cannot be compared systematically because of different data sources, concepts and definitions. Accordingly, the task facing demographers is not an easy one. Nonetheless, it may be considered essential in terms of policy support.

1. Migration, a demographic phenomenon that is particularly difficult to measure

Migration is defined as a change in the place of usual residence, and residence, in turn, is defined as the place where the person spends most daily rest periods. In the case of international migration, the place of origin and the place of destination are located in two different countries, and so international migration can be defined as a change of country of usual residence. In practical terms, it means that one or more international borders will be crossed. However, border data collection is no longer used in the EU since the abolition of internal border controls, and so alternative data collection methods have to be used. Moreover, although border-crossing data is used in non-European countries, it is usually considered to be unreliable. Consequently, even if international migration is defined with reference to borders, border-crossing data is not the best source of information.

In demography, the collection of data on international migration is a uniquely complex affair because a single phenomenon and a single event (international migration), involving the same people (international migrants), is recorded by two different countries using two completely different data collection systems. Emigration figures produced by countries of origin and immigration figures collected by countries of destination would be similar if the two data collection systems used identical definitions and the data

---

1   Expert Group Meeting on Measuring International Migration: concepts and methods, UNSD, New York, 4-7 December 2006.

were fully reliable. The idea of comparing these pairs of figures using a double-entry matrix is more than thirty years old.[2] In this double migration matrix, two figures are proposed in each cell M(i,j) for the migration flow between a specific pair of countries i and j: one on immigration to the country of destination and one on emigration from the country of origin. Low reliability is evident within the EU when comparing data on flows between pairs of EU Member States as reported by both the country of origin and the country of destination. Figure 1 shows an example of comparison of statistics for the migration flow between Italy and Germany in 2003.

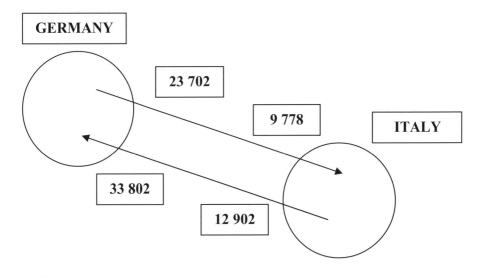

Figure 1: Migration flows between Italy and Germany in 2003: the immigration figure for Germany (33,802) may be compared to the emigration one for Italy (12,902), and the emigration figure for Germany (23,702) can be compared to immigration to Italy (9,778) (Source: Eurostat)

---

2   Such double-entry matrices have been produced annually by the UNECE since 1972 and more recently by Eurostat. The two main proponents of using this tool to estimate the level of harmonisation of international migration flows were John Kelly (1987) and Michel Poulain (1999).

The double-entry matrix is an interesting tool for studying the reliability and comparability of statistical data on a general basis, especially in cases where it is generally agreed there is a major problem with reliability. Each of the 600 cells of the intra-EU25 migration matrix[3] include, for a given migration flow from country A to country B, both the number of emigrants recorded in country A and the number of immigrants registered in country B. In this way, the two figures in the same cell are directly comparable. Here are the general conclusions based on the 2002 double-matrix (Poulain et al. 2006):

- Belgium, Estonia, Greece, France, Ireland, Luxembourg, Hungary, Malta and the UK submitted no data at all (except that Ireland and Malta provided immigration and emigration data with the UK only and Malta also provided immigration data from Italy). As a consequence 56 cells include no data at all, either for emigration or for immigration.
- By contrast, both figures are available for 277 migration flows. This means that it is possible to compare the statistics in 46% of all cases. 134 cells only include immigration data, and the remaining 133 cells only emigration data.
- In the 277 cells where both figures are available, the total number of immigrants exceeds the total number of emigrants (508,800 immigrants compared to 448,636 emigrants). This does not necessarily mean that immigration is more systematically or better recorded than emigrations, as it may also be a consequence of better recording (of both immigration and emigration flows) in traditional countries of immigration.
- A comparison of immigration and emigration figures above zero shows that 59% of the figures are higher for immigration than for the corresponding emigration but the reverse is true in 41% of the cases (none are identical).
- A difference between immigration and emigration figures of less than 25% might be considered an acceptable level of reliability. Only 16% of the 277 cells are in this favourable situation. This represents only 5% of all intra-EU migration flows.
- In 23% of the cells, the emigration figure exceeds the corresponding immigration figure by a factor of more than two, while in 38% the immigration figure is more than twice the emigration one. In total about two out of three migration flows where both figures are available are in this unfavourable situation.

---

3 This number corresponds to 25 EU Member States as sending countries, multiplied by 24 receiving countries.

The large differences observed between countries are considered to be mainly due to problems of coverage and completeness of the data collection. Differences in definition can explain only small differences between countries.[4] Accordingly, we may conclude that the harmonisation of definitions is necessary to improve the overall comparability of international migration data within the EU but is not sufficient to eradicate all the problems. The primary requirement is an overall improvement in the reliability of registration and data-collection processes.

How can the existence of such large differences between statistical figures that are supposed to describe the same migration flow be explained? Despite existing international recommendations on the harmonisation of definitions on international migration, the definitions actually used vary significantly between countries, within countries over time, and between sources of statistical information. Moreover, the definitions of immigration and emigration applied in a particular country do not necessarily match each other in terms of their time criterion. Consequently the absence of harmonisation of definitions may be responsible for the poor comparability of data. However, even if two countries use the same definitions to measure international migration flows, the problem of non-reliability of the data collection system may entail very large differences between the two figures for the same migration flow. To assess the level of reliability, we first of all have to consider the coverage of data collection by identifying all sub-populations that are involved and those that are excluded. The latter will automatically lead to differences between corresponding statistical figures. It is also important to take into consideration that international migrations are events that have to be reported by the migrants themselves to local administrations after entering or before leaving the country. For practical and financial reasons, and in the absence of strict administrative rules, it may not be in the migrants' interest to report themselves. Accordingly, the number of immigrants and emigrants will be underestimated. In some countries the level of under-registration may be as high as 90 percent for emigrations. In addition, immigration may be better registered for foreigners as some advantages may exist. For nationals returning to their home country, there is often no sense in registering their return as they did not register their emigration in the first place.

This investigation of the intra-EU double-entry migration matrix demonstrates the poor comparability of the available data. The same comparability problems probably affect data on the international migration of EU citizens outside the EU, as the same rules and practices apply. Fortunately, the legal immigration of non-EU nationals is better recorded in most EU Member States as the residence permit database is used (directly or indirectly) to measure these flows. However this is not true for emigration.

--

4   Some checks have been carried out by the THESIM team in Sweden, Denmark and Belgium that show that differences in the time criterion can be responsible only for differences of less than 25%.

In addition, a large proportion of migration may be unauthorised and consequently not registered and not included in statistical figures.

In the field of population projections and forecasts, reliable international migration data is needed and, from a European policy point of view as well, international migration is very important and reliable data is much in demand. In this context, Eurostat, the UNECE and other international bodies are paying particular attention to the improvement of the overall reliability and comparability of international migration data. To achieve this improvement, the most recent key elements are the UN Recommendations on Statistics of International Migration (UN, 1998) and the new EU Regulation on Community Statistics on Migration and International Protection (European Union, 2007).

2. The UN Recommendations and the EU Regulation

Harmonisation of these international migration statistics seems impossible to achieve, despite continuous efforts promoted by international bodies since at least 1930, under the leadership of the UN (Herm, 2006). The last revision[5] of the UN Recommendations on Statistics of International Migration (UN, 1998) proposes the following definitions for the country of usual residence and for long-term migrants:

- The country of usual residence is *the country in which a person lives, that is to say, the country in which he or she has a place to live where he or she normally spends the daily period of rest. Temporary travel abroad for purposes of recreation, holiday, visits to friends and relatives, business, medical treatment or religious pilgrimage does not change a person's country of usual residence.*
- A long-term migrant is *defined as a person who moves to a country other than that of his or her usual residence for a period of at least a year (12 months), so that the country of destination effectively becomes his or her new country of usual residence.*

In order to ensure that the definition of an international migrant was in accordance with the definition of the country of usual residence and that of an international tourist, a long-term migrant is defined by a length of stay of at least twelve months.

---

5 Different sets of international recommendations on this topic were first proposed by the ILO (in 1924) and subsequently, after the Second World War, by the UN. In the 1970s and 1980s, the UNECE initiated an in-depth data collection and analysis of the "double matrix". At the beginning of the 1990s, the UNECE, Eurostat and later the ILO, OECD and the Council of Europe joined forces to revise the 1976 UN recommendations on international migration and develop a joint data collection method.

To fulfil its objective of harmonizing international migration statistical data and ensuring the production of the requested data for policy support, the European Union has recently adopted a regulation that will oblige all Member States to produce reliable and harmonized statistics on international migration, also including asylum, residence permits, illegal migration and acquisition of citizenship.[6] This EU Regulation will require all EU Member States to produce a full set of statistics in the field, starting from 2008. It will explicitly request reliable figures and detailed metadata in order to improve the level of data comparability at EU level.

The definition of a long-term migrant, as recommended by the UN recommendations and the EU regulation, ignores the concept of short-term migration[7] and only considers long-term migrants renamed as (international) migrants. According to the UN Census recommendations, short-term migrants will still be counted as part of the resident population figure in the country of departure as their absence is for less than 12 months. This implies that short-term migration flows are disregarded when linking flows and stock figures, and that the EU definition of international migrants is complies if long-term migrants only are considered as a component of population change. Therefore, short-term migrants will need to be considered as a different category. It seems appropriate to consider these persons as seasonal workers, since they travel in relation to the labour market or as students. Another relevant group, tourists, should also be considered as international travellers who are not included among the short-term migrants group. Both groups of migrants need to be counted separately for the usual resident population and international migration statistics, and a clear distinction should be made between the two types of data in order to avoid any risk of misunderstanding when linking population stocks and migration flows. The EU decision to consider only long-term migrants in the migration data collection requested by the EU regulation is therefore appropriate and will avoid one obvious area where errors are likely. Using twelve months as a time limit for identifying international migrants as in the proposed EU regulation appears to be the most appropriate choice.

In the EU regulation, the definition of (international) migrants is based on a period *that is, or is expected to be, of at least twelve months.* This definition allows the possibility of using either an ex-post duration of twelve months or an intended duration of twelve months. In the UN Recommendations on Statistics of International Migration, the definition of long-term migration implicitly refers to a minimum period of at least 12 months after migration, and this is therefore an intended duration of stay in the

—

6   European Parliament and Council Regulation on Community statistics on migration and international protection</Titre> <DocRef>(COM(2005)0375 – C6-0279/2005 – 2005/0156(COD)]</DocRef>

7   According to the UN recommendations, a short-term migrant is defined in a similar way to a long-term migrant, but the duration of stay is between three and twelve months.

receiving country. In the implementation instructions of the same recommendations, three methods are proposed for estimating this duration of stay:

1. Asking the intended duration of stay is recommended when somebody is observed at a border crossing or when the person registers in the country of immigration, and only if that person has the right to live in the country (e.g. citizens or foreigners holding a permanent residence permit).
2. If the right to stay is not granted, the intended duration of stay is not relevant. We will then need to rely on the duration of validity of the residence permit in order to be able to identify long-term migrants as those having a residence permit for at least one year, and intending to live in the country for at least one year.
3. For asylum seekers and other foreigners who have not been granted a residence permit for at least one year, the duration of stay in the country may only be estimated one year after immigration, using population registers, registers of aliens or registers of asylum seekers. This will provide the actual, or ex-post duration of stay.

In effect, somebody entering the country with the right to stay for at least one year, but not asked intended duration of stay at the time of registration, can only be checked through population registration systems one year later, in order to identify long-term migrants. The same investigation is possible for those who are already considered as international immigrants because their intended duration of stay was at least one year and they had the right to live in the country for that minimum period. When doing this, consolidated statistics will only be available for the year t in the first semester of the year t+2. International statistical bodies will often not accept this delay, as policy-makers always request data that is as up – to - date as possible. Therefore an initial proposal could be as follows:

The declaration made on arrival of an intended duration of stay of at least twelve months, and the issue of a residence permit for one year may be seen in many countries as a possible source of information on international migration. However, this measurement needs to be confirmed by more reliable estimates of the actual duration of stay. There may be an opportunity for statistical bureaus to propose provisional figures based on a ratio observed in previous years but, in this case, the final figures should be released one year later in order to replace the provisional ones.

While there is a growing awareness of the impact of varying national definitions, the UN recommendations have not been formally adopted anywhere (Poulain et al. 2003). Until recently, national interests have taken precedence over the need for internationally comparable statistics. Obviously harmonisation at international level will occur only if focused political energy can lead to a substantial improvement in the estimation of migration flows. In the EU, there is a real prospect of this with the new regulation coming into force with the 2008 data collection.

3. Various data sources used

The availability of statistics on international migration flows is conditional upon the existence of a data collection system that has the potential to yield meaningful statistical information on changes of the usual place of residence. Data sources used to produce statistics on international migration flows in the EU countries are very diverse. The major types of sources can be summarised as follows:

- Population registration systems including centralised population registers and local population registers;
- Statistical forms completed for all changes of residence;
- Other administrative registers or databases related to foreigners, such as registers of aliens, residence permits or asylum seekers;
- Sample surveys such as special migration surveys or household surveys;
- Other sources including censuses.

Countries try to make the best possible use of national administrative data sources, since alternative statistical tools such as sample surveys have drawbacks, mainly, sampling size. Population registers are the most widely used source of statistical information on international migration among the EU Member States. The majority of those registers are centralised at national level.[8] A centralised, computerised, and comprehensive population registration system providing continuous recording of information on each member of the target population seems to be the best source of reliable statistics, provided that people obey the registration rules. However, in some countries the centralised population register does not cover the whole target population. Some foreigners are excluded as nationals and, in some countries, holders of permanent residence permits are included.[9]

---

8   Central population registers are used to produce statistics on international migration flows for both nationals and non-nationals in the following ten countries: Belgium, Denmark, Estonia, Latvia, Lithuania, Luxembourg, Austria, Finland, Spain and Sweden.

9   The Czech Republic, Hungary and Slovenia derive their statistics from the central population registers, but only on nationals. In Hungary the register does not cover the whole target population of foreigners, since only those with permanent residence permits are included. In the Czech Republic and Slovenia theoretically the population registers have full coverage, but data on foreigners are of inferior quality than in the aliens register from which they were transferred, because the transfers have not been complete. However, this state of affairs is treated as transitional and the population registers are to be used for both nationals and non-nationals in the future.

The same statistics can usually be derived from population registers run locally or based on forms (administrative or statistical) completed when registering changes of residence.[10] However, this requires additional input and introduces the possibility of errors when processing the documents, which may have a negative impact on the reliability of the data. Finally, in some countries, centralised population registers are in operation, but are not yet used for statistical purposes due to the lack, or poor quality of, some crucial characteristics .[11]

If there is no administrative data source covering the whole population, or data for some population categories is considered unreliable, more specific registers are used that contain only subsets of the population, e.g. a register of foreigners or register of residence permits. These special registers constitute a valuable source of data on international migration in the countries where the population register does not exist, or does not cover the whole target foreign population, or where the development of the population register has not been completed.[12]

–

10 Population registers that operate at the local or regional levels are used to derive statistics on international migration flows in three EU countries: Germany, Italy and the Netherlands. Details regarding preparation of statistics vary from country to country.

11 This is the case in Poland and the Slovak Republic. For instance, in the Polish central population register there is no historical information on places of residence. In the Slovak population register there are a number of persons whose former Czechoslovakian citizenship has not been replaced by the new one (Czech or Slovak), so statistics on flows cannot be produced by citizenship. However, the population register in the Slovak Republic is now being reconstructed and will be used for statistical purposes in the future.

12 In the Central European countries (the Czech Republic, Hungary, Slovenia, the Slovak Republic) the registers of aliens are centralised and both immigration and emigration statistics are derived from them. In the Slovak Republic, the register of aliens was used for the first time to produce data on international migration of foreigners disaggregated by citizenship for the reference year 2003. In Slovenia the emigration figures are estimated on the basis of changes in foreigners' stock, vital statistics and immigration data. In Portugal and France the registers of aliens are used only to produce immigration figures. Portugal has a centralised information system. In France the situation is more complex than in all other countries. The statistics on international immigration of non-nationals are produced using several sources: (i) data from the Office des Migrations Internationales (OMI) covering non-EEA citizens who have received medical certificates; (ii) data from the Ministry of the Interior (AGDREF register) for EEA nationals and certain categories of non-EEA nationals who are not counted by the OMI; (iii) data from the French Office for the Protection of Refugees and Stateless Persons (OFPRA). In Greece no statistics on international migration are currently produced, but some statistics on immigration are to be compiled from two sources managed by two different ministries: the Register of Aliens kept by the Ministry of the Interior that covers non-European nationals, and the file for residence permits issued to EU citizens run by the Ministry of Public Order.

Theoretically, the collection of statistics based on the issue of residence permits and long-stay visas can compensate for the lack of sources on international migration. However, this source is limited to foreigners only and it can only therefore be used to supplement statistics for them. In addition, in some countries, minors have no obligation to hold a residence permit. Moreover, the act of obtaining a visa or a residence permit does not mean that this person is going to use it (at least when residence permits are issued abroad before the entry) or stay until its expiry, which would allow determining the actual duration of the stay. As far as inflows are concerned, the ability to distinguish first residence permits issued (for a length of validity of at least one year) from residence permits issued for a renewal (or for a shorter period) is probably the most difficult task for the ministries of the interior frequently involved in this new statistical process.

In addition, some countries have decided to rely on statistical surveys carried out at border controls, or among households.[13] Some information on international migration flows can also be derived from population censuses, but this source has a number of well-known limitations. For instance, censuses are carried out at long intervals, accommodate only a small number of questions and are not able to capture all migration events that occurred between subsequent enumerations. Moreover, only international immigrants may be easily identified, whereas international emigrants are no longer part of the enumerated population. Therefore, censuses cannot constitute a source of annual statistics on international migration. To be comprehensive, statistics should cover immigrants and emigrants irrespective of their citizenship. However, governments attach different levels of importance to particular flows. They are more interested in controlling the migration of foreigners, in particular immigration, which is reflected in the administrative procedures and data collection systems.

---

13 Sample surveys are used to produce statistics on international immigration and emigration flows in three countries: Cyprus, Ireland and the United Kingdom. In Portugal, although this statistical tool is applied to the emigration of nationals and non-nationals and immigration of nationals, an estimation of the latter flow is prepared only for national purposes. In Portugal and Ireland the sample surveys are households surveys carried out within the country. Cyprus and the United Kingdom rely on sample surveys of border crossers. The United Kingdom also uses supplementary data sources to adjust statistics derived from surveys, namely data on asylum seekers, removals and long-term switcher visitors (visitors who became migrants) from the Home Office, and data on migration flows from Ireland provided by the Irish Central Statistical Office. Specific data sources are used in Malta. Data on international immigration comes from the Customs Department. People who intend to settle in Malta are recorded at Customs since they have to declare their personal effects. As for emigration, the only available information is that on Maltese emigrants requesting permission for permanent settlement in the United Kingdom received from the British High Commission.

All EU countries currently use the census as a source of data on stocks of foreign citizens and foreign-born population. It is rarely used to estimate international immigration and emigration flows, as it cannot supply full coverage of migration events and annual statistics.

Despite the differences that can exist between countries, methods for measuring migration may be ranked in terms of their appropriateness. The census is surely the least satisfactory solution as it can only indicate numbers of new immigrants from the time between two censuses. Cross border counting theoretically allows an estimate of exits as well as entries. However, the reliability of existing border counting systems is low and difficult to improve. Specific surveys can be considered an improvement, but the size of the sample limits their usefulness. The population register is undeniably better, as it is the only source to record both immigration and emigration The link between each individual's entry and exit can therefore be made and the real duration of the stay can be established. However, not all population registers are reliable. Only centralisation guarantees the reliability of the system, ensuring that the entries and exits are correctly recorded to avoid double counts. Even using a reliable, centralized population register does not guarantee international comparability between immigration and emigration figures, as the double matrices have shown.

4. The THESIM findings: data availability, reliability and comparability

For the years 2004-2006, the European Commission launched its 6th Framework Programme of Research. When scientific research was requested for policy support, among the key priorities, the following was proposed: "Better sources for statistics and better knowledge on migration flows to the EU". The THESIM project was selected to co-ordinate efforts by demographers from different European Research Centres.[14]

14 THESIM means Towards Harmonised European Statistics on International Migration. The project was coordinated by GéDAP-UCL (Belgium) and involved the following institutions: NIDI (The Netherlands), INED (France), ICMPD (Austria), IcSTAT (Italy) and CEFMR (Poland). All the results of that EU project have been published in Poulain et al. (2006).

The ultimate aim of THESIM was to understand why the data-collection systems for statistics of international migration do not work properly, and to supply detailed metadata on all the EU Member States as an effective support to the implementation of the EU regulation. The three key topics tackled by THESIM were availability, reliability and comparability. The main findings and recommendations of the THESIM project follow:

The first problem is the absence of data, and the main recommendation is to use all potential sources and databases related to the given topics. However, the correspondence between different data sources should be checked carefully. For example, the number of foreigners entering the country for immigration could be captured through the usual population registration system, but also by using the residence permit database for non-EU citizens. Administrative databases exist in most countries, but no statistical data collection has been developed from these databases. With this aim in mind, strengthening the cooperation between the National Statistical Offices and the Ministries in charge of these administrative databases is recommended.

The mere availability of statistics is not an end in itself. Even if statistics are available, their poor quality may render them useless. The key aspect of data quality is reliability. The concept of reliability is understood here as the compliance of statistics with the national definition, and that may substantially differ from the internationally recommended one. Therefore, even if an incorrect definition is applied, but data collection is meticulous, data are classified as reliable. In such a situation data users can trust in the available statistics – therefore, there is a clear correspondence between concepts underlying the data and the produced statistics.

There are two main factors that make international migration statistics unreliable. The first one is the under registration of migrants, which refers in particular to countries where data collection systems rely on the self-declaration of international movements. The second relates to data coverage. Some data collection systems or administrative data sources may not cover the whole target population, and as a result, some subsets are systematically excluded and will therefore not be included in the statistics. The large majority of international migration statistics in the EU countries are derived from registration systems and deficiencies in registration are the most significant influence on data reliability. People do not register or deregister because there is no obligation to do so, or even if the obligation exists, there is no effective control. The willingness to report changes of place of residence and more specifically, emigration to another country, varies from one country to another. People take into account the advantages and disadvantages of registering when deciding whether or not to do so. In general, they have more interest in reporting their arrival than departure. Therefore, immigration statistics are considered more reliable. As regards data coverage, it should be noted first of all that illegal flows of migrants, which are difficult to measure, are generally not included.[15] As for legal migrants, the most problematic group is asylum seekers. In general, asylum seekers are included only when they have been granted refugee status and received a temporary or permanent residence permit, but the situation may vary among countries.[16] Students are another example of people in this grey area.[17]

The lack of uniformity in the definitions of international migrants used in various countries has been recognized for a long time, but up to now, most efforts towards achieving international comparability of international migration statistics have not been successful. Furthermore, concepts underlying statistics of international migration flows vary significantly. Not only between countries, but also within countries over time and between different sources of statistical information. The main sources of variations in definitions used in the EU countries are the differences in the concept of place of residence and duration of stay that are applied to determine who is an international migrant. Because the datasets are usually not accompanied by detailed methodological information, these concepts remain a relatively uncharted area for most data users.

As far as the duration of stay is concerned, the threshold durations used by countries are extremely diverse. On the one hand, there are countries where duration of stay is of no relevance, any move in or out of a dwelling should be registered and this move is directly reflected in statistics. On the other hand, there are countries where only definitive movements (settlement or permanent migration) are counted. Leaving aside these extreme situations, the duration of stay criterion applied in migration statistics across the EU is usually set to a period of between three months and one year.[18] However, in all these countries the situation is far from fixed, and a convergence toward the one-year limit is seen as possible in the near future, especially in countries that currently have a short time limit.

---

15 Spain is the only EU country where illegal migrants are included in the official statistics on international migration.

16 In Germany, Spain, Austria and the Netherlands they are recorded in the population register and also included in immigration statistics at the earlier stage of the asylum procedure. In Cyprus and Ireland they are covered by statistics based on surveys. In the United Kingdom asylum seekers are not covered by the survey that is the main source for international flow statistics, but the Home Office provides the estimates. By contrast, recognised refugees are never included in migration statistics in Hungary, Portugal, Malta and Belgium.

17 For instance they are not covered by international migration statistics in France, Portugal and Finland.

18 Only Cyprus, Sweden and UK strictly apply the one-year criteria for immigration as well as emigration, whatever the person's citizenship, while Finland does so for all emigrations but only for the immigration of non-nationals.

In addition to focussing on the improvement of the availability of data, it is crucial to demonstrate that this data is sufficiently reliable. Not only from a statistical viewpoint, but from a political perspective. For the same reason, adopting the same definition and time criterion is a valuable target. Improving the reliability and the coverage of each data source, in each country is the most important task to be achieved in the short term. Only after completing these checks may the figures be interpreted and become useful for analysis and policy support. This is the reason why demographers are cooperating with all National Statistical Institutes (NSI) and with EUROSTAT to improve the situation.

The improvement of migration statistics is necessary in order to create an objective basis for a new migration policy. It should also be considered as an element of good governance in terms of efficiency, accountability and transparency. The recent regulation on Community statistics on international migration and international protection could accelerate the process (European Commission, 2007). Until now, European migration statistics have been collected on the basis of a 'gentlemen's agreement', whereby EU Member States were invited to provide data following the proposed definitions and EU standards in terms of reliability. As a result, the data provided was irregular and incomplete. Countries tended to follow national definitions and these could vary considerably from the proposed EU definitions. Moreover, it was often almost impossible to check the reliability of the figures provided. In 2008, when the new regulation comes into force, Member States will be obliged to provide data following the harmonised definitions. This data should be reliable and accompanied by detailed metadata.

5. International migration in the EU 27: What does the most recent data reveal?

The most basic figure, the total number of usual residents in each EU Member State, is problematic in terms of reliability and comparability, because of both under-counting and double counting. Figures relating to citizens who left the country on a temporary basis, or to foreigners living in the country for a variety of reasons (including asylum seekers) may or may not be included in the stock of usual residents for a given country. Every non-recording of a person entering or leaving the country may involve problems of under-registration and, within the EU territory, problems of double counting.

A non-national is someone who does not hold the citizenship of the country where he or she lives. In each EU Member State there are non-nationals who are EU-citizens and others who are not. In terms of data collection, the administrative source for identifying and characterising the non-national population is often different to that used for the total population. In several countries, discrepancies appear that are not easy to solve. In addition, some countries only provide detailed data on the non-national population at the time of the census, providing only estimated figures for the period between censuses.

The following figures are based on the EUROSTAT database,[19] with some additional information collected from the different websites of the National Statistical Institutes. Missing data has been estimated based on previous figures by the authors of this contribution. Up to now, only a few overall descriptive analyses of all international migration flows concerning the EU have been developed. The poor reliability of the aforesaid data is responsible for this and any comparative exercise would be incomplete and fragile. Accordingly, our aim here will be to enhance the main features that available statistical data on populations with a foreign background may reveal.

In order to identify the foreign population, the key variable will be citizenship, even if some comparability problems exist as explained above. The latest available data is summarised in Table 1 for the EU 27 on 1st January 2005.[20]

—

19 The Eurostat database is available online at http://epp.eurostat.ec.europa.eu/

20 The situation is shown for 1st January 2005, including Bulgaria and Romania although these countries were not yet EU Member States at the time.

Table 1: Non-national population in the EU Member States on 1st January 2005. The data are extracted from the Eurostat Database and the figures in the blue cells are our own estimations based on the only previous available figures (absolute figures are presented in thousands).[21]

↓

	Total Population	Non Nationals	% Non Nationals	Foreign EU Citizens	Non EU citizens	% Non EU Citizens	Largest foreign population	Largest non-EU population
Belgium	10 445.9	870.9	8.3%	599.7	271.2	31.1%	Italy	Morocco
Bulgaria	7 801.3	25.6	0.3%	3.9	21.7	84.9%	Russia	Russia
Czech Republic	10 220.6	254.3	2.5%	87.3	167.0	65.7%	Ukraine	Ukraine
Denmark	5 411.4	267.6	4.9%	70.0	197.6	73.8%	Turkey	Turkey
Germany	82 500.8	7 288.0	8.8%	2 212.1	5 075.9	69.6%	Turkey	Turkey
Estonia	1 347.0	250.0	18.6%	5.0	245.0	98.0%	Russia	Russia
Greece	11 075.7	900.0	8.1%	157.1	742.9	82.5%	Albania	Albania
Spain	43 038.0	3 371.4	7.8%	1 070.7	2 300.7	68.2%	Ecuador	Ecuador
France	60 561.2	3 500.0	5.8%	1 314.0	2 186.0	62.5%	Portugal	Algeria
Ireland	4 109.2	295.0	7.2%	200.0	95.0	32.2%	UK	USA
Italy	58 462.4	2 402.2	4.1%	470.9	1 931.3	80.4%	Albania	Albania
Cyprus	749.2	98.1	13.1%	58.9	39.2	40.0%	Greece	Russia
Latvia	2 306.4	487.2	21.1%	4.8	482.4	99.0%	Russia	Russia
Lithuania	3 425.3	32.3	0.9%	1.5	30.8	95.4%	Russia	Russia
Luxembourg	455.0	177.4	39.0%	152.9	24.5	13.8%	Portugal	Serbia and Montenegro
Hungary	10 097.5	143.8	1.4%	82.2	61.6	42.9%	Romania	Ukraine
Malta	402.7	12.0	3.0%	8.0	4.0	33.3%	UK	India
Netherlands	16 305.5	699.4	4.3%	233.1	466.3	66.7%	Turkey	Turkey
Austria	8 206.5	788.6	9.6%	235.1	553.5	70.2%	Serbia and Montenegro	Serbia and Montenegro
Poland	38 173.8	700.0	1.8%	16.0	684.0	97.7%	Germany	Ukraine
Portugal	10 529.3	265.0	2.5%	78.2	186.8	70.5%	Cape Verde	Cape Verde
Romania	21 712.6	40.8	0.2%	9.4	31.4	76.9%	Moldova	Moldova
Slovenia	1 997.6	44.3	2.2%	1.4	42.9	96.8%	Bosnia Herzegovina	Bosnia Herzegovina
Slovak Republic	5 384.8	22.3	0.4%	11.9	10.4	46.4%	Czech Republic	Ukraine
Finland	5 236.6	108.3	2.1%	36.2	72.1	66.5%	Russia	Russia
Sweden	9 011.4	481.1	5.3%	212.1	269.0	55.9%	Iraq	Iraq
United Kingdom	60 034.5	3 066.1	5.1%	1 173.9	1 892.2	61.7%	Ireland	India
EU 27	489 002.2	26 591.6	5.4%	8 506.1	18 085.5	68.0%		

–

21 Data presented in blue cells was not available in official statistics and we present here estimates based on previous data, mostly from censuses.

The first set of descriptive conclusions concerns foreign EU citizens living in another EU country e.g. Dutch people living in Italy or French people in Germany.

1. The smaller the country, the higher the proportion of foreign EU citizens living in this country. This is normal as in a smaller country there are automatically more international migrations compared to internal migrations, the latter being relatively more numerous in larger countries.

2. The central location of Belgium and Luxembourg and their respective roles in the European Union leads to higher numbers of foreign EU citizens living in these countries.

3. At the other extreme, countries like Greece, Portugal and Finland, which are at the periphery of the EU, have markedly lower proportions of foreign EU citizens. This may be partly explained by the fact that this external situation involves more exchanges with third countries. Ireland, which was traditionally a source of emigration, has recently experienced large immigration flows, mainly from new EU Member States. It is therefore currently experiencing an increasing proportion of foreign EU citizens compared to the proportion of non-EU citizens.

4. The numbers of citizens of a given EU country living in all other EU countries can be compared to the number of foreign EU citizens living in that particular country (Table 2). As a direct consequence of the enlargement of the EU, Germany appears to be the most attractive country within Europe for other EU Member States. France, Spain and Belgium follow, preceding the United Kingdom and Luxembourg. Sweden heads the group of countries that are attractive to a lesser extent. At the opposite end of the Table, Romania may be considered as the country of highest emigration, followed by Portugal and Poland. Italy, Bulgaria, Greece and Ireland follow, all having relatively large numbers of citizens living in another EU country compared to the number of foreign EU citizens living in these countries.

5. Finally, the preference for citizens of a given EU country to live in another EU country may be assessed by comparing actual figures with expected figures obtained through a simple bi-proportional model.[22] The larger *chi²* differences are presented in Table 3, showing that the Portuguese people in Luxembourg and France, Irish people in the United Kingdom and Finns in Sweden are the most extreme situations. Without considering neighbouring countries, we can also observe the preponderance of Italians and Greeks in Germany, Italians in Belgium and Romanians in Spain and Italy.

---

22 The estimated figure using the bi-proportional model is simply proportional to the product of the total population of the two countries concerned, so that the total number of expected figures will be equal to the total number of observed figures.

Table 2: Comparing the number of citizens of a given country living in another EU Member State and the number of foreign EU citizens living in that country.
The countries are ranked by decreasing chi2 differences between observed and expected figures.

	Citizens living in another EU country	Foreign EU citizens living in the country	Chi² differences
Immigration countries			
Germany	623 280	2 190 253	1 321
France	491 190	1 182 066	755
Spain	437 080	1 046 593	708
Belgium	180 635	599 640	671
United Kingdom	657 527	1 161 659	529
Luxembourg	17 019	136 450	431
Sweden	103 969	211 390	271
Czech Republic	65 182	87 000	79
Cyprus	29 877	36 745	38
Austria	227 325	233 795	13
Emigration countries			
Hungary	88 793	82 054	-23
Malta	7 491	4 000[23]	-46
Denmark	92 878	69 398	-82
Latvia	22 879	4 808	-154
Estonia	27 421	4 023	-187
Slovenia	31 857	1 418	-236
Netherlands	359 618	206 980	-287
Finland	137 96	36 104	-345
Lithuania	66 177	1 462	-352
Slovak Republic	116 349	11 843	-413
Ireland	409 968	146 369	-500
Greece	399 523	134 445	-513
Bulgaria	212 390	3 861	-634
Italy	1 179 657	465 698	-787
Poland	631 751	15 193	-1 084
Portugal	930 135	65 402	-1 226
Romania	773 242	5 889	-1 229

–

23 Estimated figure as no data is officially available

Table 3: The larger Chi2 differences between observed and expected figures for foreign EU citizens living in another EU country (2005).

	Country of citizenship	Country of residence	Chi² differences
1	Portugal	Luxembourg	17 121
2	Ireland	UK	13 506
3	Portugal	France	12 462
4	Finland	Sweden	7 536
5	Greec	Germany	5 948
6	Romania	Spain	5 353
7	Netherlands	Belgium	4 616
8	Italy	Germany	4 434
9	Belgium	Luxembourg	4 198
10	Italy	Belgium	4 147
11	Romania	Italy	3 973
12	Austria	Germany	3 806
13	UK	Ireland	3 760
14	Cyprus	Greece	3 487
15	Estonia	Finland	3 042

The second group of descriptive conclusions concerns the non-EU citizens living in each EU country. When comparing the proportion of non-nationals in each EU country (Table 1), the figures show a wide variation, with the highest value for Luxembourg (39%) and the lowest in Romania, Bulgaria, the Slovak Republic and Lithuania. For historical reasons, Latvia (21.1%) and Estonia (18.6%) also show high proportions due to their large Russian communities. Three traditional immigration countries – Austria (9.6%), Germany (8.8%) and Belgium (8.3%) – stand alongside Luxembourg as other major immigration countries. Greece (8.1%) and Spain (7.8%), two new immigration countries, have joined this group. France (5.8%), Sweden (5.3%), Denmark (4.9%) and Italy (4.1%), another new immigration country, come next. When considering the distribution among non-nationals of EU citizens and non-EU citizens, the proportion of non-EU citizens is very low in Luxembourg (13.8%) and relatively low in Belgium (31.1%) and Ireland (32.2%). In all other EU countries except Malta, Cyprus and Hungary, this indicator exceeds 50% and peaks above 95% in the three Baltic States, Poland and Slovenia.

When considering only non-EU citizens, the number of those who are living in any of the EU Member States can be compared with the total population of the country of origin (Table 4). Albania is clearly the country with the largest proportion of the population who live in the EU. The number of Albanian citizens in the EU is equal to one quarter of the population of Albania. All the Republics of the former Yugoslavia24 also have an average ratio of one citizen living in the EU for twelve living in their home country. Some smaller islands like Cape Verde, Sao Tome and Principe, Iceland, Mauritius, Barbados and the Seychelles also have a high ratio. Similarly, larger populations like Morocco, Ecuador and Turkey are also high in this ranking. These are clearly the three largest non-EU communities represented in the EU with 1.5, 0.5 and 2.3 million citizens respectively, or in relative numbers 4.8%, 3.9% and 3.2% of their total populations.

Table 4: Number of non-EU citizens living in the EU compared to the total population of each country in 2005.
↓

Country	Number of citizens living in the EU	Total population of the country	Ratio
Albania	784 845	3 129 678	25.1%
Cape Verde	72 088	506 807	14.2%
F.Y.R of Macedonia	194 155	2 034 060	9.5%
Bosnia and Herzegovina	337 901	3 907 074	8.6%
Croatia	332 368	4 551 338	7.3%
Serbia and Montenegro	756 911	10 502 224	7.2%
San Marino	1 831	28 117	6.5%
Iceland	18 352	294 561	6.2%
Sao Tome and Principe	8 039	156 523	5.1%
Morocco	1 522 130	31 819 881	4.8%
Ecuador	510 995	13 228 423	3.9%
Mauritius	45 581	1 244 663	3.7%
Barbados	9 450	269 556	3.5%
Seychelles	2 770	80 654	3.4%
Turkey	2 333 807	73 192 838	3.2%

Source: The number of non-EU citizens is extracted from Eurostat database while the total population figures have been found on the UN Statistical Division web site.

Finally, the number of citizens observed from each non-EU country in each EU Member State can be compared to the expected number based on a simple proportional model.[25] For example, without any specific preference, the 1.5 million Moroccan citizens could be distributed among the EU countries according to the population of each EU country. If we consider that 8% of the EU population lived in Spain in 2005, therefore, the expected number of Moroccan citizens in Spain would be about 120.000 compared to 400.000, the observed figure. Table 5 shows the larger positive chi^2 differences between observed and expected figures. These positive differences indicate the preference of people with specific foreign citizenship, to live in that EU country. Albanians have a preference for Greece, their neighbouring country, while Russian citizens are particularly numerous in Estonia for historical reasons. Turks in Germany follow, with Ecuadorians and Colombians in Spain, Algerians in France and Cape Verdeans in Portugal. Ex-Yugoslavian citizens are most numerous in Germany and Austria; Moroccans will be found in France, Belgium and the Netherlands while Indians, Pakistanis and Americans are predominant in the UK. Table 6 compares the distribution of Moroccan and Turkish citizens living in the 27 EU Member States, according to data available for 2005.

—

25 In the model, the expected number of citizens from a non-EU country within the territory of a given EU Member State is proportional to the number of citizens of that country in the whole EU and the total population of the EU Member State concerned, so that the expected total number of non-EU citizens will be similar to the one observed.

Table 5: The larger chi^2 differences between observed and expected numbers of non-EU citizens living in every EU Member States (2005).

↓

	Country of citizenship	Country of residence	Chi^2 differences
1	Albania	Greece	3151
2	Russia	Estonia	2359
3	Turkey	Germany	2186
4	Ecuador	Spain	1909
5	Algeria	France	1497
6	Colombia	Spain	1338
7	Cape Verde	Portugal	1294
8	Bosnia Herzegovina	Austria	1136
9	Serbia Montenegro	Austria	1112
10	Serbia Montenegro	Germany	1063
11	Argentina	Spain	1031
12	Morocco	Spain	897
13	Norway	Sweden	853
14	Guinea Bissau	Portugal	815
15	Senegal	Luxembourg	733

Table 6: The distribution of the Moroccan and Turkish citizens living in the 27 EU Member States.

	MOROCCO	%	TURKEY	%
Belgium	81 279	5.34%	39 885	1.71%
Bulgaria	26	0.00%	1 015	0.04%
Czech Republic	143	0.01%	520	0.02%
Denmark	2 902	0.19%	29 956	1.28%
Germany	73 027	4.80%	1 764 318	75.60%
Estonia	1	0.00%	6	0.00%
Greece	526	0.03%	7 881	0.34%
Spain	461 544	30.32%	1 347	0.06%
France	506 305	33.26%	205 589	8.81%
Ireland	161	0.01%	456	0.02%
Italy	294 945	19.38%	11 077	0.47%
Cyprus	11	0.00%	35	0.00%
Latvia	2	0.00%	38	0.00%
Lithuania	1	0.00%	56	0.00%
Luxembourg	252	0.02%	207	0.01%
Hungary	32	0.00%	629	0.03%
Netherlands	91 558	6.02%	100 574	4.31%
Austria	749	0.05%	116 882	5.01%
Poland	64	0.00%	180	0.01%
Portugal	660	0.04%	111	0.00%
Romania	0	0.00%	2 173	0.09%
Slovenia	3	0.00%	31	0.00%
Slovak Republic	11	0.00%	120	0.01%
Finland	621	0.04%	2 359	0.10%
Sweden	1 510	0.10%	12 269	0.53%
United Kingdom	5 797	0.38%	36 093	1.55%
TOTAL	1 522 130	100.00%	2 333 807	100.00%

6. A typology of the population with a foreign background

As the population with a foreign background includes the immigrant population and their descendents (even if the latter are born in the country and did not immigrate from abroad), the country of citizenship and country of birth no longer suffice as the variables for identifying them. As expressed by Extra and Gorter (2001), "collecting reliable information about the composition of immigrant groups in EU countries is one of the most challenging tasks facing demographers." Demographers are facing the problem, and the work developed by Eurostat (Krekels et al. 1998) and the Council of Europe (Haug et al., 2004) is exemplary on that issue. Nevertheless the notion of foreign background is still very complex and needs additional investigation. In order to define this concept within a statistical framework, particular objective criteria have to be selected. A combination of the following criteria is necessary to form an appropriate typology of the population with a foreign background. However, quite often some of these variables cannot be used, due to lack of basic information.

- country of citizenship
- citizenship at birth
- citizenship of parents at birth
- citizenship of grandparents and ancestors
- country of birth
- country of birth of parents
- country of birth of grandparents and ancestors
- ethnic affiliation or attachment to a distinct ethnic group
- physical characteristics such as colour of skin or race, as accepted in the US or South Africa

As mentioned above, building a typology including all these characteristics is not a realistic objective. In addition, for a specific country, some variables may be essential or, conversely, may have little impact. Being considered as a member of a distinct ethnic group may be more acceptable in some countries than others. Some of these criteria have an important negative impact on the daily life of the person(s) concerned, and their use and the development of an *ad hoc* typology could be problematic. In these cases, proposing such a typology, even for statistical purpose, would be unacceptable as it could lead to discrimination resulting from such classification. Finally, if these variables were to be collected through questions in censuses or surveys, self-reported answers may introduce a particular bias. In this situation it may even appear impossible to statistically identify populations with a foreign background.

Officially, some EU countries like France and Belgium prefer to provide and use statistics on citizenship, despite several attempts to propose a more appropriate classification. The use of the country of birth is less common. Within Europe, the Nordic countries and the Netherlands use typologies based on the country of birth including that of the parents. In the United Kingdom and the United States, race and/or ethnicity are commonly used, while in some Central European countries the concept of "ethnic nationality" is preferred. In conclusion, any typology would be specific not only to the information available in a given country, but also to the perception towards each of the variables used to build this typology.

As a scientific support for policy development and a better understanding of the diversity of the population with a foreign background we have developed the following typology for Belgium. Based on the data extracted from the *National Population Register* and the last censuses carried out in 1991 and 2001 the following variables can be obtained:
- current citizenship
- all changes of citizenship from 1991 onwards
- citizenship at birth as reported in the 1991 census if the person was enumerated
- country of birth
- year of first immigration in the country as reported in the 1991 census for those living in the country at that time
- year of first immigration in the country as recorded in the *National Population Register* for those who immigrated since 1991.

The proposed typology does not take into consideration the characteristics of parents. However, it has been possible to identify children who received Belgian citizenship at birth but who have at least one parent with a foreign background (non-Belgian citizens at birth). Based on this information it is possible to identify some groups on the basis of a distinction between:
- persons currently holding Belgian citizenship or not
- persons who held Belgian citizenship at birth or not
- foreigners who have been naturalized or not
- foreigners born abroad who immigrated to Belgium and foreigners born in Belgium
- persons who have immigrated to Belgium, according to their age at immigration and their duration of stay in the country.

Table 7 presents a comparison of the population with any foreign background and the population with a Moroccan background on the same date. A distinction is made between different types of immigrants in terms of age of arrival and duration of stay. Figure 2 shows the evolution of different sub-groups and allows one to trace the population with a foreign background in Belgium from 1991 until 2005.

Table 7: Typology of population with a foreign background developed for Belgium. Comparative figures for population with any foreign background vs. Moroccan background on 1st January 2005
↓

	All people with a foreign background	People with a Moroccan background	% All	% Moroccans
Total	2 022 548	299 283	100.0	100.0
Belgian citizenship at birth	451 525	56 448	22.3	18.9
Of whom both parents have a foreign origin	105 760	35 822	5.2	12.0
Of whom only the father has a foreign origin	196 015	15 481	9.7	5.2
Of whom only the mother has a foreign origin	149 750	5 145	7.4	1.7
No Belgian citizenship at birth	1 571 023	242 835	77.7	81.1
Of whom born in Belgium	505 756	105 004	25.0	35.1
Of whom not naturalised	173 282	16 154	8.6	5.4
Of whom naturalised	332 474	88 850	16.4	29.7
Of whom born abroad and immigrants	1 065 267	137 831	52.7	46.1
Of whom not naturalised	698 128	65 197	34.5	21.8
Immigrated during the last 5 years, aged up to 12	32 504	1 847	1.6	0.6
Immigrated during the last 5 years, aged over 12	212 056	31 482	10.5	10.5
Immigrated more than 5 years ago, aged up to 12	107 726	5 883	5.3	2.0
Immigrated more than 5 years ago, aged over 12	345 842	25 985	17.1	8.7
Of whom naturalised	367 139	72 634	18.2	24.3
Immigrated during the last 5 years, aged up to 12	4 925	566	0.2	0.2
Immigrated during the last 5 years, aged over 12	8 239	2 223	0.4	0.7
Immigrated more than 5 years ago, aged up to 12	129 006	19 510	6.4	6.5
Immigrated more than 5 years ago, aged over 12	224 969	50 335	11.1	16.8

Source of data: INS, Registre National. Typology and calculations done by GéDAP-UCL.

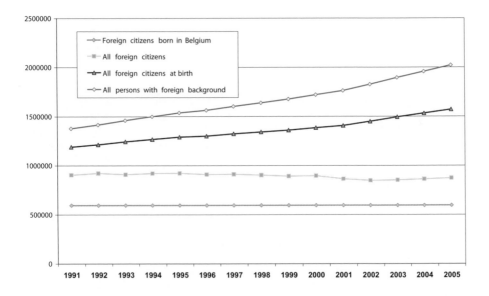

↑

Figure 2: Evolution of different sub-populations with a foreign background according to the proposed methodology.

Source of data: INS, Registre National. Typology and calculations done by GéDAP-UCL.

While the number of foreign citizens born abroad, as well as the total number of foreign citizens, is very stable in Belgium, the number of persons not holding Belgian citizenship at birth is increasing. This increase is even larger when we consider all persons with foreign background.

Finally, Figure 3 represents the age and gender structure of the foreign population not holding Belgian citizenship, compared to the total population with a foreign background. The differences, which are larger for younger people than older ones, are due to naturalisation and to the large number of children with a foreign background who received Belgian citizenship at birth.

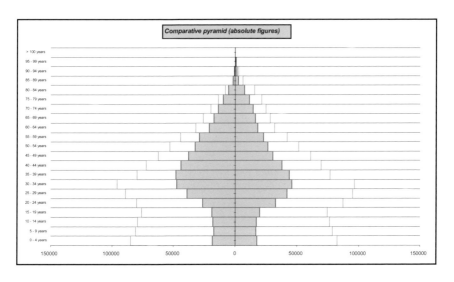

Figure 3: Age and sex structure of the foreign population not holding Belgian citizenship (in grey)
and the whole population with any foreign background on 1st January 2005.
Source of data: INS, Registre National. Typology and calculations done by GéDAP-UCL.

7. Conclusion

Statistical data is necessary to understand the evolution of migration trends more precisely and objectively. It is also necessary for population forecasts and developing migration policies. However, collecting such data may be difficult and the figures are easily misused. At present, availability is still limited, reliability is often very poor and comparability is still a remote goal at EU level. Even if data related to stocks may be considered to be relatively reliable and easily available, the poor situation concerning flow data must be recognised.

International standards exist, but the last updated UN recommendations cannot easily be followed, especially when data collection is based on a 'gentlemen's agreement'. Within the EU, the recent adoption of a regulation on Community Statistics on Migration and International Protection represents a real hope, as Member States will be forced to produce reliable statistics and associated metadata. Nevertheless, such a regulation cannot improve the situation to a satisfactory level and the key problem will be the implementation phase. The role of demographers will be essential in helping countries to fulfil the requirements of the regulation and to ensure Eurostat of the quality of the figures provided. Considering the various national situations, producing fully accurate and comparable figures seems an unattainable goal. But the total accuracy of the figures is not a goal in itself. Reliable and comparable data represents an objective that may be reached by improving the data collection systems, using different data sources in combination and estimating comparable figures with the help of ad hoc methodologies.

Stock data on population by country of citizenship provides more reliable and comparable information, and allows a description of the situation within the EU. But here we should also consider that policies granting citizenship to foreigners vary largely between countries and may result in statistics that are not strictly comparable. Several criteria may be used to define the population with a foreign background living in a country and depending which criteria are used, the size and characteristics of the corresponding population may be different. This again demonstrates that important challenges exist in the field of international migration data collection and that the scientific support expected from demographers is enormous.

8. References

European Union (2007), *Regulation of the European Parliament and of the Council on Community Statistics on Migration and International Protection*, Brussels, 14.9.2005, COM (2005) 375 final, 2005/0156 (COD).

Extra, Guus and D. Gorter, (Eds.). (2001). *The other languages of Europe. Demographic, sociolinguistic and educational perspectives.* Clevedon: Multilingual Matters.

Haug, Werner, Youssef Courbage and Paul Compton (ed.), 2002, *The demographic characteristics of immigrant populations*, Council of Europe, Strasbourg, Population studies n°38, 600 p.

Herm, Anne, 2006, Recommendations on International Migration Statistics and Development of Data Collection at an International Level, in Poulain Michel, Nicolas Perrin and Ann Singleton, *Towards Harmonised European Statistics on International Migration*, Louvain-la-Neuve, Presses universitaires de Louvain, pp. 77-106.

Kelly, John, 1987, Improving the comparability of international migration statistics: Contribution to the Conference of European Statisticians from 1971 to date, *International Migration Review*, 21, pp. 1017-1037.

Krekels, Barbara and Michel Poulain, 1998, *Stocks de migrants et population d'origine étrangère – Comparaison des concepts dans les pays de l'Union Européenne*, Luxembourg, Office de Publication des Communautés Européennes, Eurostat Working Papers, Coll. "Population et conditions sociales", 3/1998/E/N°4, 86 p.

Poulain, Michel, 1999, *Confrontation des statistiques de migration intra-européennes : vers une matrice complète ?*, Eurostat Working Paper N°3/1999/E/N°5, Bruxelles-Luxembourg, Eurostat.

Poulain, Michel and Nicolas Perrin, 2003, Can UN Migration Recommendations Be Met in Europe?, *Migration Information Source*, July 1, 2003, www.migrationinformation.org.

Poulain Michel, Nicolas Perrin and Ann Singleton (eds.), 2006, *Towards Harmonised European Statistics on International Migration*, Louvain-la-Neuve, Presses universitaires de Louvain, 744 p.

United Nations. Department of Economic and Social Affairs. Statistics Division, 1998, *Recommendations on Statistics of International Migration*, Revision 1, United Nations. Department of Economic and Social Affairs. Statistics Division, No ST/ESA/STAT/ SER.M/58/REV.1 Pub. Order No 98.XVII.14, 104p.

06 Triggering Inequality and Health Gradients: Do Health Selection Effects Matter?

Alberto Palloni, Carolina Milesi,
Robert White and Alyn Turner

1. Introduction

The main goal of this paper is to formulate an integrated theoretical framework to explain the potential existence of health selection effects as a mechanism producing observed adult socioeconomic gradient in health and mortality. We do so by bringing together literatures and findings from separate and unconnected fields, including labor economics, health and mortality, and the more recent research on the influence of early health on adult health status and economic success. The resulting theoretical framework is translated into a simplified model which, it turn, lends itself to empirical estimation. If requisite data are employed, the empirical estimates for the relations represented in the model can be used as inputs for calculations of indicators that are useful to test the main propositions of the theory.

The paper is divided into five sections. In this, the first section, we provide an overview of the problem, suggest the need to integrate separate literatures, and clarify key concepts. In the second section we review extant knowledge about adult health and mortality differentials by socioeconomic status and introduce the possible role of health selection. In the third section we identify mechanisms through which early childhood health can exert an impact on both adult health status and economic success. In section four we formulate a conventional structural equation model, identify the minimum data requirement for estimation of the model and suggest a Monte Carlo simulation procedure to calculate sufficient statistics for the falsification of the theory. We show that simple Monte Carlo simulations supply the ingredients to calculate the effects of early health status on adult socioeconomic achievement, and to evaluate the magnitude of the contribution of the direct and/or indirect influence of early health status to the observed association between adult health and socioeconomic status. Section five concludes.

1.1. Health and economic inequalities: empirical regularities

There are two apparently unconnected regularities that stand out in modern open societies. The first is that intergenerational transmission of earnings and income inequalities, far from having been eroded, is today as strong, if not stronger, than it was in the past twenty years or so. In the US, progress in intergenerational social mobility has slowed down considerably (Hauser 1998; Hout 2005). By the same token, the intergenerational correlation of income (and wealth) has not weakened significantly. Indeed, the empirically estimated elasticity of offspring income relative to parental income has remained in the range of .3-.6 for well over twenty years. The bulk of this association remains unexplained (Bowles, Gintis, and Osborne Groves 2005; Mazumder 2005). These regularities are resistant to explanations invoking differential endowments of conventional market-valued skills or unequal distribution of rents from assets– the standard explanations from neoclassic labor economics (Heckman and Rubinstein 2001).

The second regularity is the ubiquitous presence of health and mortality differentials across socioeconomic strata. Far from having disappeared, these gradients have acquired renewed salience. Although there is agreement that at least some of the observed differentials are explained by attributes associated with social class positions (from access to information and health care to life styles and behavioural management and control), there are lingering doubts about the power these factors might have to provide a complete explanation for the differentials. There is also the sometimes veiled and sometimes more explicit argument suggesting that, at least in part, the observed health and mortality gradients are the outcome of selection mechanisms whereby individuals in poor health early in life are prevented from or have more difficulty experiencing upward social mobility or, alternatively, are more likely to experience downward mobility (Adams, Hurd, McFadden, Merrill, and Ribeiro 2003; Fox, Goldblatt, and Jones 1985; Manor, Matthews, and Power 2003; Smith 1999; West 1991; Stern 1983; Illsley 1955; Power, Matthews, and Manor 1998; Fox, Goldblatt, and Adelstein 1982).

1.2. Health selection: conditions of possibility

This paper focuses on the 'health selection' conjecture. In order to evaluate its relevance we need to first verify a central proposition, namely, *that health inequalities during early childhood are a non-trivial contributor to the persistence of economic inequalities among adults.* This is a theoretically relevant possibility, and it remains to be seen whether it has any empirical significance. If it does, two consequences follow immediately, one relevant for social stratification theories and the other for theories of health and mortality. The first consequence is that an important mechanism reproducing economic inequalities is the differential allocation of health status that occurs early in life. By influencing cognitive and non-cognitive traits, early health status may contribute non-trivially to the reproduction of economic inequalities across generations.

The second consequence, and the one of most interest to us, is that further advances in our understanding of health and mortality disparities will be attained only if we explicitly model health selection processes. It is through these processes that health endowments and attributes acquired early in life could result both in different lifetime exposure to ill-health and in differential ability to harvest economic rewards throughout adulthood.

Any attempt to identify the contribution made by health selection processes to the observed association between socioeconomic status and health requires a **unified** explanation of the two empirical regularities identified at the outset, namely, persistence of social inequalities and persistence of health gradients. For this explanation to be relevant, however, we need to establish two conditions. The **first condition** is that *allocation of health status early in life is not random but is itself a function of the socioeconomic position individuals occupy at birth.* This implies that the environment and background associated with socioeconomic positions of origin and parental health status contribute significantly to a child's early health status. It is clear that this is a necessary condition, for if early health status is randomly allocated anew in each generation, it could not possibly contribute to the intergenerational transmission of inequality.

The **second condition** is that *there must be a relation between early health status and the acquisition of cognitive and non-cognitive traits that regulate the allocation of rewards in the labor market.* Together, these conditions constitute what we refer to throughout the paper as the *conditions of possibility for health selection effects.*

Section II examines the feasibility and potential conduits of health selection processes. Section III evaluates the first and second condition through a review of evidence about determinants of economic inequalities and by identifying findings in social stratification and labor economics that connect determinants of wages, earnings and income with early health status. We then identify a subset of determinants that are likely to be affected by health status in early childhood.

1.3. Conceptual fine-tuning: social class, childhood health, and adult health status

To avoid misunderstandings, we clarify at the outset two of the central concepts we will use throughout, social class and health status.

Social Class: First, to simplify terminology, we will define socioeconomic stratification as a hierarchy of positions which individuals may access and occupy for finite periods of time. Individuals belonging to a socioeconomic position will be distinguished by a key attribute, namely, the appropriation or right of collection of rewards in the form of occupational prestige (a socially constructed quantity), earnings from labor (wages), and rents from assets which, in combination, constitute sources of personal and family income. Some of these rewards, such as occupational prestige or earnings are tightly, though not perfectly, associated with education, a proxy for the presence of rent-extracting skills. These two reward systems may not always be positively correlated and may not even be directly connected to each other. In such cases, we will refer to only one of them rather than creating a more complex, multidimensional construct encompassing both.

Social sciences assign different importance and meaning to various dimensions of social stratification. In economics the standard object of study has been factor payments and, in the case of labor, wages and other types of earnings. Economists also investigate the determinants of wealth and assets as well as factors influencing income flows derived from assets. But, for the most part, most controversies surround wages and earnings to which economic sciences assign centrality as determinants of economic positions within a stratified society (Carneiro, Heckman, and Masterov 2003).

In contrast, classical sociological stratification theory pays considerable attention to occupations— as occupational prestige and as socioeconomic standing gauged by combinations of the educational and earning attributes of individuals who occupy those occupations (Duncan 1961; Hodge, Siegel, and Rossi 1966; Warren, Hauser, and Sheridan 2002). That is, sociology is concerned not just with the distribution of material rewards but also with the allocation of symbolic markers, some of which may be functions of collective evaluation. More complex conceptualizations involve the introduction of other dimensions of occupation and labor, such as control over material and human resources within the job place, degree of authority over subordinates, and location in a hierarchy of decision-making within firms (Wright 2003).

For the most part this paper focuses on material rewards embodied in wages and earnings and on symbolic rewards such as occupational prestige, and refers only superficially to other dimensions along which individuals may be positioned within a social hierarchy. An immediate advantage stemming from this simplification is that we can confine the term socioeconomic position to refer to individuals grouped by easily measurable attributes such as wages, income, assets or occupational prestige ranks. Finally, we completely eschew the relevant but somewhat distracting issue of race and ethnic stratification. While allocation of individuals into social classes may dominate the profile of a stratification system, the existence of race and ethic groups adds a layer of complication for two reasons. First, discrimination or other forms of race-based criteria may partially determine allocation into social classes, independently of individuals' market contributions. Second, and more importantly, the processes through which early health status affects adult social status may vary by race. But the evidence on this score is scant or nonexistent (Palloni and Milesi 2002). While it is clear that race-ethnic disparities in social stratification, mobility and health raise important complications, we will focus only on issues that can be assessed along the social class axis, however defined.

Child health: Child health status does not only refer to what we normally can measure (things such as birthweight, number of chronic conditions or assessment of health status by third parties). In fact, most of what child health really is remains concealed by such feasible measures. To assess child health we should also include factors that surround gestation and birth, physical growth and development, conditions that may be chronic or acute such as asthma or transient episodes of infections, many of which have rather striking long term effects, particularly if they are not treated in a timely way. We should consider mental health, not just severe or mild mental impairments, but also emotional stability and depression. Finally, importance should be given to general fitness and lack of frailty. Both of these features are sometimes visible to the naked eye and can be easily undermined by mild deficiencies in micronutrient intake, such as iron (Thomas, McKelvey, and Sikoki 2006) or more overt poorer nutrition (Popkin, Richards, and Montiero 1996; Glewwe, Jacoby, and King 2001). Although we have much to learn, traits such as physical frailty or an introverted personality exert powerful effects on children's behaviour towards others and on the behaviours of others toward them.

These are non-trivial matters in a world of open competition for economic positions. The relevance of what we, as a rule, do not measure when we refer to child health becomes obvious upon reviewing an impressive report on the science of early childhood development published by the National Research Council (National Research Council 2000). In this work a case is made that health and well-being of children depends closely on health and well-being of their parents. The authors report that health, mental or physical, of a child, the ability to develop a well-controlled, balanced temperament and a constructive personality and behaviour management style, depends on things as trivial as sleeping habits, and on much less trivial phenomena such as how discipline is taught to them. Emphasis on the possibility that these influences sculpt the health status of children is not just a quirk of the literature on child development. As it turns out, this literature is identifying processes that can imperil, impose forbidding constraints on, or enhance the development of traits valued in the job market. Maternal care, the environments children experience at home, in school and, now more than ever, in child care centers --the quality of which is associated with family income—should be understood better. Jointly, they influence nutritional status, exposure to illnesses, mental wellbeing and the occurrence of experiences that could inhibit or retard the normal development of equilibrated personalities and temperaments. All these are factors that affect the likelihood of later economic success.

Needless to say, what we conventionally measure as child health and the indicators we will use in this paper are far from reaching the core of these states and traits that apparently matter so much. *This is a very important reason why the estimated effects of early childhood health on adult socioeconomic status and on the relation between adult health and socioeconomic status underplays the true importance of early childhood health.*

Adult health status: For the most part, the literature on socioeconomic differentials in health and mortality has dealt with mortality. It is only recently that the availability of surveys providing health information has made it possible to observe that similar differentials emerge when using metrics other than mortality. One of them is given by information on self-rated or self-reported health status. Although there is disagreement about what exactly self-rating measures and the degree to which these ratings are comparable across groups (let alone across countries), there is abundant literature suggesting that they are quite consistent across individuals, reflect well actual health status as assessed by physicians, and are a very good, perhaps the best, predictor of short-term individual mortality (Idler and Kasl 1995; Idler and Kasl 1991; Idler and Benyamini 1997). In this paper we will use self-reported health assessed at two different stages in the life cycle of individuals, at age 33 and at age 41.

2. Persistence of adult health and mortality differentials

There is little doubt that health and mortality gradients by socioeconomic status have persisted and, in some cases, even increased. The evidence is particularly striking in the US but it applies much more broadly to Western European countries and, to the extent that we know, to countries in Asia and Latin America. The main difficulty in the assessment of differentials has to do with the choice of a metric to classify individuals by social strata. Due to data availability, the more expeditious way turns out to be the use of educational attainment or years of schooling. Since the landmark study of Kitagawa and Hauser (Kitagawa and Hauser 1973), mortality differentials by education have persisted in the US. Repeatedly, new studies using different data sources uncover a recurrent finding, that mortality rates among the better educated are several times lower than those who are less educated (Preston and Taubman 1994; Feldman, Makuc, Kleinman, and Cornoni-Huntley 1989; Lauderdale 2001; Preston and Elo 1995; Elo and Preston 1996). In a recent paper it was estimated that disparities in US adult mortality (over age 20) in the year 2005 are tantamount to a displacement of mortality risks equivalent to ten years: individuals with lower levels of education experience mortality risks equivalent to those experienced by their more educated counterparts when they are ten years older (Palloni 2006). A similar and striking disparity exists with regards to self-reported health status both in the US (Palloni 2006; Lynch 2003; Lynch 2005; Smith and Kington 1997a; Smith and Kington 1997b), England and Wales (Banks, Marmot, Oldfield, and Smith 2006), and even among adults in Latin America and the Caribbean (Palloni, McEnry, Wong and Pelaez, 2006). As Valkonen has shown, the gradients are strikingly similar in the US, England and Wales, Finland, Hungary, Norway, and Denmark (Valkonen 1987; Valkonen 1989; Valkonen 1992; Sorlie, Rogot, Anderson, Johnson, and Backlund 1992; Rogot, Sorlie, Johnson, and Schmitt 1992).

Using other metrics to assess social class does not alter the picture. Indeed, the gradients tend to become steeper when one uses permanent or even more transient measures of income (Lynch 2003; Pappas, Queen, Hadden, and Fisher 1993; Sorlie, Backlund, and Keller 1995; Lynch 2005; Duleep 1986; McDonough, Duncan, Williams, and House 1997; Duleep 1998). An even stronger relation and steeper gradients are obtained with measures of wealth and assets (Adams et al. 2003; Spittel 2003; Attanasio and Hoynes 2000; Attanasio and Emmerson 2001; Smith 1999; Mare and Palloni 1988; Palloni and Spittel 2004) or even poverty level (Menchik 1993). Using occupational rank—either as prestige scores or with the standard British classification- leads to similar though somewhat attenuated disparities (Kitagawa and Hauser 1973; Fox et al. 1985; Mare 1986; Marmot, Ryff, Bumpass, Shipley, and Marks 1997; Moore and Hayward 1990; Power, Manor, and Fox 1991). And, as mentioned above, just about all these differentials remain strong whether one uses mortality or self-reported health status (Palloni 2006; Lynch 2003; Lynch 2005).

This much is not controversial: the empirical evidence stubbornly suggests that gradients in health and mortality are large, persistent and somewhat insensitive to the use of diverse social class metric. What is controversial are the mechanisms producing them: are higher income, wealth, education or occupation health-protective? Of all possible mediating processes, the one that interests us is the so-called *health selection mechanism*. Because this term is used in the literature with changing and frequently inconsistent meanings and definitions, we will first define what we consider relevant health selection mechanisms (for a more detailed review see West 1991; Palloni and Ewbank 2004).

2.1. Reverse causality

This is the most frequently invoked relation whereby the gradient is generated because antecedent health status constrains the social position individuals may occupy at any given point in time. For example, to the extent that a major illness leads to dilution or liquidation of assets, a cross sectional study (and even a limited panel study) may find a negative association between health status or mortality and assets or income simply because the health deterioration process operated as a shock on assets and wealth (Adams et al. 2003; Smith 1999). A similar mechanism was invoked early on to partially explain the gradient in England and Wales though in this case the outcome affected by antecedent health status was occupational and labor force status rather than wealth or assets (Fox et al. 1982).

2.2. Heterogeneity

To the extent that the composition of a closed population changes over time (age) in ways that are directly influenced by individual frailty, levels of health and mortality in various social subgroups will converge as those who are more frail are selected out, leaving only individuals above a threshold frailty level in all social groups (Palloni and Ewbank 2004; Beckett 2000; Vaupel, Manton, and Stallard 1979). This mechanism could be responsible for weakening or even reversals of gradients at older ages. To our knowledge, the magnitude of the contribution of this type of selection to the reduction of gradients has not been conclusively estimated. In any case, only in perverse cases (during periods following wars or population crisis that change mean frailty negatively in lower status groups and positively in higher status groups) can this type of selection induce an increase in the gradient. In most empirically relevant cases individual heterogeneity generates downward biases on the observed adult health and mortality gradients.

2.3. Indirect effects of health processes

The most intriguing selection process, and also the most likely to have pervasive effects, is referred to as 'indirect selection'. Suppose individuals are allocated to various health statuses at birth and suppose also that this allocation does not occur at random but depends on parental health and/or parental social class. Suppose further that individuals located at the lower end of the health distribution are also less likely to perform well in school, to participate in social activities and, more generally, less likely to acquire traits that are both relevant for social accession and conducive to a healthier lifestyle. It may well be that membership in a lower social class gradually strengthens the adoption of unhealthy behaviours (such as drinking and smoking), but this occurs in addition to the fact that an individual who acceded to this social class is also more likely to have been drawn from the lower end of the health status distribution. The relations can proceed with feedback effects and cumulative damage and disadvantages whereby lack of health begets fewer resources and diminished resources begets unhealthy statuses. This kind of process is the one that was prominently noted in the Black report (Black, Morris, Smith, Townsend, and Whitehead 1988). It has also been the focus of a large literature both substantive and empirical (Palloni and Ewbank 2004; Kuh and Ben-Shlomo 2004; Martorell, Stein, and Schroeder 2001; Blane 1999; Vagero and Illsley 1995; Blane, Davey Smith, and Hart 1999; Manor et al. 2003; West 1991; Stern 1983; Illsley 1986; Chandola, Bartley, Sacker, Jenkinson, and Marmot 2003; Power and Matthews 1997; Illsley 1955; Power, Hertzman, Matthews, and Manor 1997; Power, Manor, Fox, and Fogelman 1990; Power et al. 1991).

Two remarks are important. First is that the effective operation of health selection does not require that early health status be allocated via a specific mechanism. It can operate even if early health is allocated randomly. However, the *intergenerational transmission of the social class gradient in health via early health status* can only take place if early health status is allocated non-randomly. That is, health selection can be a pervasive process influencing health gradients if and only if antecedent health status is distributed non-randomly.

Second, while the existence of early health effects on adult health could reinforce health selection, they are neither necessary nor sufficient for health selection to operate efficaciously. If, for example, the conjecture about a critical period is borne out by the facts and does indeed lead to higher risks of congestive heart disease or diabetes II (Barker 1998), this, by itself, cannot automatically result in health selection. By the same token, health selection does not require the existence of effects associated with a critical period type to be an effective producer of social class gradients. The necessary ingredient is that, at some point in the life course of individuals (or at multiple stages in it), accession to social classes is a tight function of antecedent health status.

It is fair to say that most of the empirical studies that evaluate indirect selection mechanisms lead to the conclusion that they are of rather muted importance, and that the bulk of the observed health gradients must be attributable to mechanisms linking attributes of the social class to an individual's health status and mortality. However, an accurate test of the existence of health selection has not yet been carried out for lack of (a) an appropriate theoretical model linking early health status and adult social stratification and (b) adequate data and/or procedures to identify health selection from feasible observable relations.

3. Early health status, transmission of economic inequalities and adult health

In this section we develop arguments in support of two ideas. First, early health status is not randomly allocated. Instead, both parental social class and parental health status contribute to it. Second, early health status is a non-trivial determinant affecting the life chances of individuals in the social stratification system. These two conditions are sufficient to generate an environment of relations in which (a) there will be intergenerational transmission of inequalities and (b) the operation of health selection effects will be promoted and this may account, albeit partially, for the social class gradient in adult health and mortality.

3.1. Non-random allocation of early health status: first condition of possibility for health selection

One of the most recurrent findings in the literature on child health is that early childhood health conditions are strongly related to a number of indicators of the socioeconomic position of family of origin. Among these are maternal and paternal education, income, poverty level, parental occupation, and receipt of economic assistance. These factors appear to have anywhere from weak to strong associations with characteristics such as birth weight, prematurity, growth retardation, stunting, children's experiences with illnesses, and other indicators of child health status. The relations are by no means uncontroversial. Indeed, close scrutiny of various studies does not eliminate ambiguities about either the magnitude of effects or the type of processes involved. Thus, for example, in a meta-analysis of 895 studies carried out between 1970 and 1984, Kramer (1987) found that several of the above mentioned socioeconomic variables had weak **direct effects** on prematurity, low birthweight and intrauterine growth retardation (IUGR). These findings applied both to developing and developed countries. On the other hand, analyzing the first wave of the Children of the National Longitudinal Survey of Youth (NLSY-C), Cramer (1995) found that while income from earnings and from family and public assistance is indeed associated with birthweight, the effects are small and often not significant at conventional statistical levels. Yet he also finds that low income accounts for much of the excess incidence of low birthweight among blacks and other racial and ethnic minorities.

Although none of these studies find strong associations between early childhood health indicators and parental income or other indicators of parental social class position, it is important to remember two issues. First, these studies refer to **direct effects** of social class, that is, those that remain *after controlling for a number of intermediate factors,* such as birth order, length of birth intervals, mother's age, mother's marital status, timing of prenatal care and the like. Our argument is that social class affects birthweight (or alternative indicators of child health status) *regardless of the nature of mediating mechanisms.* Thus the evidence of a weak **direct** relation is immaterial for our purposes. In most studies included in Kramer's review and in Cramer's work, the gross effects of income and maternal education, for example, are much larger and more significant than the direct effects.

Second, as Cramer (1995) recognized, measures of dimensions of social class or strata used in these studies are conventionally quite poor, as they leave out many factors that have significant effects. Thus, "if these other dimensions were included in the model, surely the effects of economic status would be impressive, both in predicting birth outcome and in explaining ethnic differences in birth outcomes" (Cramer 1995: 244).

The tenor of the discussion in very recent research in the U.S. and elsewhere confirms the importance of family socioeconomic background in terms of direct and indirect effects. This research has exploited large and rich data sets, uniformly confirming that social and economic characteristics of the family of origin, including but not limited to maternal education, have strong effects on child health and mortality. In a recent paper, Case and colleagues (Case, Lubotsky, and Paxson 2002) complete a review of three major U.S. surveys with a summary that aptly describes findings from similar research in the area: "We have shown that the relationship between income and health status observed for adults has antecedents in childhood. A family's long-run average income is a powerful determinant of children's health status, one that works in part to protect children's health upon the arrival of chronic conditions." More importantly: "The health of children from families with lower incomes erodes faster with age, and these children enter adulthood with both lower socioeconomic status and poorer health" (Case et al. 2002, p. 1330). Thus, the adult socioeconomic and health and mortality gradient is formerly mirrored among children (Brooks-Gunn, Duncan, and Britto 1999). There are a number of mechanisms through which this gradient can emerge and it is likely that their relative importance will vary with social context.

A somewhat different though complementary idea is that health status in early childhood may be "inherited" from parents at birth. The apparent relation of parents' and offspring birthweight suggests the possibility of genetic inheritance, although it can also be due to shared environments. In a series of papers, Conley and Bennett (Conley and Bennett 2000; Conley and Bennett 2001) document strong intergenerational correlation of birthweight for both blacks and whites in the U.S. They find that inheritance of parental birthweight "dramatically reduces the black-white gap in birthweight" (Conley and Bennett 2001). The authors interpret these findings as evidence of both inheritability of a propensity to low birthweight and the influence of environments shared by parents and offspring (Conley and Bennett 2001).

Not only are disadvantaged children at a higher risk of poor health, but research suggests their families are less likely to be able to deal with the consequences of poor childhood health than are advantaged families. In their research on the impact of early childhood health (measured by low birth weight) on educational attainment Currie and Hyson (1999) find that low birth weight has long-term effects on children from advantaged as well as from disadvantaged families. However, the authors note that disadvantaged children "suffer from double jeopardy in that they are more likely to suffer both from the effects of low socioeconomic status and from low birth weight" (Currie and Hyson 1999, p. 250). The authors argue that while children from all social backgrounds are at risk of developing health problems, advantaged families are able to assuage the disadvantage of poor health. Similar mechanisms may explain recent findings suggesting that gaps in health status of children by social class widens as they age both in countries with and without sizeable socialized medicine sectors such as Canada and the US (Currie and Stabile 2003).

In summary, there is substantial evidence indicating that, either due to early environments--conditions directly associated with parental social, economic and cultural endowments--or through inheritance of predispositions, there is a correlation between parental health status and parental economic status, on one hand, and offspring health conditions during early childhood, on the other. Thus, the research reviewed here reveals that the first condition of possibility for health selection does apply.

3.2. Determinants of stratification: second condition of possibility for health selection effects

In theory at least, payments to labor in the form of wages and salaries (earnings) ought to be a function of productive (market-related) skills, namely, traits (acquired or inherited) that contribute to the production process and, as such, are explicitly entered in a production function. Standard economic theory concedes that the importance of these factors may vary depending on market conditions but, by and large, is unconcerned with the possibility that markets may reward other traits.

The role of conventional wage-enhancing traits: Traditionally, relevant skills have been equated with educational attainment, experience, on-the-job training, and cognitive abilities. These variables have been shown consistently to exert important effects on earnings. But, equally consistently, they fail to account for more than a fraction of earning variance within the same generation (Bowles and Gintis 1976; Jencks 1979; Jencks and Phillips 1998; Heckman and Rubinstein 2001). Indeed, according to a recent survey of the empirical literature, between 67 and 80 percent of the variance of (log) earnings remains unexplained after accounting for a person's age, years of schooling, years of labor market experience, and parental socioeconomic characteristics (Bowles, Gintis, and Osborne 2000). Furthermore, there is a persistent direct effect of parental earnings (or background) on offspring earnings which is robust to model specification, and *remains so even after controlling for a host of market-relevant offspring traits, including years of schooling, cognitive ability and labor market experience* (Bowles and Nelson 1974; Mulligan 1997; Bowles et al. 2000).

The effects of standard labor market characteristics are not easily explained with conventional interpretations. In particular, while the effects of years of schooling on earnings are strong and always statistically significant, the mechanism through which they operate remains obscure. One mediating mechanism, cognitive ability is, as one would expect, quite important but it only accounts for a small fraction of the effects of education.[1] Thus, some of the effects of education on earnings may be due to high correlations between education and other, non-cognitive traits (Manor et al. 2003; Carneiro and Heckman 2003).

The puzzle is not that empirical research suggests that standard human capital variables are irrelevant for earnings, but that after fully accounting for them there is still substantial unexplained variance in (log) earning and a remarkably high degree of uncertainty about the mechanisms through which standard factors realize their effects (Palloni and Milesi 2006).

In sum, current conventional accounting of labor earnings is not satisfactory. Not only does it explain only a small fraction of the variance of earnings, but also signals that variables that are presumed to be irrelevant turn out to be important, and that those that we expect to perform do so but only up to a point. And in these cases we are not always able to explain or interpret their effects.

Why should other individual traits matter at all either as direct predictors of earnings or as mediating factors between years of schooling and earnings? What exactly are these factors, what are they useful for, how are they acquired, how is it that they become beneficial for employers?

The role of "soft-skills": Microeconomic models that include consideration of unconventional traits are not standard fare. Yet those that have been formulated do shed light on conditions under which the demand for these traits may grow, thus fostering mechanisms to reward individuals who possess them. Perhaps the most important theoretical insight comes from the literature on microeconomic markets with asymmetric information, where employment relationships are contractually incomplete and associated with potentially significant enforcement costs (Bowles et al. 2000). Bowles and colleagues start with a conventional (Walrasian) model but proceed to do away with assumptions regarding mechanic equilibrium and invoking exogenous effort in the work place. The new situation is one of asymmetrical information and subject to incentive problems, since workers' effort is not fixed and can vary according to the work situation. Enforcement of contractual relations is costly and employers will choose to reward employees' characteristics or traits that minimize such enforcement costs while ensuring their full cooperation. Bowles and colleague baptize these traits as "incentive enhancing preferences" (IEP). They refer to personal traits that facilitate the timely flow of quality labor inputs into the production process. Examples of such

---

1   According to estimates drawn from an extensive review by Bowles et al. (2000) cognitive scores account for no more than 20 percent of the effects of education on earnings.

IEPs are loyalty, predisposition to telling the truth, low disutility of effort, low time discount rate, "selfdirectedness," sense of efficacy, perception of being in control, low fatalism, and ability to function in groups and establish social networks. The degree to which these traits matter --that is, the degree of deviation from a Walrasian world — could vary and depend on local market conditions, type of industry or commercial establishment, technological change, and legal environments, among other factors. Thus, the degree to which earnings are responsive to IEPs and/or more conventional market skills will also vary according to these conditions.

Some of these traits are undoubtedly shaped through school experience and will thus be captured by years of schooling. Some are learned or acquired outside school and other informal settings. Yet others, as suggested recently by Farkas (2003), may be part of a set of habits with which individuals are endowed as a result of prolonged learning and early socialization. These are traits sculpted early on in childhood, through parents' involvement, hands-on-teaching, mentorship, and participation in extracurricular activities. Some could contribute to educational attainment and cognitive performance; others may be unrelated to either. Many of these factors, however, are most definitely not the result of a limited stay in high school or of transient participation in a job training setting (Heckman 2000).[2]

The evidence that IEPs are important contributors to human capital and that, just as other production factors do, they can facilitate rent extraction, is somewhat recent and does not yet amount to a well-established body of literature. However, the findings are so ubiquitous as to encourage reexamination of standard human capital theories and to encourage revisions of the foundations of public policy. In a sweeping account of conditions that could improve the effectiveness of policies designed to enhance human capital, Heckman (2000) suggests that a broader view of skills and the processes that produce them is called for. In particular, Heckman points out that exclusive preoccupation with cognition and academic performance, as assessed by test scores, educational attainment or adult-on the job training, is misguided, and that models and policies must make room for conditions associated with "motivation" and "social adaptability" (Heckman 2000). Evidence for this "shadow" reward system comes to us from very different traditions: one emphasizing personality traits (Jencks 1979; Osborne 2000; Dunifon and Duncan 1998), another focusing on attitudinal and motivational traits (Heckman, Hsee, and Rubinstein 1999; McClelland and Franz 1992; Nollen and Gaertner 1991; Cameron and Heckman 1993) and yet a third one focusing on physical

---

2   If the most important among these traits were a function of early environment and family socioeconomic background only, their effect would vanish once a control for the latter is introduced. We are unaware of models including good measures for either.

characteristics, such as obesity among women (Gortmaker, Must, Perrin, Sobol, and Dietz 1993; Harper 2000; McLean and Moon 1980; Register and Williams 1990; Sargent and Blanchflower 1994) and height among males (Loh 1993; Persico, Postlewaite, and Silverman 2001; Judge and Cable 2004; Scrimshaw 1997; Sargent and Blanchflower 1994). Importantly for the health selection argument, what matters about physical traits such as height and obesity is not their value during adulthood but their value early in the individual's life: it is not weight or height at age 30 *per se* that matters but what *they reflect about height and weight during early childhood or adolescence* (Persico et al. 2001). Adult height appears to have an effect on wages only because it is related to early height. And the latter's effects are interpreted by invoking the idea that early stature could facilitate or contribute to the acquisition of traits, such as leadership, responsibility, working habits, that are later demanded in the labor markets. Height and weight may simply act as signals to employers that reveal the possible existence of such desirable qualities, much more than diplomas or other formal credentials do.

A growing literature in labor economics attempts to identify the market conditions under which traits not conventionally included in standard accounts of labor market theory acquire importance (Bowles et al. 2005). Admittedly the evidence available so far is tenuous and does not constitute a proper body of work on which the relevance of IEPs could rest. But it is highly suggestive and, more importantly for the main argument in this paper, it establishes a mechanism through which early health status may influence social stratification, allowing us to identify the two conditions of possibility for the existence of health selection. For example, it is well-known that both early obesity and childhood height are strongly influenced by birthweight. On the one hand, if birthweight is partly inherited and partly shaped by parental social background and, on the other, if height and obesity of adolescents depends on birthweight and itself affects adult socioeconomic status, we have a mediating mechanism through which early health (here reflected by birthweight) operates to maintain or reproduce health and socioeconomic inequalities across generations.

3.3. Enduring effects of early childhood health and other conditions: integrating the first and second condition of possibility

The foregoing establishes that there are a number of factors influencing adult earnings that may be plausibly related to early health status. We will now discuss if there is any evidence substantiating the claim. If so, then early health exerts an influence on later economic success, either directly or indirectly.

The bulk of the effects we refer to below are not direct but instead mediated by other factors and they can be classified into two classes: first, those that influence individuals' cognitive abilities at various ages, ultimate educational attainment, and on-the-job acquisition of skills and, second, those that shape, constrain or facilitate the acquisition of IEPs or "soft-skills."

Effects operating through conventional traits: By and large, the influence of early childhood health status is likely to be indirect. The literature documenting their existence focuses almost exclusively on cognition and educational attainment as potential conduits. Thus, findings from the 1946 British cohort study reported by Wadsworth (Wadsworth 1999; Wadsworth 1991; Wadsworth 1986) indicate that the experience of serious illness during childhood is directly and indirectly associated with decreased educational attainment and increased risks of downward social mobility. Similar evidence has surfaced in other studies (Rahkonen, Lahelma, and Huuhka 1997; Behrman and Rosenzweig 2002; Lichtenstein, Harris, Pedersen, and McClearn 1993; Power, Li, and Manor 2000; Lundberg 1991). With few exceptions these findings are fragile, as are those that establish direct links between health status in early adolescence and mature educational attainment (Koivusilta, Rimpela, and Rimpela 1995; Koivusilta, Rimpela, and Rimpela 1998).

Other mechanisms could alter individuals' ability and motivation to learn, school performance and attainment and ultimately labor market success. Exposure to unfavorable conditions **in utero**, subsequent low birthweight, illnesses and poor growth and development during the first years of life modify the growth of brain tissue and through it alter the functioning of one or more neuro-physiological centers of hormonal balance and activation. These, in turn, will affect behaviour, motivation, individual choices, resilience, frailty, and immune status (see the collection of essays in Hack, Klein, and Taylor 1995 and Hertzman 1999b). These processes have the potential to induce a wholesale shift in lifelong health (and mortality risks) of individuals exposed to them and to shape and mold cognitive experiences and learning capacity early in life.

For example, recent studies show that cognitive scores and educational attainment among low birthweight (less than 2,500 grams) children are significantly lower than among normal birthweight children, even when comparisons are made between siblings (Matte, Bresnahan, Begg, and Susser 2001; Boardman, Powers, Padilla, and Hummer 2002; Conley and Bennett 2000). Other studies replicate this finding in other contexts and extend it to include influences of other birthweight categories, such as very low birthweight children (less than 1,500 grams) or different ranges within the normal birthweight distribution (Richards, Hardy, Kuh, and Wadsworth 2001; Elgen and Sommerfelt 2002; Jefferis, Power, and Hertzman 2002; Hack et al. 2002; Seidman et al. 1992). Behrman and Rosenzweig (2002) analyze data on female twins from a sample of the Minnesota Twin Registry. Using within monozygotic twin estimators, they show that augmenting a child's birthweight by one pound increases schooling attainment by about a third of a year, and boosts adult earnings by over 7 percent. More generally, the evidence shows that, however measured, early health status has a direct impact on early cognition, school performance, late cognition, and educational attainment (Edwards and Grossman 1979; Korenman, Miller, and Sjaastad 1994; Richards et al.

2001; Rosenzweig and Wolpin 1994; Shakotko, Edwards, and Grossman 1981; O'Brien Caughy 1996; Hack et al. 1995; Ricciuti and Scarr 1990; Scarr 1982; Taubman 1975a; Grossman 1972; Taubman 1975b).

A more distal mechanism of influence can occur if events experienced early in life determine individuals' choices and life course, locking them into a reduced set of possible paths. If these career pathways are endowed with different conditions, require the exercise of different abilities, and expose individuals to different opportunities, educational and occupational attainment will vary. Thus, the occurrence of earlier events through which individuals are selected into those life courses or pathways can be thought of as triggers that largely determine subsequent social and economic experiences (Hertzman 1999a). An example of this is when early health problems influence early education and thus limit educational attainment and foreclose a number of occupational and career paths. Take the case of apparently trivial events, such as early chronic otitis media. It has been shown that this condition may be influential in determining cognitive ability, but particularly the acquisition and development of verbal skills (Shriberg, Friel-Patti, Flipsen Jr., and Brown 2000). If so, exposure to the condition during a critical period in the life of the individual will simply foreclose some developmental paths. These types of health shocks at critical periods are important as triggers of processes such as those illustrated by Lubotsky (2001) who suggests the emergence of cascading spirals whereby early failures to rank well in cognition, for example, leads to higher subsequent disadvantages, a confirmation in reverse of Heckman's idea that "skills beget skills."

Effects operating through "soft-skills": Another set of mechanisms by which early health status could impact social stratification is through its influence on "soft-skills" or IEPs, by affecting physical characteristics, such as height and weight, which enhance (depress) the chances of acquiring "soft-skills." Relevant to the effect of early health on "soft-skills" is a large body of literature documenting the influence of early health and nutritional status on adolescent and adult weight and height (Blane 1995; Scrimshaw 1997; Floud, Wachter, and Gregory 1990; Fogel and Costa 1997; Fogel 1994). It is complemented by growing research on the existence of a relation between income and wages, on one hand, and adult height and weight, on the other (Behrman and Rosenzweig 2002; Loh 1993; Persico et al. 2001; Hamermesh and Biddle 1994; Martel and Biller 1987; Sargent and Blanchflower 1994; Averett and Korenman 1996; Thomas and Strauss 1997).[3] This evidence provides at least one conduit linking early health status with adult earnings and economic inequality.

---

3 Although "soft-skills" not reflected in height or weight could also be associated with early health status, we are not aware of literatures documenting these effects.

Through what mechanisms do adult height and weight, partial outcomes of early health status conditions, confer advantages (disadvantages) in the labor market? Both with regard to height (Persico et al. 2001) and weight (Sargent and Blanchflower 1994; Averett and Korenman 1996), the key advantage does not seem to reside on the adult physical characteristics, but on appearance during adolescence. This suggests that being a tall man and a non-obese woman facilitates the acquisition of traits that are highly valued by employers but prior to entrance in the labor market. Thus, these skills, not adult physical appearance per se, are what make early height and weight relevant for labor market success.

In summary, when conventional and "soft-skills" traits are considered jointly, we find strands of research bridging literatures on early health status, on the one hand, and on determinants of labor markets and socioeconomic success, on the other. This literature is not conclusive and much remains to be elucidated but by itself it provides sufficient empirical evidence on which the plausibility of the second condition of possibility mentioned before rests, namely, that there are mechanisms through which early health may influence traits that are relevant for economic success and achievement.

In the following section we translate the relations identified before into a structural equation model. The model includes relationships covering a large section of the life cycle of individuals. We then propose the use of a data set to estimate the parameters of the model. These estimates can then be deployed in conventional path analysis decompositions. More importantly, however, they can be the inputs of a simple Monte Carlo simulation to generate statistics summarizing two dimensions of the process: (a) the degree to which early health accounts for the intergenerational transmission of inequalities and (b) the degree to which selection mechanisms triggered by early health conditions account for the adult social class differentials in health status.

4. Models, data requirements and estimation

We formulate a parsimonious model capturing the most important relations for which we found empirical evidence in the discussion above. The model can be translated into a path diagram that applies very generally.

4.1. Model and data requirements

Figure 1 displays the dimensions of the model and the principal relations involved. Parental social class and parental health are on the left side of the diagram. These conditions influence health conditions early on and these, in turn, affect cognitive and non-cognitive (soft) skills. Added to educational attainment, these are the main inputs for the production of offspring adult social class. The paths leading to adult social class sufficient to represent relations involved in the intergenerational transmission of social class. By adding adult health, the model also allows us to represent the social class gradient in health and, furthermore, the contribution of early health to this gradient. The figure translates into a standard set of non-recursive structural equations (no feedback effects). The parameters of the system can be estimated using conventional maximum likelihood procedures to enable us to handle discrete dependent variables.

To estimate the model represented in Figure 1 it is necessary to use data from a study that follows individuals throughout their life course, from birth up to adulthood (and ideally until death). Furthermore, it is necessary to have information on a wide array of factors including parental health and socioeconomic background prior to the individual's birth; individual's health conditions at birth and during childhood; measures of individual's cognitive and non-cognitive development; their educational attainment; adult socioeconomic conditions; and, finally, information on their adult health status. In the U.S. there are no datasets that meet these requirements. In the U.K, the set of birth cohort studies provide the type of information necessary to estimate our proposed model. These studies have prospectively followed, up to adulthood, individuals born in a particular week of 1946, 1958, and 1970. A major challenge associated with using these data regards the substantive amount of attrition and, even

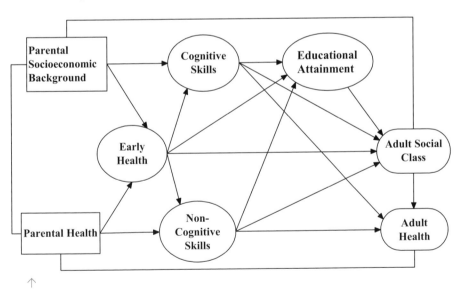

↑
Figure 1: Simplified path diagram representing the relations between early child health conditions and adult social class

more, the selective attrition of respondents from particular socioeconomic and health conditions. For example, males who belong to the lowest social classes and who are in the poorest early health status are more likely to attrite (for example, through death, a phenomenon that accounts for about one fifth of the total attrition among males). It is likely that discarding these cases leads to overall attenuation of effects of interest. We have proposed how to deal with this issue elsewhere (Palloni et al., 2006). A different problem associated with using these British cohort studies has to do with their generalizability. In countries such as the UK around 1958, conditions surrounding the lives of the most deprived in the population were in all likelihood vastly superior to the conditions of the most deprived in low income countries. In these early malnutrition, child stunting, limited growth and development, and insufficiency of micronutrients among children and young adults, are rampant and consequently the room for early health status to leave a marked imprint is much larger and so is the number of routes through which it can sculpt adult socioeconomic achievement and adult health inequalities

4.2. Estimation and analyses

We suggest analyses divided in two stages. In the first stage one can produce results that pertain to the intergenerational transmission of social class. The question being asked here should be as follows: how much of the observed relation between paternal and offspring social class is attributable to mechanisms involving early health conditions? The second stage of analysis should focus on the social class health gradient during adulthood. The main question is as follows: what is the contribution of early health status to the association between adult social class and adult health status?

In both stages the analysis proceeds in three steps: (a) first one must summarize the results obtained from the path model; (b) second, we should decompose the paths that account for the correlation between the main variables of interest and estimate the contribution of paths associated with early health status; and, finally, (c) we need to use the estimates of the structural equation model as inputs to a Monte Carlo simulation describing the trajectory of a population that initially has all the characteristics observed in a population. This population is then assumed to experience a life course 'governed' by the path model. For the analysis of socioeconomic inequality one estimates a mobility matrix that combines class of origin and class of destination and we study its steady-state behaviour. In the analysis of social class health gradients we obtain a mobility matrix that combines social class and health status of origin with social class and health status of destination and, as before, we study its properties in steady state. In what follows we briefly discuss the details in each of the three steps proposed above.[4]

---

4   The procedure suggested here has been applied elsewhere and shown to perform fairly well. See Palloni et al., 2006

4.2.1. Examining estimated path coefficients.

A standard statistical package can be used to estimate the non-recursive set of equations. But perhaps the most useful and convenient is M-plus which can handle a number of alternative variants of the models portrayed in figure 1. These set of estimates provides some important information about social stratification and mobility. First, one can evaluate the degree to which effects of parental social class continue to affect class of destination even after all other factors are controlled. Second, one can determine which of the many pathways linking parental social class and social class of destination is most important. Third, we can assess the degree to which early health factors affect social class of destination and identify the main pathways. A key issue here is to trace the importance of effects that are transmitted via non-cognitive traits and their relative magnitude vis a vis those transmitted via cognitive effects. Fourth, the most important task in this step is to evaluate the strength of the paths linking adult social class and adult health status and the degree to which is accounted for other factors, including indicators of early childhood health. A fundamental issue here is the following: if one verifies that indicators of early health are not associated with statistically significant effects on either social class or adult health status, one should not jump to the conclusion that they do not matter at all. They may not have direct effects but their total contribution may still be substantial. What matters for the theory we propose here is their total effects. Similarly, if the observed association between lagged social class and health status is only marginally affected after controlling for early health indicators, one should not conclude that selection effects are unimportant. As in the case before, selection effects may be present in complicated and indirect ways that are not easily rendered or manifested in the magnitude of paths coefficients.

4.2.2. Decomposing the overall association into contributing paths

A standard procedure when using path analysis is to decompose a total correlation between two variables into components attributable to different paths. In particular, our model produces sufficient information to know how much of the total, gross correlation between parental social class and social class of destination is attributable to pathways involving cognitive traits, non cognitive traits or early health factors. By the same token, we can estimate how much of the total correlation between lagged social class and adult health status is associated with pathways that involve early health conditions. These are much better measures on which to base an assessment about either the dynamics character of the stratification system (how much of the correlation between parents and offspring' social class can be explained by various factors present in the model) or, alternatively, how much of the association between lagged social class and health status can be explained by pathways involving early health status.

4.2.3. The Monte Carlo simulation

Despite the substantial advances one can make through path's decomposition, the procedure does have an important flaw: it only depends on the size of the estimated path coefficients. It totally ignores the distribution of the population of offspring by characteristics identified in the model. In order to account for this we propose a third step. It consists of transforming the estimates form the structural equations into suitable statistics that combine the joint influence of the magnitude of the path coefficients and the distribution of the population by traits. We start with the individual members of the cohort for whom we have full information[5] and then simulate what would have been their class of destination assuming they are exposed to the regime of transitions and attainment embedded in the estimated structural equations.

We envision the process as one where people are born to a social class and are then endowed with a health status which is partially dependent on social class of origin and partially determined by a random process. The degree to which health status of offspring and parents is related can vary and should capture both the inheritability of health status (via genetic predisposition) as well as the processes through which health status is conferred via parental investments. Apart from a random component, social mobility is a function of acquisition of cognitive and non-cognitive skills reflecting parental endowments and investments, and health status at birth. There might conceivably be some room for adding the influences of parental influences that work neither through health status nor through acquisition of skills and abilities but through social networks, for example, to account for additional "stickiness" of social classes.

To simplify even more, assume there are only two social classes determined by wages and two health status determined by birthweight. It follows that the entire system can be represented in a 4x4 matrix with High and Low social class and Good and Bad health:

		Low Social Class		High Social Class	
		Bad Health	Good Health	Bad Health	Good Health
Low Social Class	Bad Health	p11	p12	p13	p14
	Good Health	p21	p22	p23	p24
High Social Class	Bad Health	p31	p32	p33	p34
	Good Health	p41	p42	p43	p44

---

5   See our comments on the magnitude and likely impact of sample attrition and, more generally, missing data.

The entries are probabilities that a person born in a certain social/health class makes it to some other social/health class. For the time being we ignore fertility and assume that fertility differentials, if they exist at all, are neutral with respect to social and health class.If we knew the values of p_{ij}'s we could study the steady state distributions by raising the matrix to successively high powers until there is convergence. Studying different specification of the p_{ij}'s is sufficient to shape the steady state matrix and to answer the questions of interest. Thus, the most important issue revolves around the identification of p_{ij}'s.

This simulation includes the role of chance as one can utilize the residual variance for continuous variables and a simple Bernoulli process for discrete variables. Finally, to account for fertility we only need to determine a value of Net Reproduction Rate for each one of the cells in the matrix. Using first principles and all the estimates supplied above one can calculate the degree to which a social class system in one generation mirrors the previous one and how much of it is only due to early health status. The resulting algebra is analogous to that of Leslie matrices in stable populations. A full description can be found elsewhere (Preston and Campbell 1993; Lam 1986; Keyfitz 1977).[6]

The resulting matrix can answer a number of questions of interest. For example, given the estimated structural equation model, what would the steady state distribution by social classes be? Is this unique or are they multiple steady states? What proportion of individuals who start out in a social class will produce offspring trapped in the same social class? What is the steady state correlation between social class of origin and destination? Because we can manipulate the estimates of the structural equations (by eliminating selected paths) and the fertility differentials by social class (by altering the fertility gradient by social class) these questions can be answered under alternative scenarios. For example, one can choose the following: (a) a scenario in which early health effects are as estimated by our structural equation model, (b) a scenario in which early health effects are set to zero, (c) a scenario in which the effects of selected mediating mechanisms, such as cognitive and non-cognitive skills are set to zero, (d) a scenario in which the fertility gap between the highest and lowest social class is doubled.

Systematic comparison between statistics calculated from these scenarios is sufficient to capture the joint influence of the strength of relations in the model (both direct and indirect) and the changing distribution of individuals by characteristics throughout the very stylized life cycle simulated by the Monte Carlo exercise.

---

6   In all the exercises with matrices we assume complete homogamy. This ensures that we maximize the effects of both parental social class and original health status. Introducing homogamy would lead to downplay some of the effects we uncover.

Elsewhere (Palloni et al., 2006), we show that the Monte Carlo exercise suggests that while early childhood health contributes to intergenerational transmission of social class, the contribution is small, possibly in the range of 5 to 10 percent. Similarly, it also plays a fairly small role in explaining the socioeconomic gradient of adult health status. This is in part because direct effects are quite small and because, as mentioned above, the indirect paths-those working by affecting the social class position of individuals—are somewhat marginal to the entire process.

5. Summary and conclusion

The main goal of this paper is theoretical, namely, to review in a systematic way the question of whether health selection effects have much or anything to do with the observed adult socioeconomic gradient of health (and mortality). In order to pose the right questions and to derive testable propositions we elaborate a framework connecting literatures in labor economics and social mobility with research findings from epidemiology and demography regarding extant adult gradients and the role of early health status. We show that this preliminary framework is the basis for a simplified path model representing in a stylized way the life cycle of individuals. The set of structural equations embedded in this model can then be estimated using a suitable data sets retrieving a cohort's history. We then suggest the utilization of these estimates as input in a Monte Carlo simulation study of social stratification and health. This can be done estimating steady state mobility matrices and associated statistics that can then be used to test the significance of the role played by early health status as an explanation for observed adult social class differentials in health status.

But there are a number of important gaps, issues mentioned in passing that deserve more thorough treatment, and others we simply neglected to address altogether that need to be reintroduced. Although the skeleton of a cogent theory may exist, it needs to be propped considerably to become useful. The lacunae are many and too glaring. We identify them briefly.

First, the matter of race and ethnicity is urgent and daunting. It is likely that there are differentials by ethnic and race groups in mobility that deserve special attention since the various patches of theory we used to weave the final arguments do not always concern themselves with ethnic and racial differences. Surely, some of these differences will vanish once we take into account factors identified above. But, it would be truly astonishing if unexplained residuals vanish. The degree to which this will happen has much to do with the political and institutional contexts being studied, those that provide the raw materials within which populations create ideologies about and deal with race and ethnicity.

Second, the conduits through which early child health influences adult health and earning potential need to be explored better. Early health status is strongly related to parental decision-making and investments in child health during infancy and subsequent years. Surely these have effects that are independent of health status at birth. Just as parental cultural, economic or social investments are ongoing processes, so are parental health investments spread over the life of a child.

Third, to understand better the exact contribution of intergenerational transmission of income we need to model more thoroughly the dynamics of assortative mating with respect to earning-relevant characteristics. All calculations implied by the simplified set up introduced in the last section of the paper will always depend on the degree of similarity between parents' traits that must be *a priori* assumed. Information on parent-specific characteristics would be an improvement but it is plainly not enough. We need to understand couple formation and childbearing practices as a function of earning-relevant parental characteristics.

6. References

Adams, Peter, Michael D. Hurd, Daniel McFadden, Angela Merrill, and Tiago Ribeiro. 2003. "Healthy, Wealthy and Wise? Tests for Direct Causal Paths Between Health and Socioeconomic Status." *Journal of Econometrics* 112(3-56):57-63.

Attanasio, Orazio and Hilary Hoynes. 2000. "Differential Mortality and Wealth Accumulation." *Journal of Human Resources* 35(1):1-29.

Attanasio, Orazio P. and Carl Emmerson. 2001. "Differential Mortality in the UK." NBER Working Series Paper No. 8241, Cambridge, Massachusetts.

Averett, Susan and Sanders Korenman. 1996. "The Economic Reality of the Beauty Myth." *Journal of Human Resources* 31(2):304-30.

Banks, Michael, Michael Marmot, Zoe Oldfield, and James P. Smith. 2006. "Disease and Disadvantage in the United States and in England." *Journal of the American Medical Association* 295:2037-45.

Barker, D. J. P. 1998. *Mothers, Babies and Health in Later Life*. Edinburgh, Scotland: Churchill Livingstone.

Beckett, Megan. 2000. "Converging Health Inequalities in Later Life- An Artifact of Mortality?" *Journal of Health and Social Behavior* 41(1):106-19.

Behrman, Jere R. and Mark R. Rosenzweig. 2002. "The Returns to Increasing Body Weight." PIER Working Paper 01-052. Penn Institute for Economic Research, University of Pennsylvania http://papers.ssrn.com/sol3/papers.cfm?abstract_id=297919.

Black, D., J. N. Morris, C. Smith, P. Townsend, and M. Whitehead. 1988. *Inequalities in Health: The Black Report: The Health Divide*. London: Penguin.

Blane, David. 1995. "Editorial: Social Determinants of Health-Socioeconomic Status, Social Class, and Ethnicity." *American Journal of Public Health* 85(7):903-4.

Blane, David. 1999. "The Life Course, the Social Gradient, and Health." Pp. 64-80 in *Social Determinants of Health*, eds. Michael Marmot and Richard G. Wilkinson. New York: Oxford University Press.

Blane, David, George Davey Smith, and Carole Hart. 1999. "Some Social and Physical Correlates of Intergenerational Social Mobility: Evidence From the West of Scotland Collaborative Study." *Sociology* 33(1):169-83.

Boardman, Jason D., Daniel A. Powers, Yolanda C. Padilla, and Robert A. Hummer. 2002. "Low Birth Weight, Social Factors, and Developmental Outcomes Among Children in the United States." *Demography* 39(2):353-68.

Bowles, Samuel and Herbert Gintis. 1976. *Schooling in Capitalist America: Educational Reform and Contradictions of Economic Life.* New York: Basic Books.

Bowles, Samuel, Herbert Gintis, and Melissa Osborne Groves, eds. 2005. *Unequal Chances: Family Background and Economic Success.* Princeton: Princeton University Press.

Bowles, Samuel, Herbert Gintis, and Melissa Osborne. 2000. "The Determinants of Earnings: Skills, Preferences, and Schooling." *Working Paper No. 2000-07, Department of Economics, University of Massachusetts.*

Bowles, Samuel and Valerie Nelson. 1974. "The 'Inheritance of IQ' and the Intergenerational Reproduction of Economic Inequality." *Review of Economics and Statistics* 56(1):39-51.

Brooks-Gunn, Jeanne, Greg J. Duncan, and Pia R. Britto. 1999. "Are Socioeconomic Gradients for Children Similar to Those for Adults? Achievement and Health in the United States." Pp. 94-124 in *Developmental Health and the Wealth of Nations Social, Biological, and Educational Dynamics*, eds. Daniel P. Keating and Clyde Hertzman. New York: Guilford Press.

Cameron, Steven and James Heckman. 1993. "The Non-Equivalence of the High School Equivalents." *Journal of Labor Economics* 11(1):1-47.

Carneiro, Pedro and James Heckman. 2003. "Human Capital Policy." NBER Working Series Paper No. 9495, Cambridge, Massachusetts.

Carneiro, Pedro, James J. Heckman, and Dimitriy V. Masterov. 2003. "Labor Market Discrimination and Racial Differences in Premarket Factors." NBER Working Paper No. 10068: Cambridge, Massachusetts.

Case, Anne, Darren Lubotsky, and Christina Paxson. 2002. "Economic Status and Health in Childhood: The Origins of the Gradient." *American Economic Review* 92(5):1308-34.

Chandola, T., M. Bartley, A. Sacker, C. Jenkinson, and M. Marmot. 2003. "Health Selection in the Whitehall II Study, UK." *Soc Sci Med* 56(10):2059-72.

Conley, Dalton and Neil G. Bennett. 2000. "Is Biology Destiny? Birth Weight and Life Chances." *American Sociological Review* 65(3):458-67.

Conley, Dalton and Neil G. Bennett. 2001. "Birth Weight and Income: Interactions Across Generations." *Journal of Health and Social Behavior* 42(4):450-465.

Cramer, James C. 1995. "Racial and Ethnic Differences in Birthweight: The Role of Income and Financial Assistance (in Determinants of Mortality)." *Demography* 32(2):231-47.

Currie, Janet and Rosemary Hyson. 1999. "Is the Impact of Health Shocks Cushioned by Socioeconomic Status? The Case of Low Birthweight." *The American Economic Review* 89(2):245.

Currie, Janet and Mark Stabile. 2003. "Socioeconomic Status and Child Health: Why Is the Relationship Stronger for Older Children?" *The American Economic Review* 93(5):1813-1823.

Duleep, H. O. 1986. "Measuring the Effect of Income on Adult Mortality Using Longitudinal Administrative Record Data." *Journal of Human Resources* 21(2):238-51.

Duleep, H. O. 1998. "Has the US Mortality Differential by Socioeconomic Status Increased Over Time?" *American Journal of Public Health* 88(7).

Duncan, Otis D. 1961. "Socioeconomic Index for All Occupations." Pp. 109-38 in *Occupations and Social Status*, ed. Albert J. Reiss. New York: The Free Press.

Dunifon, Rachel and Greg J. Duncan. 1998. "Long-Run Effects of Motivation on Labor-Market Success." *Social Psychology Quarterly* 61 (1):33-48.

Edwards, Linda N. and Michael Grossman. 1979. "The Relationship Between Children's Health and Intellectual Development." Pp. 273-314 in *Health, What Is It Worth? Measures of Health Benefits*, eds. Selma J. Mushkin and David W. Dunlop. New York: Pergamon Press.

Elgen, I. and K. Sommerfelt. 2002. "Low Birthweight Children: Coping in School?" *Acta Paediatrica* 91(8):939-45.

Elo, Irma T. and Samuel H. Preston. 1996. "Educational Differentials in Mortality: United States, 1979-85." *Social Science and Medicine* 42(1):47-57.

Farkas, George. 2003. "Cognitive Skills and Noncognitive Traits and Behaviors in Stratification Processes." *Annual Review of Sociology* 29:541-62.

Feldman, J. J., D. M. Makuc, J. C. Kleinman, and J. Cornoni-Huntley. 1989. "National Trends in Educational Differentials in Mortality." *American Journal of Epidemiology* 129(5):919-933.

Ferri, E., ed. 1993. "*Life at 33: The Fifth Follow-Up of the National Child Development Study.*" London: National Children's Bureau.

Floud, R., K. Wachter, and A. Gregory. 1990. *Height, Health and History: Nutritional Status in the United Kingdom*, 1750-1980. Cambridge: Cambridge University Press.

Fogel, Robert W. 1994. "Economic Growth, Population Theory, and Physiology: The Bearing of Long-Term Processes on the Making of Economic Policy." *American Economic Review* 84(3):369-95.

Fogel, Robert W. and Dora L. Costa. 1997. "A Theory of Technophysio Evolution, With Some Implications for Forecasting Population, Health Care Costs, and Pension Costs." *Demography* 34(1):49-66.

Fox, A. J., P. O. Goldblatt, and A. M. Adelstein. 1982. "Selection and Mortality Differentials." *Journal of Epidemiology and Community Health* 36:69-79.

Fox, A. J., P. O. Goldblatt, and D. R. Jones. 1985. "Social Class Mortality Differentials: Artefact, Selection or Life Circumstances?" *Journal of Epidemiology and Community Health* 39(1):1-8.

Glewwe, Paul, Hanan G. Jacoby, and Elizabeth M. King. 2001. "Early Childhood Nutrition and Academic Achievement: a Longitudinal Analysis." *Journal of Public Economics* 81:345-368.

Gortmaker, Steven L., Aviva Must, James M. Perrin, Arthur M. Sobol, and William H. Dietz. 1993. "Social and Economic Consequences of Overweight in Adolescence and Young Adulthood." *The New England Journal of Medicine* 329(14):1008-12.

Grossman, Michael. 1972. "On the Concept of Health Capital and the Demand for Health." *Journal of Political Economy* 80(2):223-55.

Hack, Maureen, Daniel J. Flannery, Mark Schluchter, Lydia Cartar, Elaine Borawski, and Nancy Klein. 2002. "Outcomes in Young Adulthood for Very-Low-Birth-Weight Infants." *The New England Journal of Medicine* 346(3):149-57.

Hack, Maureen, Nancy K. Klein, and H. G. Taylor. 1995. "Long-Term Developmental Outcomes of Low Birth Weight Infants." *The Future of Children* 5(1):176-96.

Hamermesh, Daniel S. and Jeffrey E. Biddle. 1994. "Beauty and the Labor Market." *American Economic Review* 54(1):1174-94.

Harper, Barry. 2000. "Beauty, Stature and the Labour Market: A British Cohort Study." *Oxford Bulletin of Economics and Statistics* 62(Special Issue):771-800.

Hauser, Robert M. 1998. "Intergenerational Economic Mobility in the United States: Measures, Differentials, and Trends." Working Paper no. 98-12. University of Wisconsin-Madison, Center for Demography and Ecology.

Heckman, James, Jingjing Hsee, and Yona Rubinstein. 1999. "The GED As a Mixed Signal: The Effect of Cognitive Skills and Personality Skills on Human Capital and Labor Market Outcomes." Unpublished Manuscript, University of Chicago.

Heckman, James and Yona Rubinstein. 2001. "The Importance of Noncognitive Skills: Lessons From the GED Testing Program." American Economic Review 91:145-49.

Heckman, James J. 2000. "Policies to Foster Human Capital." *Research in Economics* 54 (1):3-56.

Hertzman, Clyde. 1999a. "The Biological Embedding of Early Experience and Its Effects on Health in Adulthood." Pp. 85-95 in *Socioeconomic Status and Health in Industrial Nations*, ed. Nancy E. Adler, Michael Marmot, Bruce S. McEwen, and Judith and Stewart. New York, New York: New York Academy of Sciences.

Hertzman, Clyde. 1999b. "Population Health and Development." Pp. 21-40 in *Developmental Health and the Wealth of Nations*, eds. Daniel P. Keating and Clyde Hertzman. New York: Guildord Press.

Hodge, Robert W., Paul M. Siegel, and Peter H. Rossi. 1966. "Occupational Prestige in the United States: 1925-1963." Pp. 322-34 in *Class, Status, and Power: Social Stratification in Comparative Perspective*, 2nd ed. eds. Reinhard Bendix and Seymour Martin Lipset. New York: The Free Press.

Hout, Michael. 2005. "Educational Progress for African-Americans and Latinos in the United States From the 1950s to the 1990s: the Interaction of Ancestry and Class." Pp. 262-87 in *Ethnicity, Social Mobility, and Public Policy*, ed. Glen C. Loury, Tariq Modood, and Steven M. and Teles. New York: Cambridge University Press.

Idler, Ellen L. and Yael Benyamini. 1997. "Self-Rated Health and Mortality: a Review of Twenty-Seven Community Studies." *Journal of Health and Social Behavior* 38:21-37.

Idler, Ellen L. and Stanislav V. Kasl. 1991. "Health Perceptions and Survival: Do Global Evaluations of Health Status Really Predict Mortality?" *Journal of Geronotology* 46(2):S55-S65.

Idler, Ellen L. and Stanislav V. Kasl. 1995. "Self-Ratings of Health: Do They Also Predict Change in Functional Ability?" *Journal of Gerontology* 50B(6):S344-S353.

Illsley, Raymond. 1955. "Social Class Selection and Class Differences in Relation to Stillbirths and Infant Death." *British Medical Journal* 2:1520-1526.

Illsley, Raymond. 1986. "Occupational Class, Selection and the Production of Inequalities in Health." *The Quarterly Journal of Social Affairs* 2(2):151-65.

Jefferis, Barbara, Chris Power, and Clyde Hertzman. 2002. "Birth Weight, Childhood Socioeconomic Environment, and Cognitive Development in the 1958 British Birth Cohort Study." *British Medical Journal* 325(7359):305-8.

Jencks, Christopher. 1979. *Who Gets Ahead?* New York: Basic Books.

Jencks, Christopher and Meredith Phillips, eds. 1998. *The Black-White Test Score Gap*. Washington, D.C.: Brookings Institution Press.

Judge, Timothy A. and Daniel A. Cable. 2004. "The Effect of Physical Height on Workplace Success and Income: Preliminary Test of a Theoretical Model." *Journal of Applied Psychology* 89(3):428-41.

Keyfitz, Nathan. 1977. "The Demographic Theory of Kinship." *Applied Mathematical Demography*, ed. Nathan Keyfitz. New York: John Wiley & Sons.

Kitagawa, Evelyn and Philip M. Hauser. 1973. *Differential Mortality in the United States*. Cambridge, Massachusetts: Harvard University Press.

Koivusilta, Leena, Arja Rimpela, and Matti Rimpela. 1995. "Health Status: Does It Predict Choice in Further Education?" *Journal of Epidemiology and Community Health* 49(2):131-38.

Koivusilta, Leena, Arja Rimpela, and Matti Rimpela. 1998. "Health Related Lifestyle in Adolescence Predicts Adult Educational Level: a Longitudinal Study From Finland." *Journal of Epidemiology and Community Health* 52(12):794-801.

Korenman, Sanders, Jane E. Miller, and John E. Sjaastad. 1994. "Long Term Poverty and Child Development in the United States: Results From the NLSY." IRP Discussion Paper No. 1044-94. Madison: Institute for Research on Poverty, University of Wisconsin.

Kramer, M. S. 1987. "Determinants of Low Birth Weight: Methodological Assessment and Meta-Analysis." *Bulletin of the World Health Organization* 65(5):663-737.

Kuh, D. and Y. Ben-Shlomo, Editors. 2004. *A Life Course Approach to Chronic Disease Epidemiology*, 2nd Ed. Oxford: Oxford University Press.

Lam, David. 1986. "The Dynamics of Population Growth, Differential Fertility, and Inequality." *The American Economic Review* 76(5):1103-16.

Lauderdale, D. S. 2001. "Education and Survival: Birth Cohort, Period, and Age Effects." *Demography* 38(4):551-61.

Lichtenstein, Paul, Jennifer R. Harris, Nancy L. Pedersen, and G. E. McClearn. 1993. "Socioeconomic Status and Physical Health, How Are They Related? An Empirical Study Based on Twins Reared Apart and Twins Reared Together." *Social Science and Medicine* 36(4):441-50.

Loh, Eng S. 1993. "The Economic Effects of Physical Appearance." *Social Science Quarterly* 74(2):420-38.

Lubotsky, Darren. 2001. "Family Resources, Behavior, and Children's Cognitive Development." Unpublished Manuscript. Research Program in Development Studies, Woodrow Wilson School of Public and International Affairs, Princeton University.

Lundberg, Olle. 1991. "Childhood Living Conditions, Health Status, and Social Mobility: A Contribution to the Health Selection Debate." *European Sociological Review* 7(2):149-162.

Lynch, Scott M. 2003. "Cohort and Life-Course Patterns in the Relationship Between Education and Health: a Hierarchical Approach." *Demography* 40(2):309-31.

Lynch, Scott M. 2005. "Explaining Life Course and Cohort Variation in the Relationship Between Education and Health: The Role of Income." Unpublished manuscript. Princeton University.

Manor, Orly, Sharon Matthews, and Chris Power. 2003. "Health Selection: the Role of Inter- and Intra-Generational Mobility on Social Inequalities in Health." *Social Science and Medicine* 57:2217-27.

Mare, Robert D. 1986. "Socioeconomic Careers and Differential Mortality Among Older Men in the United States." Presented at seminar on comparative studies of mortality and morbidity, July 1986.

Mare, Robert D. and Alberto Palloni. 1988. "Couple Models for Socioeconomic Effects on the Mortality of Older Persons." Center for Demography & Ecology Working Paper 88-07, University of Wisconsin-Madison.

Marmot, Michael, Carol D. Ryff, Larry L. Bumpass, Martin Shipley, and Nadine F. Marks. 1997. "Social Inequalities in Health: Next Questions and Converging Evidence." *Social Science Medicine* 44(6):901-10.

Martel, Leslie F. and Henry B. Biller. 1987. Stature and Stigma: the Biopsychosocial Development of Short Males. Lexington, Massachusetts: Lexington Books.

Martorell, R., A. Stein, and D. Schroeder. 2001. "Early Nutrition and Later Adiposity." *Journal of Nutrition* 131:874S-80S.

Matte, Thomas D., Michaeline Bresnahan, Melissa D. Begg, and Ezra Susser. 2001. "Influence of Variation in Birth Weight Within Normal Range and Within Sibships on IQ at Age 7 Years: Cohort Study." *British Medical Journal* 323(7308):310-314.

Mazumder, Bhashkar. 2005. "Fortunate Sons: New Estimates of Intergenerational Moblility in the United States Using Social Security Earnings Data." *The Review of Economics and Statistics* 87(2):235-55.

McClelland, David C. and Carol E. Franz. 1992. "Motivational and Other Sources of Work Accomplishments in Mid-Life: A Longitudinal Study." *Journal of Personality* 60(4):679-707.

McDonough, Peggy, Greg Duncan, David Williams, and James House. 1997. "Income Dynamics and Adult Mortality in the United States, 1972-1989." *American Journal of Public Health* 87(9):1476-83.

McLean, Robert A. and Marilyn Moon. 1980. "Health, Obesity, and Earnings." *American Journal of Public Health* 70(9):1006-9.

Meaney, Michael J. 2001. "Maternal Care, Gene Expression, and the Transmission of Individual Differences in Stress Reactivity Across Generations." *Annual Review of Neuroscience* 24:1161-92.

Menchik, Paul L. 1993. "Economic Status As a Determinant of Mortality Among Black and White Older Men: Does Poverty Kill?" *Population Studies* 47(3):427-36.

Moore, David E. and Hayward Mark D. 1990. "Occupational Careers and Mortality of Elderly Men." *Demography* 27(1):31-53.

Mulligan, Casey. 1997. *Parental Priorities and Economic Inequality.* Chicago: University of Chicago Press.

National Research Council. 2000. *From Neurons to Neighborhoods. The Science of Early Childhood Development.* Washington, D.C.: National Academy Press.

Nollen, Stanley D. and Karen N. Gaertner. 1991. "Effects of Skill and Attitudes on Employee Performance and Earnings." *Industrial Relations* 30(3):435-55.

O'Brien Caughy, Margaret. 1996. "Heath and Environmental Effects on the Academic Readiness of School-Age Children." *Developmental Psychology* 32(3):515-22.

Osborne, Melissa. 2000. "The Power of Personality: Labor Market Rewards and the Transmission of Earnings." Ph.D. Dissertation, University of Massachusetts.

Palloni, A., C. Milesi, R. White, and A. Turner. 2006. "Early Childhood Health, Reproduction of Economic Inequalities and the Persistence of Health and Mortality Differentials." Paper presented at the International Seminar on Early Life Conditions, Social Mobility, and Other Factors that Influence Survival to Old Age, International Union for the Scientific Study of Population, Lund, Sweden, June 8-10.

Palloni, Alberto. 2006. "Childhood Health and the Reproduction of Inequalities." *Demography* 43(4):587-615.

Palloni, Alberto and Douglas Ewbank. 2004. "Selection Effects in the Study of Ethnic and Race Differentials in Adult Health and Mortality." *Ethnic Differences in Health in Later Life*, eds. N.A. Anderson, R. Bulatao, and B. Cohen. Washington D.C.: The National Academy Press.

Palloni, Alberto and Carolina Milesi. 2002. "Social Classes, Inequalities and Health Disparities: The Intervening Role of Early Health Status." *Conference on "Ethnic Variations in Intergenerational Continuities and Discontinuities in Psychosocial Features and Disorders"* (Marbach Castle, Switzerland.

Palloni, Alberto and Carolina Milesi. 2006. "Economic Achievement, Inequalities, and Health Disparities: The Intervening Role of Early Health Status." *Research in Social Stratification and Mobility* 24(1):21-40.

Palloni, Alberto and Melissa Partin. 1994. "Trends and Determinants of Black-White Differentials in Infant Mortality in the United States Since 1964." Robert M. La Follette Institute of Public Affairs Working Paper 23. University of Wisconsin, Madison, Wisconsin.

Palloni, Alberto and Michael Spittel. 2004. "Wealth, Health and Mortality in the US: 19671993." Center for Demography and Ecology, University of Wisconsin-Madison.

Pappas, Gregory, Susan Queen, Wilbur Hadden, and Gail Fisher. 1993. "The Increasing Disparity in Mortality Between Socioeconomic Groups in the United States, 1960 and 1986." *New England Journal of Medicine* 329(2):103-9.

Persico, Nicola, Andrew Postlewaite, and Dan Silverman. 2001. "The Effect of Adolescent Experience on Labor Market Outcomes: The Case of Height." PIER Working Paper 01050. Penn Institute for Economic Research, University of Pennsylvania http://papers.ssrn.com/sol3/papers.cfm?abstract_id=293122.

Popkin, B. M., M. K. Richards, and C. A. Montiero. 1996. "Stunting Is Associated With Overweight in Children of Four Nations That Are Undergoing the Nutrition Transition." *Journal of Nutrition* 126(12):3009-16.

Power, C., O. Manor, and A. J. Fox. 1991. *Health and Class: the Early Years.* London: Chapman and Hall.

Power, C., O. Manor, A. J. Fox, and K. Fogelman. 1990. "Health in Childhood and Social Inequalities in Health in Young Adults." *Journal of the Royal Statistical Society, Series A (Statistics in Society)* 153(1):17-28.

Power, C. and S. Matthews. 1997. "Origins of Health Inequalities in a National Population Sample." *Lancet* 350(9091):1584-9.

Power, Chris, Clyde Hertzman, Sharon Matthews, and Orly Manor. 1997. "Social Differences in Health: Life Cycle Effects Between Ages 23 and 33 in the 1958 British Birth Cohort." *American Journal of Public Health* 87(9):1499-503.

Power, Chris, Leah Li, and Orly Manor. 2000. "A Prospective Study of Limiting Longstanding Illness in Early Adulthood." *International Journal of Epidemiology* 29(1):131-39.

Power, Chris, Sharon Matthews, and Orly Manor. 1998. "Inequalities in Self-Rated Health: Explanations From Different Stages of Life." *The Lancet* 351:1009-14.

Preston, S. H. and Irma T. Elo. 1995. "Are Educational Differentials in Adult Mortality Increasing in the United States?" *Journal of Aging and Health* 7(4):476-96.

Preston, Samuel H. and Cameron Campbell. 1993. "Fertility and the Distribution of Traits: The Case of IQ." *American Journal of Sociology* 98(5):997-1019.

Preston, Samuel H. and Paul Taubman. 1994. "Socioeconomic Differences in Adult Mortality and Health Status." Pp. 279-318 in *The Demography of Aging*, eds. L. Martin and S. Preston. Washington, D.C. National Academy Press.

Rahkonen, O., E. Lahelma, and M. Huuhka. 1997. "Past or Present? Childhood Living Conditions and Current Socioeconomic Status As Determinants of Adult Health." *Social Science and Medicine* 44(3):327-36.

Register, Charles A. and Donald R. Williams. 1990. "Wage Effects of Obesity Among Young Workers." *Social Science Quarterly* 70(1):130-41.

Ricciuti, Anne E. and Sandra Scarr. 1990. "Interaction of Early Biological and Family Risk Factors in Predicting Cognitive Development." *Journal of Applied Developmental Psychology* 11(1):1-12.

Richards, Marcus, Rebecca Hardy, Diana Kuh, and Michael E. J. Wadsworth. 2001. "Birth Weight and Cognitive Function in the British 1946 Birth Cohort: Longitudinal Population Based Study." *British Medical Journal* 22(7280):199-203.

Rogot, E., P. D. Sorlie, N. J. Johnson, and C. Schmitt. 1992. "A Study of 1.3 Million Persons by Demographic, Social and Economic Factors: 1979-1985 Follow-Up." National Institute of Health Publication No. 92-3297.

Rosenzweig, Mark R. and Kenneth I. Wolpin. 1994. "Are There Increasing Returns to the Intergenerational Production of Human Capital? Maternal Schooling and Child Intellectual Achievement." *Journal of Human Resources* 29(2):670-693.

Sargent, J. D. and D. G. Blanchflower. 1994. "Obesity and Stature in Adolescence and Earnings in Young Adulthood - Analysis of a British Birth Cohort." *Archives of Pediatrics and Adolescent Medicine* 148(7):681-87.

Scarr, Sandra. 1982. "Effects of Birth Weight on Later Intelligence." *Social Biology* 29 (34):230-237.

Scrimshaw, Nevin S. 1997. "Nutrition and Health From Womb to Tomb." *Food and Nutrition Bulletin* 18(1):1-19.

Seidman, Daniel S., Arie Laor, Rena Gale, David K. Stevenson, Shlomo Mashiach, and Yehuda L. Danon. 1992. "Birth Weight and Intellectual Performance in Late Adolescence." *Green Journal - Obstetrics And Gynecology* 79(4):543-46.

Shakotko, Robert, Linda Edwards, and Michael Grossman. 1981. "An Exploration of the Dynamic Relationship Between Health and Cognitive Development in Adolescence." Pp. 305-26 in *Health, Economics, and Health Economics*, eds. J. van der Gaag and M. Perlman. New York: North-Holland.

Shriberg, Lawrence D., Sandy Friel-Patti, Peter Flipsen Jr., and Roger L. Brown. 2000. "Otitis Media, Fluctuant Hearing Loss, and Speech-Language Outcomes: A Preliminary Structural Equation Model." *Journal of Speech, Language, and Hearing Research* 43(1):100-120.

Smith, J. P. and R. S. Kington. 1997a. "Demographic and Economic Correlates of Health in Old Age." *Demography* 34(1):159-70.

Smith, J. P. and R. S. Kington. 1997b. "Race, Socioeconomic Status, and Health in Late Life." Pp. 105-62 in *Racial and Ethnic Differences in the Health of Older Americans,* ed. L.G. Martin and B. J. Soldo. Washington DC: National Academy Press.

Smith, James P. 1999. "Healthy Bodies and Thick Wallets: The Dual Relation Between Health and Economic Status." *Journal of Economic Perspectives* 13(2):145-66.

Sorlie, P. D., E. Backlund, and J. B. Keller. 1995. "U.S. Mortality by Economic, Demographic, and Social Characteristics: The National Longitudinal Mortality Study." *American Journal of Public Health* 85(7):949-56.

Sorlie, Paul, Eugene Rogot, Roger Anderson, Norman J. Johnson, and Eric Backlund. 1992. "Black-White Mortality Differences by Family Income." *The Lancet* 340:346-50.

Spittel, Michael L. 2003. "A Study of Inequalities in Health: The Role of Wealth Differences and Social Context." Thesis, University of Wisconsin-Madison.

Stern, Jon. 1983. "Social Mobility and Interpretation of Social Class Mortality Differentials." *Journal of Social Policy* 12(1):27-49.

Suomi, Stephen J. 1999. "Developmental Trajectories, Early Experiences, and Community Consequences." Pp. 185-201 in *Developmental Health and the Wealth of Nations: Social, Biological, and Educational Dynamics*, eds. Daniel P. Keating and Clyde Hertzman.

Taubman, Paul. 1975a. "Determinants of Earnings in 1955 and 1969." Pp. 29-64 in Sources of Inequality in *Earnings: Personal Skills, Random Events, Preferences Toward Risk and Other Occupational Characteristics*, ed. Paul Taubman. Amsterdam: North-Holland Pub Co.; NY: American Elsevier Pub Co.

Taubman, Paul. 1975b. Sources of Inequality in *Earnings: Personal Skills, Random Events, Preferences Toward Risk and Other Occupational Characteristics*. Amsterdam: North-Holland Pub Co.; NY: American Elsevier Pub Co.

Thomas, Duncan, C. McKelvey, and B. Sikoki. 2006. "Immediate and Longer-Term Effects of Health on Socioeconomic Success." Paper presented and the Population association Meeting, Los Angeles, March 30-April 2, 2006.

Thomas, Duncan and John Strauss. 1997. "Health and Wages: Evidence on Men and Women in Urban Brazil." *Journal of Econometrics* 77(1):159-85.

Vagero, Denny and Raymond Illsley. 1995. "Explaining Health Inequalities: Beyond Black and Barker. A Discussion of Some Issues Emerging in the Decade Following the Black Report." *European Sociological Review* 11:219-41.

Valkonen, Tappani. 1987. "Social Inequalities in the Face of Death." *Plenaires/Congres Europeen De Demographie. Scenances Plenaires.* Helsinki, Finland: International Union for the Scientific Study of Population/European Association for Population Studies and Finland Central Statistical Office.

Valkonen, Tappani. 1989. "Adult Mortality and Level of Education: a Comparison of Six Countries." Pp. 142-60 in *Health Inequalities in European Countries*, Fox, John ed. Aldershot, United Kingdom: Gower.

Valkonen, Tappani. 1992. "Social Inequalities in Health in Europe: Evidence and Trends." Paper presented at the Seminario dei Laghi, Baveno, Italy.

Vaupel, J., K. Manton, and E. Stallard. 1979. "The Impact of Heterogeneity in Individual Frailty on the Dynamics of Mortality." *Demography* 16(3):439-54.

Wadsworth, M. E. J. 1991. *The Imprint of Time; Childhood, History and Adult Life.* Oxford: Oxford University Press.

Wadsworth, Michael E. J. 1986. Serious Illness in *Childhood and Its Association With Later-Life Achievement.* New York: Tavistock Publications.

Wadsworth, Michael E. J. 1999. "Early Life." Pp. 44-63 in *Social Determinants of Health*, eds. Michael Marmot and Richard G. Wilkinson. New York: Oxford University Press.

Warren, J. R., R. M. Hauser, and J. T. Sheridan. 2002. "Occupational Stratification Across the Life Course: Evidence From the Wisconsin Longitudinal Study." *American Sociological Review* 67(3):432-55.

Wells, Thomas, Gary D. Sandefur, and Dennis P. Hogan. 2003. *What Happens After the High School Years Among Young Persons With Disabilities?* Population Studies Center, Brown University.

West, Patrick. 1991. "Rethinking the Health Selection Explanation for Health Inequalities." *Social Science and Medicine* 32(4):373-84.

WESTAT. 2000. "Measurement of Activity Limitation Among Children: An Analysis of National Surveys." *Measurement Workshop on Child Disability.* Washington, D.C..

Wright, Erik O. 2003. "Social Class." *Encyclopedia of Social Theory*, ed. George Ritzer. Thousand Oaks, CA: Sage Publications.

–

07 The relationship between childhood conditions and older-age health: disease specificity, adult life course, and period effects.

Commentary on
"Early childhood health, reproduction of economic inequalities and the persistance of health and mortality differentials" by A. Palloni, C. Milesi, R. White, and A. Turner

Vladimir M. Shkolnikov and Dmitri Jdanov

1. Summary of the Palloni study

Persisting socioeconomic inequalities in mortality and health constitute the most challenging health threat in industrialized countries. Although the average level of mortality is continuously declining, differences in mortality within countries tend to be sustained or even increase (Valkonen, 2001, Machenbach, 2006). In spite of a proliferating number of studies, the reasons behind the remarkable continuity are not well understood.

The study by *Alberto Palloni, Carolina Milesi, Robert White, and Alyn Turner* (hereafter the Palloni study) is devoted to mechanisms of the transmission of health inequalities from parents to children. It provides a theoretical framework and a mathematical model connecting socioeconomic position (SEP) and health in early childhood with SEP and health at ages 30-40. The study is primarily interested in the role the *health selection process* plays in the transmission of socioeconomic position and health from parents to offspring and from younger to older age.

Two path models are developed. According to the first model, early life (or parental) SEP is correlated with children's health, which in turn influences educational, cognitive, and communication abilities at later childhood ages. These individual traits induce educational and occupational careers and finally the adult SEP. The second model connects SEP at age 30 (including the entire explanatory path-scheme of the first model) with the health status at age 40.

Importantly, the two models capture not only the described pathways of the central interest, but also a variety of other possible causal chains. In agreement with the classification by Ben-Shlomo and Kuh (2002), they include biological links between childhood health and later life health, social links between childhood and adult socioeconomic positions, socio-biological links between conditions in childhood and adverse health exposures and behaviours in adulthood; and bio-social links between childhood health and educational performance and social status in adulthood. Although the Palloni study primarily focuses on bio-social pathways, the two path models account for other SEP-health, health-SEP, and SEP-SEP links.

The two path models are expressed mathematically as systems of simultaneous equations. Panel data of the British Cohort Study-58 (BCS-58) are used for the parameter estimation. In BCS-58, about 17 thousand men are followed up from birth in 1958 until they reached age 41-42. The estimated parameters of the models allow to calculate the contributions of childhood health to the observed relationships between SEP and health at birth and SEP and health at adult age. The model parameters are then used in the Monte-Carlo simulations to evaluate matrices of the probabilities of parent-offspring mobility in respect to SEP and health at population level.

It was found that childhood health can explain about 10% of the overall relation between parental SEP and offspring SEP. At the same time, the childhood health selection can account for not more than 10% of the overall relationship between SEP at age 30 and health status at age 40. These empirical results are important. The mathematical model provides a good and (perhaps) underexploited opportunity to play with various assumptions and scenarios for a look ahead.

The Palloni study further enhances to research on health inequality. So far, the vast majority of life course epidemiological studies were limited to simple regressions linking SEP to mortality or health outcomes that do not capture a range of inter-relations.

The Palloni study is not free of problems. Although the two path models look plausible, it may be possible to develop alternative models fitting the same data. There are also certain data problems acknowledged by the authors. In particular, the measures of health, especially of childhood health, as well as the data on educational and communicational skills are insufficient. A substantial 30-percent attrition of the cohort over the 40-year follow up constitutes another data problem.

The next section provides two reflections on issues that remain outside the scope of the Palloni study, but nevertheless are relevant to understand the relationship between childhood conditions and health at older ages. The first has to do with the disease-specificity of the relationship between SEP and health. The second looks at the plasticity of adult health in respect to childhood experiences and pertains to variability in cohort mortality trajectories depending on period conditions.

2. Reflections

2.1. Specificity in the relationship between health and SEP

Is it important to take into consideration cause-specific explanations of health inequalities or does it suffice to observe just general "health" (as the Palloni study does)? The question has to do with two approaches in explaining socioeconomic health inequalities and their relations with early life conditions. The first approach emphasizes the shared risk of many forms of ill-health characteristic of less favored SEPs. This "general susceptibility" to disease has been linked to poor diet, psycho-social stress, inadequate coping resources, and genetic differences (Najman, 1980; Valkonen, 1987). The psychosocial stress caused by perceived relative deprivation and effort-reward imbalance (Marmot, Shipley, Rose, 1984; Wilkinson, 1992; Siegrist, 2000) has been put forward as the principal cause of general vulnerability. A certain set of biomedical indicators was proposed to express the multi-system burden caused by stresses cumulated over the life course (Karkamangla et al., 2002).

This view, however, has been complemented and partly challenged by a more "material" approach considering multiple relations between specific exposures in childhood and adulthood on the one side and disease-specific risks on the other (Davey Smith et al., 1994; Davey Smith, 2003; Galobardes, Lynch, Davey Smith, 2004). This approach emphasizes the importance of changing structures of exposures and epidemiologic profiles and helps to explain many empirical findings. In particular, it explains why in certain periods of mankind's history mortality differences across social strata did not exist (Antonovski, 1967; Kunitz, 1987; Davey Smith, 2003). It also explains the substantial variation in the magnitude of the socioeconomic differences across causes of death seen today. In particular, especially large socioeconomic differences have been observed in causes closely related to alcohol, smoking, and other adverse behaviours such as lung cancer, various accidents, suicide, and homicide (Pensola and Valkonen, 2000; Pensola and Valkonen, 2002; Siahpush et al., 2007; Chervyakov et al., 2003). A marked diversity in socio-economic differentials is also seen among cancer sites. For example, the Whitehall Study found the highest low-to-high grade relative mortality rates (about 2.7-3.0) for cancers of the liver, of the lung, and of the stomach, while the lowest relative rates (about 0.5-0.7) were observed for melanoma, cancers of the prostate and of the brain (Davey Smith et al., 1991).

The cause-specificity of socioeconomic differentials in health suggests the importance of changeable disease patterns. Today's magnitude and structures of socioeconomic mortality and morbidity differentials are largely shaped by the structures of predominant diseases and cause-specific exposures either current or past. The relative importance of early-life and adult-life determinants of adult-life health differs by type of disease. In particular, both population- and individual-level studies suggest that stomach cancer, respiratory TB, and hemorrhage stroke are connected with early life conditions (Leon, Davey Smith; 2000, Galobardes, Lynch, Davey Smith, 2004). At the same time, many major causes of death, including coronary heart disease and lung cancer, are less dependent on childhood conditions and more closely related to risks accumulated over the adult life course (see Table 1 reproduced from Leon, 2001).

Table 1: Correlation coefficients (p-values) of adult mortality ages 65-74 in 1991-3 with infant mortality at time of birth and at time of death for 27 countries

	Infant mortality 1921-1923		Infant mortality 1991-1993	
	Males	Females	Males	Females
Pearson correlation coefficients				
All causes	0.52(0.005)	0.51(0.007)	0.58(0.002)	0.63(<0.001)
Respiratory TB	0.77(<0.001)	0.73(<0.001)	0.40(0.04)	0.33(0.09)
Stomach cancer	0.83(<0.001)	0.82(<0.001)	0.39(0.04)	0.44(0.02)
Lung cancer	-0.10(0.61)	-0.48(0.01)	-0.02(0.91)	-0.23(0.24)
Coronary heart disease	-0.05(0.81)	0.16(0.42)	0.13(0.53)	0.28(0.16)
Stroke	0.66(<0.001)	0.63(<0.001)	0.61(<0.001)	0.64(<0.001)
Partial correlation coefficients (see note at end of Table)				
All causes	0.32(0.11)	0.28(0.17)	0.42(0.03)	0.50(0.009)
Respiratory TB	0.71(<0.001)	0.69(<0.001)	0.01(0.96)	-0.07(0.72)
Stomach cancer	0.8(<0.001)	0.77(<0.001)	-0.08(0.71)	0.04(0.87)
Lung cancer	-0.10(0.60)	-0.43(0.03)	0.04(0.86)	0.02(0.92)
Coronary heart disease	-0.13(0.52)	0.03(0.90)	0.18(0.39)	0.23(0.27)
Stroke	0.51(0.008)	0.45(0.02)	0.42(0.03)	0.48(0.01)

Note: Sex and cause-specific correlations of adult mortality with infant mortality in one period adjusted for infant mortality in the other period. The 27 countries analyzed are: Australia, Austria, Belgium, Bulgaria, Canada, Chile, Czechoslovakia, Denmark, Finland, France, Greece, Hungary, Japan, Netherlands, New Zealand, Norway, Poland, Portugal, Romania, Russian Federation, Spain, Sweden, Switzerland, the UK, and the US.

This suggests that there is further variability in the health trajectories of individuals with the same level of "general" health and SEP according to the presence or absence of specific exposures related to specific diseases and health conditions. During adult life, alcohol, smoking, dietary habits, occupational risks, the effectiveness of medical treatment, and prevention have the potential to modify the influence of health inherited from childhood. In the next section and with the help of the Human Mortality Database, we will demonstrate some population-level manifestations of the plasticity of middle and old-age mortality in respect to earlier life experiences.

2.2. The plasticity of mortality trajectories over adult ages

Mortality from causes with a predominately early-life determination (TB, stroke, rheumatic heart disease, and stomach cancer) have been declining at about the same speed over many decades, with a remarkable insensitivity to contemporary circumstances. These secular trends were induced by continuous improvements in the childhood environment and have resulted in a significant change in balance between causes of death toward greater role of causes, sensitive to adulthood health determinants such as lung cancer, coronary heart disease, breast cancer, accidents, and violence (Davey Smith, Gunell and Ben-Shlomo, 2001).

This epidemiological shift is probably responsible for the growing unevenness in respect to age in mortality change across cohorts. Figure 1 shows how progress in the reduction of mortality in female cohorts in England and Wales was distributed by age. The rate of change in the age-specific mortality rates in the figure is less variable by age for older cohorts (1890 vs. 1870) compared to the younger ones (1910 vs. 1890 and 1930 vs 1910). It looks as if younger cohorts had to face a greater number of variable health problems over their life course compared to the older cohorts. For example, mortality in the English female cohort of 1930 is 50% lower at ages 0-14 than it is in the cohort of 1910; this compares to 70% and 15% at ages 20-34 and 45-59, respectively. This variation in the rate of improvement by age reflects the relative success gained in the fight against childhood infections, maternal death, and the relative lack of success in the battle against chronic diseases (especially cancers).

In a number of cases, the mortality trajectories of many cohorts were simultaneously distorted by the effects of specific periods. Figure 2 shows the ratios of age-specific death between successive cohorts of Swedish males similar to those in Figure 1. The shape of the curves suggests a major slow-down in mortality progress taken place in 1965-75. Despite the fact that various cohorts entered this period at different ages, all of them made no progress in mortality reduction during that time. Very similar patterns can be found in 20 other industrialized countries (analysis not shown here). The phenomenon can be attributed to temporary crisis of transition from the fight against infectious diseases at young ages to the battle against cardiovascular and man-made diseases at middle and old ages (Meslé and Vallin ,1993).

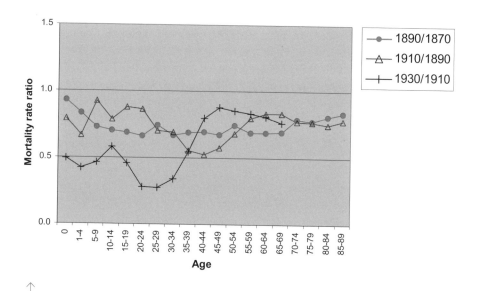

↑

Figure 1: Age-specific ratios of mortality rates between successive female cohorts in England and Wales.

Source: Human Mortality Database (www.mortality.org).

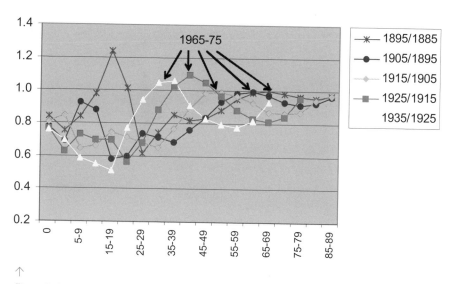

↑

Figure 2: Age-specific ratios of mortality rates between successive male cohorts in Sweden.

Source: Human Mortality Database (www.mortality.org).

The experience of the last two decades of the twentieth century provides examples of extraordinary period effects that caused unexpected changes in mortality and differential mortality that could not be predicted from what has happened in earlier life of the involved cohorts. For example, in 1984-93, there was an unexpected increase in mortality of black men in the US that led to a widening in the black-white gap in male life expectancy from 6 to 8 years. An analysis has shown that the health problem was caused by the excess mortality of African Americans from HIV/AIDS and homicide (Kochanek et al., 1994).

In Russia, a major anti-alcoholic campaign produced a sharp drop in mortality at ages 15-60 by many principal causes of death except cancer (Leon et al., 1997). In the first half of the 1990s, a rapid return of alcohol abuse combined with the psychological shock pertaining to sudden and poorly planned economic reforms caused a steep mortality increase to levels unprecedented in the absence of war and famine. During this period, mortality increase was most pronounced among the least educated and qualified population groups (Shkolnikov, Andreev, Maleva, 2000; Shkolnikov et al., 2006).

At the same time, the political and economic transitions of the 1990s in many Central and Eastern European countries coincided with significant mortality decreases, somewhat unexpectedly in view of the prior experiences of living under an oppressive communist regime. These improvements were largely caused by decreasing cardiovascular mortality at old ages (Meslé, 2004; Richtaryková, 2004). In spite of the adverse past experience, elderly people benefited from a higher quality of life and better medical technologies. The impressive mortality decrease of the 1990s in the East German cohorts born around 1900 was used by Vaupel, Carey, and Christensen (2003) as an illustration of the potential for improvements in survival even at very advanced ages.

3. References

Adler N.E., Boyce W.T., Chesney M.A., et al. Socioeconomic inequalities in health. No easy solution. JAMA 1993; 269: 3140-5.

Antonovsky A. Social class, life expectancy and overall mortality. Milbank Memorial Quarterly 1967; 45: 31-73.

Ben-Shlomo Y. and D. Kuh. A life course approach to chronic disease epidemiology: conceptual models, empirical challenges and interdisciplinary perspectives. International Journal of Epidemiology 2002; 31: 285-293.

Chervyakov, V.V., Shkolnikov, V.M., Pridemore, W.A., McKee, M. The changing nature of murder in Russia. Social Science and Medicine 2002; 55(10): 1713-24.

Davey Smith G., Leon D., Shipley M., Rose G. Socioeconomic differentials in cancer among men. International Journal of Epidemiology 1991; 20: 339-45.

Davey Smith G. Health inequalities: life course approaches. Bristol, UK: Policy Press, 2003.

Davey Smith G., Blane D., Bartley M. Explanations for socio-economic differentials in mortality in Britain and elsewhere. European Journal of Public Health 1994; 4: 131-44.

Davey Smith G., Gunell D., Ben Shlomo Y. Life-course approaches to socio-economic differentials in cause-specific mortality. In: Poverty, Inequality, and Health ed. by Leon, D.A., Walt, G., 2001; Oxford University Press: 88-124.

Galobardes B., Lynch JW, Davey Smith G. Childhood socioeconomic circumstances and cause-specific mortality in adulthood: systematic review and interpretation. Epidemiologic Reviews 2004; 26: 7-21.

Kochanek K.D., Maurer J.D., Rosenberg H.M. Why did black life expectancy decline from 1984 through 1989 in the United States? Am J Public Health 1994; 84: 938–44.

Kunitz S. Making a long story short: a note on men's height and mortality in England from the first to the nineteenth centuries. Med Hist 1987; 31: 269-80.

Leon D.A., Chenet L., Shkolnikov V., Zakharov S. et al. Huge variation in Russian mortality rates 1984-1994. Artefact, alcohol or what? Lancet 1997; 350: 383-388.

Leon D.A. and Davey Smith G. Infant mortality, stomach cancer, stroke, and coronary heart disease: ecological analysis. British Medical Journal 2000; 320: 1705-6.

Leon D.A. Common threads: underlying components of inequalities in mortality between and within countries. In: Poverty, Inequality, and Health ed. by Leon, D.A., Walt, G., 2001; Oxford University Press: 58-87.

Mackenbach J.P. Health Inequalities: Europe in Profile. Report of the project "Tackling Health Inequalities: Governing for Health", The European Commission, 2006.

Marmot M.G., Shipley M.J., Rose G. Inequalities in death – specific explanations of a general pattern? Lancet 1984; i: 1003-6.

Meslé F. and Vallin J. Devéloppement économique et esperance de vie: la transition sanitaire au tournant des anées soixante. XXII General IUSSP Conference, Montreal, Aug 24-Sept 1, 1993.

Najman J.M. Theories of disease causation and the concept of general susceptibility: a review. Social Science and Medicine 1980: 14A: 231-237.

Pensola T.H. and Valkonen T. Effect of parental social class, own education and social class on mortality among young men. European Journal of Public Health 2002; 12: 29-36.

Pensola T.H., Valkonen T. Mortality differences by parental social class from childhood to adulthood. J. of Epidemiol. Community Health 2000; 54: 524-9.

Shkolnikov V.M., Andreev E.M., Jasilionis D., Leinsalu M, Antonova O.I, McKee M. The changing relation between education and life expectancy in central and eastern Europe in the 1990s. Journal of Epidemiology and Community Health 2006; 60: 875-81.

Shkolnikov, V.M., Andreev, E.M., Maleva, T. ed. Neravenstvo i smertnost v Rossii. [Inequality and Mortality in Russia] 2000; Signal, Moscow, 107 p.

Siahpush M., English D., Powles J. The contribution of smoking to socioeconomic differentials in mortality: results from Melborne Collaborative Cohort Study, Australia. J. of Epidemiol. Community Health 2006; 60: 1077-9.

Siegrist J. Place, social exchange and health: proposed sociological framework. Social Science and Medicine 2000; 51(9): 1283-93.

Valkonen T. Social inequality in the face of death. In: European Population Conference. Helsinki: Central Statistical Office of Finland, 1987: 201-261.

Valkonen T. Trends in differential mortality in European countries. In.: J. Vallin & F. Meslé (Eds.), *Trends in mortality and differential mortality* 2001:185-322. Council of Europe Publishing, Strasbourg.

Vaupel J.W., Carey J.R., Christensen K. It's never too late. Science 2003: 301: 1679-80.

Wilkinson R.G. Income distribution and life expectancy. Br Med J 1992; 304: 165-8.

–

08 The Challenges of Ageing: Prospects for the family support of older people in 21st Century Europe.

Emily Grundy

1. Introduction

"Forget the population bomb. The rich countries, and possibly the entire world, will soon be grappling with a new problem: population ageing and population decline. In *The Empty Cradle*, Phillip Longman offers a wealth of insight into what is arguably the biggest – and least appreciated- challenge of our time"
Richard Jackson, 2004.

As indicated by this quotation from a cover review of a book published in 2004, population ageing is widely regarded as one of, if not the, most important demographic challenges facing Europe in the 21st Century. The book in question, *'The empty cradle: how falling birthrates threaten world prosperity'* was written by an American, Philip Longman [1], and his primary concerns are to do with the USA, however the book is global in its coverage and draws heavily on demographic studies, particularly those concerning family and family formation. Longman views population ageing attendant on sub-replacement level fertility as a disaster in the making and his policy recommendations include increased rewards for parents, a return to a family based economy, and initiatives to promote and preserve the health status and economic participation of older people. These latter aims are shared by the author of another book published early in this century which, like Longman's, was addressed to an audience beyond academia and drew heavily on demographic sources of various kinds. However, as the title suggests, the thesis of *'The imaginary time bomb: why an ageing population is not a social problem'* [2] by Phil Mullan, a British economist, is very different from that of Longman. Mullan argues that the sense of panic surrounding population ageing is largely due to growing individualism leading to feelings of social fragmentation, insecurity and uncertainty for which demographic change has become a convenient scapegoat.

Despite their widely divergent views on the implications of population ageing, (particularly the economic implications), these books by the two Philips have certain elements in common. Both recognise that reduced fertility is the predominant cause of population ageing and both recognise that this shift is associated with economic, social, and ideational change. In short, although neither explicitly considers the concept of 'The Second Demographic Transition' as developed by Ron Lesthaeghe, Dirk Van da Kaa and others [3,4], both books reflect the diffusion of this concept into discourse beyond that of academic demographers.

The concept of the second demographic transition is centrally intertwined with the debates about population ageing and the implications it will have in the 21st century. Not only is very low fertility (accelerated by increased longevity) driving further population ageing, but additionally family related behaviour and values impinge not just on relationships between men and women of reproductive age and their decisions about childbearing and rearing, but also on relationships between older parents and adult children and wider social and kin interactions. In this chapter I therefore focus particularly on current patterns and future prospects for family support of older people in Europe, considering first some of the demographic changes in availability of particular kin and secondly patterns of interaction. This is prefaced with a brief review of overall trends in population ageing in Europe.

2. Population ageing in Europe

In a number of Northern and Western European countries, the first demographic transition involving a shift from relatively high to low fertility was set in motion towards the end of the 19th century resulting in population ageing in the first half of the twentieth century. In England and Wales, for example, the proportion of the population aged 65 and over doubled from 5% to 10% between 1901 and 1941. In Southern and Eastern Europe fertility fell later – but the further fall to very low fertility identified by Lesthaeghe and colleagues as constituting part of the phenomena termed the Second Demographic Transition, followed more closely on the heels of the first than in Northern and Western Europe. Largely as a result of these trends, by 2020 a quarter of the population in many European countries will be aged 65 and over and by 2050 it is highly probable that those aged 80 and over will constitute at least one in ten of the population in all the largest European countries, including Britain, France, Germany, Italy, and Spain [5]. Continuation, or amplification, of the 'lowest low' fertility levels recently observed in some Southern and Eastern European countries, would result in even greater age structure change.

Improvements in mortality rates are also contributing to accelerated population ageing. In most European countries (other than for men in the former Eastern bloc) survival to at least age 65 is the normal expectation. The official Government Actuary's Department period mortality schedule for England and Wales in 2002-4, for example, implies survivorship to age 65 for 84% of boys and 90% of girls born then, even in the absence of any further improvement throughout their lifetimes. The vast majority of deaths occur at older ages and reductions in the overall level of mortality are being achieved through improved survival beyond the age of 65. Such improvement has been considerable (except in Eastern Europe) and in several countries has recently been greater for men than for women, a reversal of a long previous trend towards increasing female advantage in mortality. In England and Wales, by no means an exceptionally low mortality country, male life expectancy at age 65 increased by over four years between 1971 and 2001 (from 11.9 to 16.0 years). For women, the gain over the same period was just over three years (from 15.8 to 19.1 years) [6].

Most people aged 65 and over do not have disabling health problems (nor is there any biological reason for choosing 60, 65 or any other particular birthday as marking the onset of old age) but current patterns of economic activity and strong associations between age, morbidity, disability and use of health services have all raised concerns about the economic, social and even political implications of population ageing [7]. In OECD countries health care expenditure is typically three to five times as high for those aged 65 and over as for those aged under 65 and more detailed information available for some countries shows a continuing rising gradient in costs with increasing age. However there is considerable variation in the proportion of GDP devoted to health care spending for older people which bears little obvious relationship to the proportion of older people in the population concerned. Expenditure relative to GDP is much higher in the USA than in European countries, for example, even though the USA has a younger population. Moreover analyses by health economists have identified the growing costs of new technological innovations in medicine as a far greater influence than population ageing on past growth in health care expenditures [8,9]. Needs for, and expenditure on, long term care of various kinds is, however, more clearly linked with demographic changes as in later old age rates of disability and needs for assistance are high. For example, a quarter of women aged 85 and over in Britain are unable to bathe or shower without assistance and half are unable to manage one or more locomotion activities without help [6]. Even projections which assume falling rates of disability suggest large increases in the number of older people with limitations in Activities of Daily Living ((ADLs) –tasks such as bathing, dressing and transferring to and from bed) as a result of growth in the size of the age groups in which the prevalence of disability is greatest [10].

Within Europe there are large variations in the extent to which the state contributes to the provision of this assistance but even in the most generous welfare states, family provision of care and support (including provision by elderly family members such as spouses) is pre-eminent [11-13]. It is important to note that older people are important providers of support, and indeed within families the balance of transfers tends to flow downward from older generations at least until the age of 70 or 75 [14,15]. These downward transfers include both money and provision of practical help, including help with grandchildren. The greater availability of older generation relatives thus brings benefits, as well as potential costs, for their children and grandchildren.

Although family support, both upward and downward, is a major, mechanism for redistribution of resources between generations (and so in some senses across the life cycle), many have suggested that such arrangements may falter in the future. Ron Lesthaeghe and colleagues identified recent changes in fertility as part of a wider constellation of change in family related behaviour involving shifts from familial towards more individualistic orientations. These, it has been argued, reflect shifts in values and aspirations involving a greater emphasis on meeting higher order needs, such as self-actualisation. Thus whereas fertility changes in the first demographic transition were driven partly by desires for 'higher quality child life' requiring greater investment in the nurture and education of a smaller number of children, changes during the second demographic transition may reflect desires for 'higher quality adult life', in some cases untrammelled by familial obligation. 'Second Demographic Transition' type behaviour may thus result not only in accelerated population ageing, but may carry a further sting in its tail- reduced family support for older people. Such a change would have implications both for older people's needs for state or market provided services and for their well-being more generally, as family ties form a major element of many older people's social environment. Extensive evidence indicates that this social environment, including social participation and social support, is an important component of ageing well [16].

2.1. Availability of family support: demographic elements

Assessing demographic availability of close family – spouses and children who are the most important potential supporters of older people- requires consideration of past as well as current trends, and these in fact indicate favourable prospects in many European countries for the next twenty to thirty years. Marriage rates (especially for women) were much higher, and proportions never married much lower, in cohorts born in the late 19th and early 20th century than in cohorts born in the 1930s and 1940s [17,18]. In England and Wales, for example, 16% of women aged 85 and over were in 1971 were never-married, compared with 10% in 2001 and a projected low of 6% in 2021. Moreover, falling mortality and the recent narrowing of gender differences in mortality seen in several European countries, has served to postpone widowhood. Partly as a consequence of these trends in marriage, levels of fertility were also higher, and levels of childlessness lower, among women born in the 1930s and 1940s than in earlier (or later) cohorts. This appears counter intuitive given the role of falling fertility in driving population ageing, but as already noted, in a number of European countries the initial shift to lower fertility occurred in the late 19th or early twentieth century. Although fertility levels have never returned to pre transition levels, there have since then been periods of higher fertility (for example during the post-war baby boom). The distribution of family sizes has also changed with fewer very large families but also lower levels of childlessness.

These trends are illustrated in Figures 1a and b which show Cohort Total Fertility Rates and proportions of women who were nulliparous for cohorts born between 1905 and 1945 in nine European countries. The data used were assembled from official international and national sources by members of the European Science Foundation Network on Family Support for Older People: Determinants and Consequences (FAMSUP). In the Netherlands, Ireland and Portugal – all of which had late initial declines in fertility- cohorts included in the range considered had successively lower fertility, but in several other countries (England and Wales, Germany and Sweden) fertility was slightly higher among cohorts born in the 1930s than in some preceding ones ones. In nearly all countries shown, the proportions of childless women were higher in cohorts born early in the twentieth century than among those born thirty or so years later.

Demographic modelling also taking mortality into account, has shown that in England and Wales some 90% of women born in 1946 will have at least one child still alive when they reach the age of 80 (in 2026), compared with 82% among those born in 1926 who constitute today's population of 80 year olds [19]. Similar patterns have been demonstrated for a number of other European countries [20].

Projections of marital and parenthood status among the population aged 75 and over were undertaken as part of the Future Elderly Living Conditions in Europe (FELICIE) project, which included nine European countries (Belgium, Britain, the Czech Republic, Finland, France, Germany, Italy, the Netherlands and Portugal). Results showed that although the number of unmarried older people (especially unmarried older men), will increase substantially in the next thirty years, there will be even more substantial growth in the number of married women. Overall the size of the married population will grow faster than that of the unmarried and the numbers with a child faster than the numbers of childless. These results are illustrated in Figure 2. One further change will be the much more rapid growth in the numbers of unmarried and childless men than women. Currently the proportion of childless people in the population aged 75 and over is higher among women than men, but this will reverse by 2015 (Figure 3). As a consequence of this, and associated changes in marital status, the composition of the childless population is likely to change considerably between 2000 and 2030, as shown in Figure 4. In 2000 women accounted for over two-thirds of the childless population aged 75 and over in these countries (combined); but in 2030 it is likely half the childless will be men.

2.2. Availability of family support: co-residence, contact and help

These demographic trends mean that in the next twenty to thirty years the potential family support available to older people will tend to increase. Longer term prospects for the demographic availability of close kin are, however, much less favourable as cohorts born since the mid 1950s have experienced high rates of divorce, as well as a return to higher levels of childlessness and lower nuptiality. Moreover, in order to assess possible changes in the availability of family support for older people, we also need to consider the effects of possible changes in the extent to which family members actually provide support of various kinds.

Concerns about possible changes in the willingness, or ability, of younger generations to provide support for older relatives have arisen partly because of the kind of changes in behaviour associated with the Second Demographic Transition, such as rises in divorce, cohabitation and non-marital childbearing, and also because of observed changes in the living arrangements of older people. In the 1950s and 1960s it was quite common for older widowed people to live with a child, even in Scandinavia, other North West European countries and North America [12], now even in very old age groups, living alone is the most usual arrangement for women without a spouse, at least in Northern and Western Europe. However, although trends towards greater residential independence among older people are common throughout, and beyond, Europe, large differentials persist [21-24]. This is illustrated in Figure 5 which shows the proportions of people aged 60 and over and aged 80 and over by living arrangement and European region. The data are drawn from the 2002-4 rounds of the European Social Survey (ESS) and relate to 18 countries here grouped by region. The Northern group comprises Denmark, Finland, Norway and Sweden; West refers to Austria, Belgium, Germany, The Netherlands and the UK; East to the Czech Republic, Estonia, Hungary, Poland and Slovakia and South to Greece, Spain and Portugal. (A number of other countries were represented in the ESS but have not been included in this analysis because of poor response rates). The categorisation used distinguishes those living alone; those living just with a spouse; those living with a spouse and others, and those living with people other than a spouse (usually children). As can be seen, differences were marked. Thus among men aged 60 and over in Northern and Western regions well over 80% lived alone or just with a spouse compared with 60% in Eastern and Southern regions. Seventy six per cent of women aged 80 and over in the Northern region lived alone compared with 20% in the South. In analyses for the married and unmarried populations separately, we estimated odds of living with a spouse and others versus living alone (for the married) or with others versus alone (for the unmarried) taking into account age, level of education, income, feelings about income and self rated health, in both cases relating other regions to the North. Results shown in Figures 6 and 7 demonstrate that these large variations are not due to compositional differences in the characteristics of the older population in different regions of Europe. Compared with those in the Northern region, married men and women in the East and South were much more likely to be living with a spouse and at least one other person (in the case of women in the East, over ten times as likely). Among the unmarried, those in the South and West were far more likely to be living with someone else rather than alone than was the case in the North or West.

Living alone does not in itself indicate an absence of family contact or support. Although intergenerational co-residence has fallen, extensive survey evidence points to high levels of contact and mutual support between older people and their families, even if living separately [12-15, 25]. Frequent contact is more common in Southern than Northern European countries. Results from the Surveys of Health and Retirement in Europe (SHARE) have shown that in the Southern European countries included at least three-quarters of parents aged 80 and over were in touch with a child daily. This proportion was much lower in the Netherlands, Sweden and Denmark, but was still at least 20-40% (being lower among men) [26]. Older people and their relatives are also involved in frequent exchanges of help, often reciprocal, with tasks and activities such as shopping, paperwork, household chores and, in the case of help provided by older people, care of grandchildren [14,15].

Within countries, those from more highly educated groups tend to have less contact with relatives and also different patterns of support exchanges, with help from younger to older generations being more pronounced in less advantaged groups [26-29]. Analyses for three of the FELICIE countries with suitable data (Finland, France and Italy) [27] (Table 1) showed that parental divorce, parental health status, number of children and level of education were all associated with differentials in the extent of frequent contact between elderly parents and their children. In all countries men who were divorced had lower odds of at least weekly contact with a child than married or widowed men and in Finland this association was also apparent for women. Number of children was positively associated with frequent contact in France and Italy and in all countries higher levels of education were negatively associated with contact for either mothers or fathers. In analyses reported elsewhere [27] we estimated future scenarios based on these coefficients and changes in the composition of the older population by marital status and history, level of education and number of children. These scenarios showed very little effect of compositional changes in Italy where essentially all parents see a child weekly regardless of their circumstances. However changing parameters of interest had a large effect in Finland and France. For example, if the proportion of parents divorced were set to 25% in Finland, the proportion having weekly contact with a child would fall from 0.64 to 0.57 for fathers and from 0.77 to 0.57 for mothers, effects substantial enough to be important in terms of policy. However such scenario modelling rests on the assumption of current associations remaining fixed which is unlikely to be the case.

Apart from help with everyday tasks and sharing of activities, some mid-life children provide more extensive care for disabled older parents. Ogg and Renault [30] found that between 6 and 13% of people aged 50-59 included in the SHARE surveys who had a parent alive were providing help with aspects of personal care such as bathing. Detailed country studies have shown that higher educated people are less likely to be providers of substantial amounts of care (20 or more hour per week), as are women in full time employment or women who in the past have had more engaged employment histories. One study from England and Wales also found that women who had returned to work within a few years of having a child were subsequently less likely to be caregivers than women who had responded to childbearing by curtailing or withdrawing from market work [31]. This finding, and similar results from other studies, is consistent with theories that see the growing involvement of women in the labour market –

something advocated by policy makers concerned about the labour supply implications of population ageing –as encroaching upon 'traditional' roles as both mothers and caregivers. It is also consistent with theories, such as those related to the concept of the Second Demographic Transition, which suggest that underlying attitudinal and aspirational changes may be associated with change in a range of behaviours.

It seems from the evidence reviewed above that in the short term future, relatively more of the older population in many European countries will have the potential support of a spouse or child to draw on than has been the case in the past (or will be the case in the longer term future), and that although intergenerational co-residence has become much less usual, levels of contact and mutual help between older parents and their children (and grandchildren) are high, although with variations between and within countries. In the final sections of this chapter, the implications of these conclusions are considered in terms of influences on older people's health, well-being and access to care when needed.

3. Implications for older people's wellbeing

Given the important role of family members as confidantes, helpers and members of social networks, it would seem an obvious conclusion that family support and engagement should also contribute positively to the health and well-being of older people. Evidence for this is strongest in the case of availability of a spouse. Numerous studies have indicated that marriage seems to be associated with clear health benefits for older men, with married men generally having the best health and lowest mortality [32]. Results for older women are less clear cut with some studies finding no advantage for the married, or indeed advantages for the never-married women [32, 33]. This may be because women have stronger links with friends and other relatives and so are less reliant on spouses for emotional support; never-married women in particular may be able to draw on alternative social networks cultivated over a lifetime.

Some studies also point to effects of relationships with children and other relatives on health and well-being, [34, 35] but these, and the effects of living arrangements, are harder to interpret, due to the complexity of various selective influences. It is also likely that associations between family interaction, including co-residence, and indicators of well-being vary between populations and strata within populations. Different pathways to specific types of living arrangement also make it difficult to unravel possible effects on health. Most studies (for a review see Grundy [36]) which have looked at this, find that in older groups those living with a spouse have the best health, consistent with the literature on marital status differences in health, and that, especially among the older old, those living alone are in better health than those living with relatives. However, this is presumably because serious disability makes living alone very difficult (except perhaps in countries with particularly good support services) and is an important driver of changes in living arrangements. Some recent longitudinal studies conducted in Scandinavia and the USA which have controlled carefully for initial health status, have found some indications of health damaging effects of living alone (the usual option for the unmarried in Northern European and American populations), including cognitive decline, especially in groups with serious impairments at baseline [37,38]. Higher risks of cognitive decline have also been reported among those with no close social ties, those with unsatisfactory relationships with close relatives and those with few social activities [37,39].

Married people potentially have access to practical help and care from a spouse, as well as emotional support, and children are also potential care providers for older people with disabilities. The proportion of married older people in, or entering, institutional care is much lower than that of older people of other marital statuses, particularly the never-married (who in current older cohorts are generally childless). Availability of a child is itself associated with differentials in use of institutional care and other formal services [40, 41]. Living with a spouse or other co-resident (usually an adult child), especially a spouse in good health, is also associated with a greater chance of dying at home – a preferred option among older decedents [42].

Availability of children is of course also a pre-requisite of co-residence with a child. Whether or not this is regarded as a desirable (or least undesirable) option for older people with serious disabilities and major assistance needs will depend on a range of personal and cultural preferences and circumstances, and the availability and quality of alternatives, such as nursing home care. In Southern European countries older people who live with their adult children report higher levels of satisfaction than other women, [43] whereas a study conducted in Wales found that older people living with relatives were the most likely to report loneliness and poor morale [44]. This may reflect both cultural differences in preferences and different pathways to co-residence; in countries, such as Britain, where residential independence is valued, co-residence with a child may more often be a last resort than a positive choice. If so, we might expect that elderly people living with relatives in Southern European countries might be happier than those living alone, while the reverse might be true in Northern countries. As shown in Table 1, based on analysis of the ESS for the 18 European countries already identified, older people living with a spouse, whether with or without additional persons, reported being happier than those living alone (as expected), but there were no differences between those living without a spouse but with others and those living alone. Happiness was also positively associated with having no worries about money; with social activities and meetings and someone to discuss intimate matters with; with increasing age and, more surprisingly, with lower levels of education. Older people in the North (Nordic countries) and Western Europe reported being happier than those in the South and, most particularly, those in Eastern Europe. Stratified analyses showed similar patterns within each region; that is we did not find noticeable regional differences in the association between living arrangements and happiness (or reported satisfaction with life). This analysis of course has a number of limitations; the regional groupings may obscure important differences between and within countries; there may be cultural variations in how people report happiness and the data are cross-sectional. Additionally, sampling errors and non response bias need to be considered.

4. Discussion

Older people rate relationships with family members high among the domains of life important to them and the available empirical evidence shows that most people are in close contact with family members and engaged in various, generally reciprocal, exchanges of support. Emotional support and social engagement are known to be important dimensions of a healthy old age and, as we have seen, happiness, and it seems highly probable that family links form a major component of these, although empirical evidence on this (apart from evidence on the role of marriage) is sparse.

Increases in the proportion of older people with a spouse and at least one child, projected for the next twenty to thirty years, are therefore positive developments for older people and society as a whole. The demographic context in the longer term future, when the post 1950 cohorts reach later life is less favourable as these cohorts will have experienced more diverse partnership histories and a return to higher levels of childlessness. These cohorts, who have led The Second Demographic Transition, will undoubtedly have different aspirations and values, as well as different family related behaviours. These trends suggest an urgent need during the relatively auspicious next couple of decades to research and establish the best means of enabling older people to maintain and develop supportive relationships and social activities; the best balance between formal and unpaid care for those with disabilities (which may involve evaluating the impact of encouraging greater work participation), and, of course, the best means of promoting and maintaining health in later life. Additionally Europe needs to find ways of further developing and using the many contributions older Europeans continue to make. Innovative research spanning both geographic and disciplinary boundaries and including due attention to concepts as well as data, of the kind exemplified in Lesthaeghe's distinguished scientific contributions on the Second Demographic Transition, is now needed to prepare for the longer term consequences of that Transition.

5. Acknowledgments

This chapter draws on research carried out under the auspices of the European Science Foundation funded Network on Family Support in Later Life, Determinants and Consequences (FAMSUP);as part of the Future Elderly Living Conditions in Europe (FELICIE) project funded under the European Union 5th Framework Research Programme (reference QLRT-2001-02310) and research funded by the UK Economic and Social Science Research Council (Grant reference RES-163-25-0024). The author is very grateful to these funders and to the many collaborators involved in these projects particularly Karen Glaser, Cecilia Tomassini, Patrick Festy, Joelle Gaymu and Harriet Young.

6. Appendix

Countries and data included in comparative data presented.
European Social Survey (2002 and 2004). Countries included in the analysis: North: Denmark, Finland, Norway, Sweden; West: Austria, Belgium, Germany, Netherland, UK; South: Greece, Spain, Portugal; East: Czech Republic, Estonia, Hungary, Poland, Slovakia, Slovenia, Ukraine. Analysis carried out as part of UK ESRC funded project (Harriet Young and Emily Grundy).
FAMSUP (Family support of older people: determinants and consequences). European Science Foundation Network including members from Austria, Belgium, Britain, Germany, Italy, Netherlands, Portugal and Sweden which assembled a database of comparable national statistics. http://www.lshtm.ac.uk/cps/famsup/
FELICIE. (Future Elderly Living Conditions in Europe). EU Framework Five project co-ordinated by INED and University of Louvain and including members from Belgium, Britain, Czech Republic, Finland, France, Germany, Netherlands and Portugal. Assembled comparable databases and undertook analyses, including projections of the population aged 75 and over by important characteristics. http://www.felicie.org/

7. References

1. Longman P. *The empty cradle: how falling birthrates threaten world prosperity [and what to do about it]*. New York, Basic Books, 2007.

2. Mullan P. *The imaginary time bomb: why an ageing population is not a social problem*. London, I.B. Taurus & Co. Ltd., 2000.

3. Lesthaeghe R. A century of demographic and cultural change in Western Europe: An exploration of underlying dimensions. *Population and Development Review*, 9, 411-35, 1983.

4. van Da Kaa D. *Europe's Second Demographic Transition*. Population Bulletin 41, Population Reference Bureau, Washington DC, 1980.

5. United Nations. *World population prospects, the 2000 revision: Highlights*. United Nations, New York, 2001.

6. Grundy E. Gender and healthy ageing, in: *Longer Life and Healthy Ageing*, Zeng Yi et al. Eds., Springer, Dordrecht, 2006, 173-99.

7. OECD. *Maintaining prosperity in an ageing society*. OECD, Paris, 1999.

8. Appelby J, Harrison A. Spending on health care: how much is enough? Annex to Wanless D. *Securing good care for older people: taking a long-term view*. King's Fund, London, 2006.

9. Normand C. Ageing, health and welfare: an economic perspective. In: Dangour A, Grundy E, Fletcher A. (Eds). *Ageing well: nutrition, health and social interventions*. CRC Press, London, 2007, 117-126.

10. Jacobzone S, Cambois E, Chaplain E, Robine JM. Long Term Care Services to Older People, A Perspective of Future Needs. *The Impact of An Improving Health of Older Persons*, OECD, Paris. 1998.

11. Sundström G, Malmberg B, Johansson L. Balancing family and state care: neither, either or both? The case of Sweden, *Ageing & Society*, 26, 767-782, 2006.

12. Sundström G. Care by families: an overview of trends. In Organisation for Economic Co-operation and Development, *Caring for frail elderly people*, OECD, Paris, 1994.

13. Royal Commission on *Long Term Care. With respect to old age: Long term care rights and responsibilities*. Research volume 1, The context of long-term care policy, Cm 4192-II/1, The Stationery Office, London, 1999.

14. Attias-Donfut C, Ogg J, Wolff FC. European patterns of intergenerational financial and time transfers, *Eur J Ageing*, 2, 161-73, 2005.

15. Grundy E. Reciprocity in Relationships: Socio-economic and Health Influences on Intergenerational Exchanges between Third Age Parents and their Adult Children in Great Britain, *The British Journal of Sociology*, 56, 233-255, 2005.

16. Bath PA, Deeg D. Social engagement and health outcomes among older people: introduction to a special section, *Eur J Ageing*, 2, 24-30, 2005.

17. Coleman D (Ed.) *Europe's population in the 1990s*, Oxford University Press, Oxford, 1996, chap. 1.

18. Grundy E. Population ageing in Europe, in D, Coleman. (Ed.) *Europe's population in the 1990s*, Oxford University Press, Oxford, 1996, chap. 8.

19. Murphy M, Grundy, E. Mothers with Living Children and Children with Living Mothers: The Role of Fertility and Mortality in the Period 1911-50, *Population Trends* 112, 36-45, 2003.

20. Murphy M, Martikainen P, Pennec S. Demographic change and the supply of potential family supporters in Britain, Finland and France in the period 1911-2050, *European Journal of Population*, 22, 219-40. 2006.

21. Pampel, F. C. Trends in living alone among the elderly in Europe, in *Elderly Migration and Population Redistribution*, A, Rogers. Ed., Belhaven Press, London, 1992, chap. 6.

22. Grundy E. The living arrangements of elderly people. *Reviews in Clinical Gerontology* 2, 353-361, 1992.

23. Iacovou M. Patterns of family living, in Social Europe, Berthoud R, Iacovou M, (Eds.), Edward Elgar, Cheltenham, 2004, chap. 2.

24. Tomassini C, Glaser K, Wolf, D. Broese van Grenou M, Grundy E. Living arrangements among older people: an overview of trends in Europe and the USA. *Population Trends* 115, 24-34, 2004.

25. Daatland S.O, Lowenstein A. Intergenerational solidarity and the family-welfare state balance, *Eur J Ageing*, 2, 174-182, 2005.

26. Hank K. Proximity and contacts between older parents and their children: A European comparison. *J Marriage Family*, 69, 157-173, 2007.

27. Tomassini C, Grundy E, Kalogirou S, Gaymu J, Binet, A, Martikainen P, Karisto A. Rencontres entre parents âgés et enfants: quelles différences en Europe? *Retraite et Société* 46: 10-27, 2005.

28. Grundy E, Shelton N. Contact between adult children and their parents in Great Britain 1986-1999, *Environment and Planning A*, 33, 685-697, 2001.

29. Henretta J, Grundy E, Harris S. The influence of socio-economic and health differences on parents' provision of help to adult children: A British -United States comparison, *Ageing and Society*, 22, 441-458, 2002.

30. Ogg J, Renault S. The support of parents in old age by those born during 1945-1954: a European perspective, *Ageing & Society*, 26, 723-743, 2006.

31. Young H, Grundy E, Jitlal M. *Care providers, care receivers: a longitudinal perspective.* Joseph Rowntree Foundation, York, 2006.

32. Goldman N, Korenman S and Weinstein R. Marital status and health among the elderly. *Soc Sci Med*, 40, 1717, 1995.

33. Grundy, E., Sloggett A. Health inequalities in the older population: the role of personal capital, social resources and socio-economic circumstances. *Soc Sci Med*, 56, 935-47, 2003.

34. Antonucci, Arjouch J, Janevic M. R. The effect of social relations with children on the education-health link in men and women aged 40 and over, *Soc Sci Med*, 56, 949-60, 2003.

35. Barefoot et al. Social network diversity and risks of ischemic heart disease and total mortality: findings from the Copenhagen City Heart Study, *Am. J Epidemiol*, 161, 960-7, 2005.

36. Grundy E. Living arrangements and the health of older persons in developed countries. *Population Bulletin of the United Nations*, Special Issue, Living arrangements of older persons: critical issues and policy responses. 42/43: 311, 2001.

37. Fratiglioni L, Wang H, and Ericsson K. Influence of social networks on occurrence of dementia: a community- based longitudinal study. *Lancet*, 355, 1315-19, 2000.

38. Sarwari, A.R. et al. Prospective study on the relation between living arrangement and change in functional health status of elderly women. *Am J Epidemiol*, 147, 370-78, 1998.

39. Glei et al. Participating in social activities helps preserve cognitive function: an analysis of a longitudinal, population-based study of the elderly, *Int. J Epidemiol*, 34, 864-71, 2005.

40. Carrière et al. Socio-demographic factors associated with the use of formal and informal support networks among elderly Canadians, in *Longer Life and Health Ageing*, Zeng Y., et al. (Eds.), Springer, Dordrecht, 2006, chap.17.

41. Grundy E, Jitlal M. Socio-demographic variations in moves to institutional care 1991-2001: a record linkage study from England and Wales. *Age and Ageing* 36: 1-7, 2007.

42. Grundy E. et al. Living arrangements and place of death of older people with cancer in England and Wales: a record linkage study. *Br J Cancer*, 91, 907-912, 2004.

43. Zunzunequi MV, Nunez O, Durban M, Garcia de Yebenes MG, Otero A. Decreasing prevalence of disability in activities of daily living, functional limitations and poor self-rated health: a 6-year follow-up study in Spain. *Aging Clinical Experimental Research* 18: 352-8, 2006.

44. Wenger, G.C. *The Supportive Network: Coping With Old Age*, Allen and Unwin, London, 1984.

45. Grundy, E. Ageing and vulnerable elderly people: European perspectives. *Ageing & Society* 26: 1-30, 2006.

46. Tomassini C, Grundy E, Kalogirou S. Potential family support for older people 2000-2030. in: Gaymu J, Festy P, Poulain M, Beets G (eds). *Future elderly living conditions in Europe*. INED, Paris, forthcoming.

Table 1: Results from logistic regression analysis of variations in the proportion of fathers and mothers with at least weekly face-to-face contact with a child.
Coefficients and (standard errors).

	Fathers			Mothers		
	Finland	France	Italy	Finland	France	Italy
Intercept	0.87 (0.17)	2.79 (0.51)	3.32 (0.17)	1.29 (0.19)	1.52 (0.11)	3.31 (0.17)
Age ref. 65–74						
Aged 75+		0.01(0.10)	−0.21 (0.15)		0.28** (0.09)	0.00 (0.15)
Aged 72+	−0.13 (0.16)			−0.11 (0.18)		
Education (ref. low)						
High	−0.64 (0.28)*	−1.01 (0.15)	−0.20 (0.19)	0.14 (0.35)	−1.02 (0.18)**	−0.31 (0.22)
Medium	−0.36 (0.24)	−0.17 (0.11)	0.03 (0.21)	0.00 (0.24)	−0.40 (0.09)**	−0.63 (0.21)**
Number of children (ref. 3+)						
1	0.22 (0.23)	−1.14 (0.12)**	−1.04 (0.19)**	0.32 (0.25)	−1.08 (0.10)**	−1.11 (0.17)**
2	−0.01 (0.18)	−0.66 (0.12)**	−0.55 (0.18)*	−0.02 (0.19)	−0.57 (0.10)**	−0.42 (0.18)*
Marital Status (ref. married)						
Widowed	−0.55 (0.37)	0.07 (0.15)	−0.12 (0.20)	−0.26 (0.21)	0.45 (0.09)**	0.21 (0.15)
Single, separated, / divorced	−1.82 (0.33)**	−1.16 (0.23)**	−1.83 (0.29)**	−0.90 (0.24)**	−0.09 (0.18)	−0.35 (0.31)
Not home owner (ref. home owner)	0.286 (0.28)	0.14 (0.13)	−0.22 (0.17)	0.47 (0.28)	0.10 (0.10)	−0.32 (0.15)*
Presence of disability (ref. not disabled)	−0.25 (0.23)	0.13 (0.12)	−0.10 (0.18)	0.12 (0.27)	−0.15 (0.10)	−0.16 (0.16)

Source: FELICIE data in Tomassini, Grundy, Kalogirou et al 2005 [27]. *P<0.05, **P<0.01

Table 2: Results from ordinal logistic regression analysis of happiness scores (higher = better) among people aged 60 and over in 18 European countries.

	Men		Women	
	OR	95% CI	OR	95% CI
Living arrangement (ref: alone)				
Spouse only	1.75***	1.38,2.22	1.85***	1.55,2.21
Spouse and others	1.68***	1.28,2.22	1.81***	1.42,2.31
Others only	0.99	0.68,1.43	1.67***	1.38,2.03
region (ref: North)				
West	0.73	0.65,0.83	0.70***	0.62,0.78
South	0.39	0.32,0.46	0.36***	0.30,0.43
East	0.25	0.21,0.31	0.28***	0.23,0.34
Age	1.02***	1.01,1.03	1.02***	1.01,1.03
Income (ref: high/intermediate)				
Low	1.06	0.92,1.23	0.95	0.83,1.10
Missing	0.90	0.76,1.07	0.68***	0.59,0.78
Education (ref: upper 2ry and more)				
Lower	1.36***	1.19,1.55	1.19**	1.05,1.34
Feelings about income (ref: comfortable)				
Coping	0.55***	0.48,0.63	0.69***	0.60,0.80
Difficult	0.26***	0.21,0.32	0.33***	0.27,0.40
Social meetings (ref: > 1 per week)				
< 1/week	0.71***	0.61,0.83	0.68***	0.59,0.78
Social activities (ref: same/more than most)				
Less than most	0.83**	0.73,0.94	0.69***	0.61,0.77
Anyone to discuss intimate matters (ref: yes)				
No	0.52***	0.43,0.64	0.58***	0.49,0.69
Currently widowed (ref: no)				
Yes	0.77	0.58,1.02	0.86	0.73,1.02
Limiting long term illness (ref: yes)				
No	1.65	1.45,1.87	1.79	1.59,2.02
N				

Source: Analysis of ESS data.

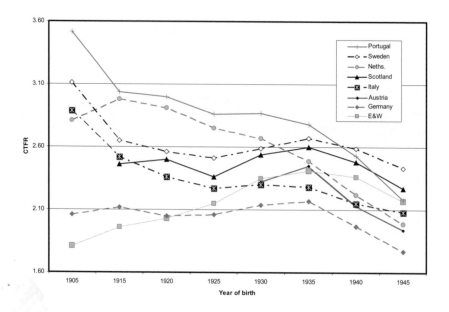

Figure 1a: Cohort Total Fertility Rate; selected countries, birth cohorts 1905-1945

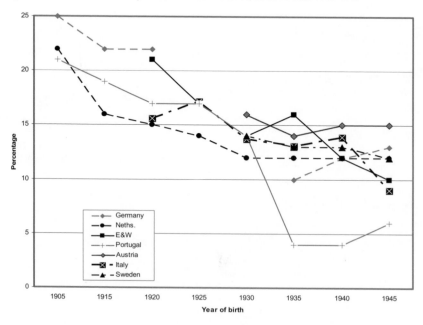

Figure 1b: Proportions of women nulliparous at age 45, by birth cohort.
(Source: FAMSUP data in Grundy 2006 [45]).

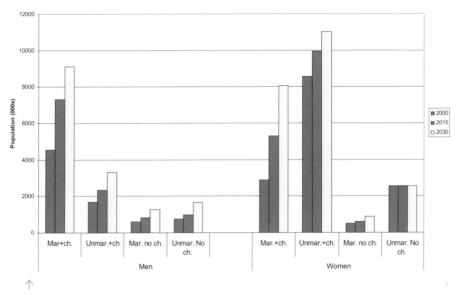

Figure 2: Numbers and projected numbers of men and women aged 75 and over by marital and parenthood status, 2000-2030, all FELICIE countries combined.
Source: FELICIE data on Belgium, Britain, Czech Republic, Finland, France, Germany, Italy, Netherlands and Portugal. (Tomassini, Grundy and Kalogirou, [46]).

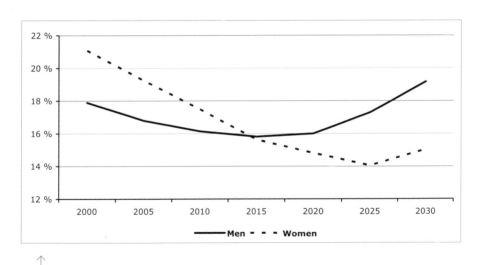

Figure 3: Proportion of men and women without children alive, age 75+, %
Source: FELICIE data on Belgium, Britain, Czech Republic, Finland, France, Germany, Italy, Netherlands and Portugal. (Tomassini, Grundy and Kalogirou, [46]).

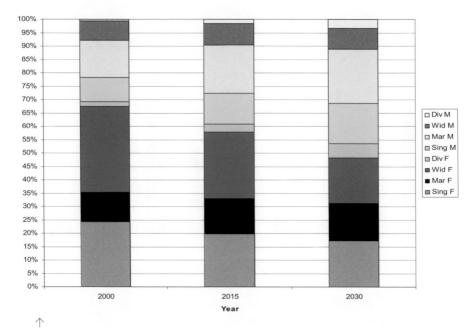

↑

Figure 4: Distribution of the childless population aged 75 and over by gender and marital status, 2000-2030, all FELICIE countries combined.

Source: FELICIE data on Belgium, Britain, Czech Republic, Finland, France, Germany, Italy, Netherlands and Portugal. (Tomassini, Grundy and Kalogirou, [46]).

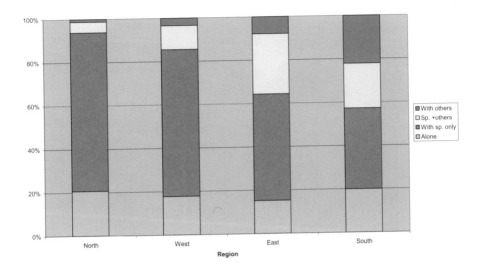

Women 60+

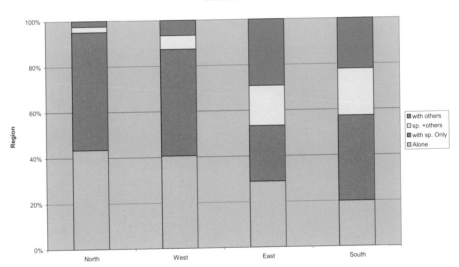

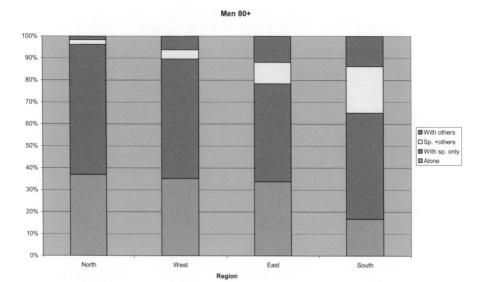

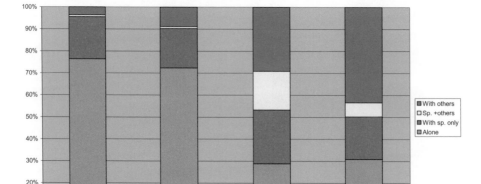

↑

Figure 5: Living arrangements of older Europeans by region, 2002/4. (Source: analysis of ESS, 2002-4).

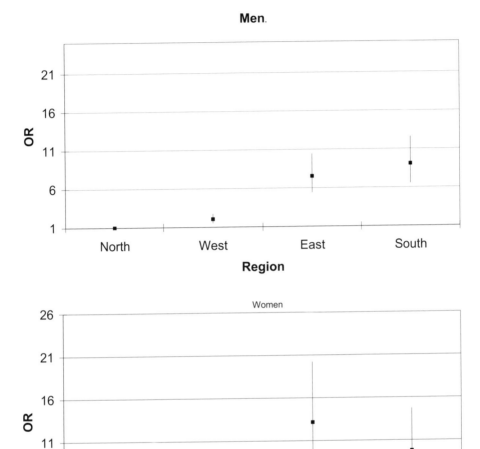

Figure 6: Odds of living with a spouse and others versus living with a spouse only by European region (reference category North), married people aged 60 and over, 2002-4 (controlling for age, education, income, feelings about income and self-rated health).

Men

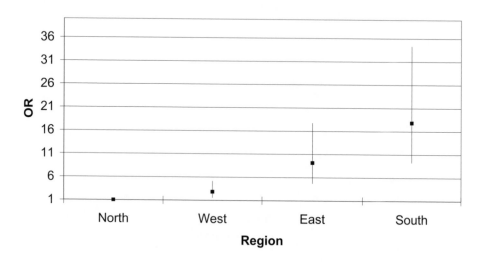

Women

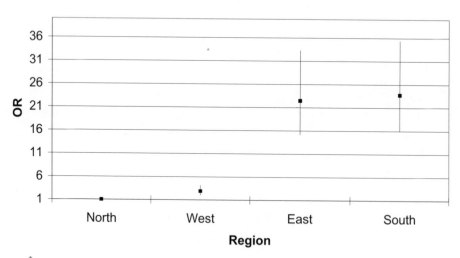

Figure 7: Odds of living with others versus living alone only by European region (reference category North), unmarried people aged 60 and over, 2002-4 (controlling for age, education, income, feelings about income and self-rated health).

–
Abstracts

Laudation for Ron Lesthaeghe
Frans J. Willekens

Ron Lesthaeghe is among the 10 most influential demographers of the past half century worldwide. Since 1988, he has been cited close to 1,000 times in top journals (Social Science Citation Index). About 50 percent of these citations are in demography journals and about 40 percent in sociology journals. These indicators of creativity, innovation and energy quantify the large impact of Ron had and continues to have on both demography and sociology. The prizes and rewards confirm the status and impact. Ron's professional career should inspire junior scholars. It is shown that events and experiences in early stages of his professional life are strong predictors of achievements later in life.

Does Persistent Low Fertility Threaten the Future of European Populations?
Tomáš Sobotka

This contribution looks at selected trends and cross-country differences in fertility, many of which are commonly seen as the main 'causes' of the envisioned future demographic decline of Europe. I analyse fertility changes in conjunction with migration, discussing their impact on likely future population trends in Europe. Many evolving fertility trends are assessed with an eye on addressing the following hypotheses:

- Extremely low period total fertility rates, observed at present in many parts of Europe, are linked to the rapid postponement of childbearing and are likely to be temporary;
- Very low fertility rates are often related to various economic, cultural and institutional constraints which may be reduced in the future;
- The second demographic transition is closely linked to fertility postponement, but not necessarily to below-replacement fertility level;
- If migration is taken into account, population replacement rates are close to the threshold necessary for stable or increasing population in most regions of Europe

In conclusion, this article discusses findings on the current positive association between the second demographic transition and period fertility level and summarises reasons why European fertility rates might increase in the future. When fertility trends are considered jointly with migration, very low fertility and the possibility of a marked population decline constitute a regional problem rather than a threat for Europe as a whole.

Education and Permanent Childlessness: Austria vs. Sweden. A Research Note
Gerda Neyer, Jan M. Hoem

In this research note we extend our previous study of the association between educational attainment and permanent childlessness in Sweden (Hoem et al., 2006) to cover Austria, and we make comparisons between the two countries. In both investigations we have defined educational attainment in terms of both educational level and educational field. We find largely the same pattern of childlessness by educational field in both countries; in particular at each educational level women educated for teaching jobs or for health occupations typically have lower childlessness than other lines of education. However, for most groups childlessness is higher in Austria, and for academic educations it is much higher. We attribute these differences to institutional differences in the two countries which may bring about a different culture of reproductive behaviour.

Recent Trends in Demographic Attitudes and Behaviour: Is the Second Demographic Transition Moving to Southern and Eastern Europe?
Aart C. Liefbroer, Tineke Fokkema

As one of the 'founding fathers' of the concept of the Second Demographic Transition (SDT), Ron Lesthaeghe has demonstrated convincingly that demographic change in many Western countries is related to changes in attitudes and values regarding family life. It is less clear, though, whether the SDT is spreading to Eastern and Southern Europe. The aim of this chapter is to shed light on this issue by tracing attitudinal change and demographic change throughout Europe from the mid-1990s onwards. We use data on family-relevant attitudes from the 1994 and 2002 International Social Survey Program and data on cohabitation and parenthood drawn from the Labour Force Surveys held in EU countries since the mid-1980s. The results suggest that the SDT is indeed spreading to Eastern and Southern Europe, but also pose some challenging new puzzles for future research.

Measuring International Migration: A Challenge for Demographers
Michel Poulain, Nicolas Perrin

Demographers consider international migration to be a topic of increasing importance for their discipline. However, policy-makers dealing with international migration show limited interest in the work of demographers. This paradox is particularly apparent in Europe, a setting where the issue of migration has become a key priority for European policy-makers. Specifically, in order to support the development of a common migration policy, the European Union is faced with an urgent need for better statistics on migration and asylum and the international migration statistics are frequently unreliable, not only in Europe, but in all countries around the world. A recent meeting organised by the UN's Statistical Division in New York[1] concluded firstly: the most recent set of recommendations on international migration statistics is not being followed, secondly: the requested data is often unavailable, and where it is available, is often unreliable and finally: that all the available data considered sufficiently reliable cannot be compared systematically because of different data sources, concepts and definitions. Accordingly, the task facing demographers is not an easy one. Nonetheless, it may be considered essential in terms of policy support.

Early Childhood Health, Reproduction of Economic Inequalities and the Persistence of Health and Mortality Differentials
Alberto Palloni, Carolina Milesi, Robert White, Alyn Turner

The persistence of adult health and mortality socioeconomic inequalities and the equally stubborn reproduction of social class inequalities are salient features in modern societies that puzzle researchers in seemingly unconnected research fields. Neither can be satisfactorily explained with standard theoretical frameworks.

In the domain of health and mortality, it is still unknown if and to what an extent adult health and mortality inequalities across the socioeconomic ladder are entirely the product of attributes of the socioeconomic positions themselves and/or the partial result of health conditions established earlier in life that influence **both** adult health and economic success.

In the domain of social stratification, the persistence of inequalities across generations in various domains, such as educational attainment, wages, income, and wealth, has proven to be remarkably resistant to satisfactory explanations. Although the literature on social stratification is by and large notoriously silent about the role played by early health status in shaping adult social and economic opportunities, new research on human capital formation contains plenty of hints suggesting that this is a serious error of omission.

This chapter is mostly about theory, models and alternative ways of obtaining empirical estimates. We first propose a model representing some of the aforementioned relations. We then suggest the use of a novel methodology to falsify the main propositions derived from the theory. In practice this methodology will enable the investigator to formulate simple procedures to estimate (a) the degree to which social mobility, or lack thereof, is influenced by early health conditions and (b) the contribution of early health status to observed adult health differentials. The model is novel insofar as it incorporates both early conditions as determinants of traits that enhance (inhibit) social mobility

---

1   Expert Group Meeting on Measuring International Migration: concepts and methods, UNSD, New York, 4-7 December 2006.

as well as conventional factors affecting adult health and socioeconomic status. This formulation enriches current social stratification theory as an explanatory tool for social and economic inequalities; it also strengthens theories that attempt to explain adult health and mortality differentials.

The Relationship Between Childhood Conditions and Older-age Health: Disease Specificity, Adult Life Course, and Period Effects.
Vladimir M. Shkolnikov and Dmitri Jdanov

We review the study by Palloni and colleagues which models transition mechanisms of socioeconomic and health inequalities from parents to children. Two reflections are relevant for further understanding the relationship between childhood conditions and health at older ages. The first concerns the disease-specificity in this relationship. Evidence suggests that childhood conditions are especially important for some causes of death such as respiratory TB, stomach cancer, and stroke, whereas other major causes such as CHD, lung cancer, and external causes are more sensitive to adulthood health determinants. The second reflection is related to the growing plasticity of cohort mortality trajectories in response to changing period conditions. The last fifty years provide numerous examples of period effects that have unexpectedly but significantly changed mortality trajectories of cohorts and have modified influences cumulated over their earlier life.

The Challenges of Ageing: Prospects for the Family Support of Older People in 21st Century Europe.
Emily Grundy

Europe is ageing and by 2020 close to a quarter of the population in any European countries will be aged 65 and over. By 2050 it seems most probable that people aged 80 and over will account for one in ten people in several of Europe's largest countries, including Britain, France, Germany, Italy and Spain. The relatively old populations of many European countries today are the long-term consequence of historical changes in birth and death rates known as the first demographic transition. However, in many European countries the process of population ageing has been accelerated and accentuated by more recent changes in family related behaviour identified by Professor Lesthaeghe and others as constituting a Second Demographic Transition. These changes seem to have involved a shift to more individualistic aspirations and behaviours and a weakening of traditional family bonds. This has led to concerns that family support for older people in need of assistance may be eroding just as the numbers potentially needing such support are increasing. Moreover, pressures on state financed and mediated transfers to the older population will be challenged by changes in the ratio of 'workers' to 'pensioners' and associated changes in economic productivity and the costs of pensions. Does this mean that population ageing is a disaster for Europe? In this paper I examine short and longer term prospects with a particular focus on demographic change and the family support of older people – and the support provided by older people and its implications both for society as a whole and for the well-being of older people. I argue that in many respects short term prospects are highly favourable, although in the longer term rather less so.